AMERICAN MODELS OF REVOLUTIONARY LEADERSHIP:

GEORGE WASHINGTON AND OTHER FOUNDERS

Edited by
Daniel J. Elazar and Ellis Katz

UNIVERSITY
PRESS OF
AMERICA

Lanham • New York • London

Center for the
Study of
Federalism

Copyright © 1992 by
University Press of America®, Inc.
4720 Boston Way
Lanham, Maryland 20706

3 Henrietta Street
London WC2E 8LU England

Co-published by arrangement with the
Center for the Study of Federalism

Managing Editor: Mark Ami-El
Typesetting: Custom Graphics and Publishing, Ltd., Jerusalem

Library of Congress Cataloging-in-Publication Data

American Models of Revolutionary Leadership:
George Washington and Other Founders
/ edited by Daniel J. Elazar and Ellis Katz.
p.   cm.
1. Political leadership—United States—History.
2. United States—Politics and government—1783-1865.
3. United States—Politics and government—Revolution,
1775-1783.   4. Political culture—United States—History.
I. Elazar, Daniel Judah.   II. Katz, Ellis.
E302.1.A47   1992
306.2' 0973—dc20   91-30470 CIP

ISBN 0-8191-8350-4 (cloth : alk. paper)
ISBN 0-8191-8351-2 (pbk. : alk. paper)

 The paper used in this publication meets the minimum requirements of
American National Standard for Information Sciences—Permanence
of Paper for Printed Library Materials, ANSI Z39.48–1984.

This book is dedicated to the memory of
J. David Greenstone,
friend and colleague,
whose sparkling and incisive analysis
made us all his students.

ACKNOWLEDGMENTS

Several of the chapters in this book were originally prepared as papers for a colloquium on Models of Revolutionary Leadership sponsored by Liberty Fund, J. Charles King, Executive Director and Kenneth S. Templeton, Jr., Program Officer, and conducted by the Center for the Study of Federalism at Temple University in 1983 in commemoration of George Washington's relinquishment of command of the Continental Army at the close of the Revolutionary War. As in so many other cases, Liberty Fund made possible stimulating conversation and improved understanding on the part of the participants in the conference and also enabled the Center for the Study of Federalism to generate the first written material for this book: the chapters by Daniel J. Elazar, Gary Wills, Forrest McDonald, Morton J. Frisch, J. David Greenstone, and Steven L. Spiegel. Hopefully, the result will have an influence beyond the confines of the conference itself.

Another two chapters, by Gary J. Schmitt and Rozann Rothman, appeared in *Publius: The Journal of Federalism*, published by the Center for the Study of Federalism as part of its continuing concern for leadership in federal systems. The chapter by Barry Schwartz was originally published in the *American Sociological Review* (Vol. 48; February 1983). We thank them for permission to reprint the article in this collection. Moshe Hazani's chapter is an original piece prepared for this volume.

Publication of this book was made possible by the Earhart Foundation, David Kennedy, President and Dr. Antony T. Sullivan, Secretary. Over the years, the Earhart Foundation has been a major contributor to the Center and has done much to make its work possible. Lately it has also assisted us in publishing important materials that would otherwise not see the light of day. They not only have our continuing gratitude but special thanks for their support.

As always, this book would not have been possible without the staff of the Center for the Study of Federalism, including head secretaries Mary Duffy and Marian Wolf, and Joseph M. Marbach, research assistant during the time the book was being prepared, later Earhart Fellow and now Assistant Director of the Center. Mark Ami-El of the Jerusalem Center for Public Affairs was responsible for the copy editing and oversaw the typesetting for this book in his usual competent manner. He, too, has our thanks. Temple University, which houses the Center for the Study of Federalism, has continued to play the role we have come to expect in making the Center's work, and therefore this book, possible.

Daniel J. Elazar
Ellis Katz
Philadelphia
February 1991

CONTENTS

INTRODUCTION

Daniel J. Elazar

Quite properly, the bicentennial commemorations in the United States have focused on American institutions — how the American people established a federal democratic republic, the first of its kind in the world, with a constitution that embodied the principles of the new science of politics developed in the seventeenth century and subsequently, and applied them in innovative ways through a set of institutional inventions that constituted the greatest step forward in political innovation since ancient times, to launch an experiment of world-shaking import. Missing in this celebration and reassessment of American institutions has been a similar celebration and assessment of the political leadership which brought this American experiment about, for in leadership as well as in institution-building, the American revolution offered a new and different model.

The interrelationship between a polity and its leaders is the key to an effective and successful politics. A good leader diagnoses the situation properly, formulates a way to deal with it, and mobilizes the public to respond. In essence, civil society provides the potential, but leaders make the difference. They do so in part through possessing formal authority, but that authority becomes real only where they can exercise power and do so in such a way that the polity continues to accept their authority.

In democratic republics this power means the mobilization and allocation of resources in the maintenance and fostering of republican norms. In any polity, but most particularly in the democratic republic, a good leader combines engineering and bargaining in determining and developing the means to act, in his understanding of cause and effect as it relates to his actions, and in applying a technology of action. Such leaders can only be effective to the extent that they have character; in democratic republics, that they stand for a proper sense of republican virtue, both in their reputation and in their behavior. This is the source of the charisma of leadership in democratic republics beyond whatever personal charisma individuals may command. Charisma in this sense constitutes a commanding presence in light of the principles and expectations of republican virtue.

The United States was thrice blessed at its founding with that kind of leadership, with men who instinctively understood what was required of leaders in the emerging democratic republic and what was especially required of founders whose every action would set precedents and models for the future. Of those leaders, George Washington stands out head and shoulders above the rest. So he was perceived at the time and so he is again perceived today, after his reputation has gone through the twin distortions of saintlike veneration and debunking. The real George Washington, with his weaknesses as well as his greatness put on the table for all to see, remains the man he appeared to be to his colleagues in the slightly more than two decades that he lead the American cause. Any man who can command the awe of John Adams, Alexander Hamilton, Thomas Jefferson, and James Madison and the enduring respect of Benjamin Franklin has to have been very special indeed.

One need not make Washington more than human to understand how he was a paragon for his generation and for all subsequent generations of Americans. Washington should be more than that. He was a model of what republican revolutionary leadership should be anywhere in the world. In this respect his reputation has not had the circulation it deserves. Just as the American revolution is often viewed by non-Americans as so uniquely an American phenomenon that it has little to teach the rest of the world (a distinctly different view than that prevalent in the world prior to the rise of revolutionary socialism in Europe — 1848 may be considered a turning point — when it served as a model from Chile to Hungary), so, too, has Washington been dismissed as an important American figure but no more.

We argue in this volume that this is a mistaken view, that it is time for the world to seek out the lessons of the American revolution and its leadership, particularly George Washington, to strengthen democratic republicanism in the present postmodern epoch. Here our argument regarding the importance of leadership becomes crucial. Since the events of the late eighteenth century, virtually the entire world (the exceptions being a few Arab states like Saudi Arabia) has come to honor democratic republicanism, at least in the breach. No country today, especially none where a revolution has taken place, claims to be other than democratic and republican. Yet we all know that while the number of true democratic republics is growing again, many of the world's independent states are sheer hypocrites, claiming to be democratic republics, yet having no intention of being anything of the sort. The rest, especially since the upheavals in the Communist bloc, seem to be either groping toward democratic republicanism or confused.

The fate of the contemporary regimes that aspire but do not achieve is not for lack of formal democratic institutions. In this respect they have borrowed well, even drawing from some aspects of the American experience in the postmodern epoch. The difference seems to be to a great extent a problem of leadership. Without leaders able to foster democratic republicanism and republican virtue, the best institutions in the world will come to naught. Thus the subject of appropriate leadership, including in our time appropriate revolutionary leadership, is of vital importance. It is too easy for most of the world to continue to follow the path of revolutionary France of the 1790s, the path of least resistance, and to watch the bright hopes of a democratic dawn descend into one or another form of tyranny and exploitation. If the peoples of the world can learn from the American experience and if the leaders of the world or at least the future leaders can be inspired by it, then the bicentennial commemoration will have far broader implications than merely being an American affair.

This book is designed to be a contribution to that end, exploring the political leadership in American and other democratic societies. The emphasis is on the transition from revolutionary to stable democratic leadership. It begins with an overview by this writer dealing with "Contrasting Models of Revolutionary Leadership" in which the special character and contribution of the American revolution is spelled out. It then turns to George Washington as a revolutionary leader with chapters by Garry Wills on "Power Gained by Surrender"; Forrest McDonald, "Washington, Cato and Honor: A Model for Revolutionary Leadership"; and Barry Schwartz, "George Washington and a Whig Conception of Heroic Leadership." Wills looks at the style of Washington's leadership, McDonald at the sources of Washington's inspiration, and Schwartz on the impact of Washington on the civil society which he led.

In Part Two we turn to the contrasting models themselves, beginning with an article by Moshe Hazani on Samuel Adams and Saint-Just as contrasting examples of professional revolutionaries in the American and French revolutions. Hazani takes the two men considered in their time the most extreme of the significant revolutionary leadership of their respective revolutions and contrasts their world views and actions in fostering revolution and dealing with it when it came; to show how Adams' contribution was to move from the stability of the old regime to revolution to a new democratic stability, while Saint-Just sought to move from the old regime to revolutionary turbulence as a means of social transformation without considering what came after — in other words, a kind of permanent revolution. Hazani's piece is followed by that of Morton Frisch on "Revolutionary Leadership and the Problem of Power," which focuses on Thomas Jefferson and Alexander Hamilton, the two rivals for Washington's favor, each of whom represented a different view of organizing power in a revolutionary context for a post-revolutionary regime.

The final two selections in this section are Gary Schmitt's "Jefferson and Executive Leadership: Revisionism and the 'Revolution of 1800,'" and Rozann Rothman's "Albert Gallatin: Political Method in Leadership." Both men were leaders of the second American revolution — the "Revolution of 1800" or the first peaceful turnover of government from one party to another. As Henry Adams has deftly portrayed in his *History of the Administrations of Thomas Jefferson*, the latter took office with the intention of conducting a democratic revolution to overthrow the entrenched Federalist elite. His style of executive leadership was designed to foster a new spirit of democratic republicanism while systematically dismantling the Federalist power bases. Yet he, too, had to take extraordinary actions as chief magistrate to serve American interests. In this, he was amply assisted by Gallatin, who brought a special wisdom to bear for the Jeffersonians. Dr. Schmitt traces Jefferson's response to the dilemma of executive power in a democratic republic, beginning with his differences with Hamilton during Washington's presidency and continuing through his own. The chapter brings out the contradictions in Jefferson's thought and behavior brought on by the realities of governing. Dr. Rothman considers the revolutionary leader as organizer of government, which was Gallatin's special role at the end of the revolutionary period. Gallatin, the only major figure of the founding generation born on the European continent (he was Swiss), made his mark first in the organization of the legislative branch of the new federal government of the United States in the 1790s and then, after the election of Jefferson to the presidency, on the executive branch between 1801 and 1809. In those two decades he became one of the architects of post-revolutionary stability that embodied rather than rejected the ends of the revolution.

Part Three focuses on issues of leadership in subsequent generations. In his famous speech to the Young Men's Lyceum in Springfield, Illinois, a young Abraham Lincoln recognized the special nature of revolutionary leadership, of those people who "belong...to the family of the lion or the tribe of the eagle" and whose ambitions require that they be given special challenges rather than being asked to trod already beaten paths. Then he poses the question of how do democratic republics deal with such vaulting ambition? Perhaps he was thinking of himself in his remarks. Certainly he rose to a challenge similar to that of Washington and the founders in his struggle to maintain the Union, an event which he acknowledged in his Gettysburg Address as nothing less than the equivalent of the revolution itself. J. David Greenstone explores the grounding of Lincoln's leadership in "Lincoln's Political Humanitarianism: Moral Reform in the Covenant Tradition in American Political Culture." Finally, Steven Spiegel brings us up to date in "Where Have All the Leaders Gone? Ruling Elites and Revolution Since World War II," in which he explores the contemporary situation and how, even in the United States today, it so often stands in sharp contrast to the model of revolutionary leadership provided by the American founders.

PART ONE:

THE TRANSITION FROM REVOLUTIONARY TO STABLE DEMOCRATIC LEADERSHIP

CONTRASTING MODELS OF
REVOLUTIONARY LEADERSHIP

Daniel J. Elazar

No dimension of the revolutions of the modern world has been more crucial to their outcome than leadership. Think of Cromwell, Washington, Napoleon, and Lenin; of Samuel Adams, Robespierre, and Trotsky. The mere mention of the names clarifies the question. In an age of revolutions, in which every revolution at least pretends to democratic ends, it is the leadership of each that has made the difference.

In March 1783, George Washington assembled the officers of his army at Newburgh, New York, in a manner that most clearly expressed the standard for American revolutionary leadership. At one time every American schoolchild knew the story and at least the gist of Washington's words. The Continental Army, fresh from its victory over the British and in the aftermath of the peace treaty signed between the newly recognized United States of America and Great Britain, was instructed to disband without soldiers and officers receiving the pay due them. Feeling was running high in certain circles in the army that the Confederation Congress was unable to govern and that the only way to save the country was for the army to take power and install Washington as the head of a new government — to transform Washington into a Cromwell. Washington, rejecting all such thoughts, used his farewell to his officers to drive the point home, beginning so dramatically by pulling out his spectacles to read his farewell address with the comment, "Gentlemen, you will permit me to put on my spectacles, for I have not only grown gray but almost blind in the service of my country," thereby bringing tears to the eyes of his companions and winning the day before he read a word of his text.[1] The myth alone has inspired generations of Americans to respect their democratic institutions even when they seem to be functioning less than adequately.

In every aspect of his career George Washington set a new and special example of revolutionary leadership. His leadership was assured through his commanding moral posture rather than through any particular brilliance. His principal talent was in

3

holding together semi-voluntary coalitions, military and political. Every office he held was gained through legitimate means, either election or appointment. Although he was personally ambitious, his ambitions were all directed to achieving position within a constitutional framework. Radical in his opposition to British encroachments on American liberties and in his advocacy of American independence, he was conservative in his emphasis on maintaining constitutional processes and institutional continuity as far as possible. Perhaps the best single word to describe his leadership is "sober." In this respect he is the exemplar of Martin Diamond's definition of the American Revolution as a "revolution of sober expectations.[2]

Unfortunately, Washington's standard for revolutionary leadership has not been widely emulated outside the United States, just as the American Revolution has been emulated far less than the French Revolution by other modern revolutionary movements. The standard for revolutionary leadership for most of the world has been set by Robespierre and Napoleon, not by Washington and his compatriots. Robespierre reflects the impatience of the ideologist fanatically committed to his cause with any restraints that might prevent him from achieving total social and political revolution. Napoleon is the model opportunist of great ambition and talent who emerges out of the wreckage of revolution to inherit power by brilliantly combining a certain lip-service to revolutionary ideals with implementation of those aspects of the original revolutionary program that advance his popularity and legitimacy while aborting all the others. What Robespierre and Napoleon were to France, Lenin and Stalin were to Russia. And the Russian Revolution is only the most prominent example of the repetition of the French revolutionary pattern. In this contrast the American Revolution gains even greater luster.

The Problem: Revolution and Great Ambition

Political ambition, like other kinds of ambition, is a basic human appetite. John Adams went so far as to suggest that ambition was *the* basic human appetite, which may have reflected more upon him than upon humanity but is not entirely wide of the mark.[3] Like other human appetites, ambition is not evenly distributed among the population, but enough people with substantial political ambition are naturally drawn to political careers to make the problem of controlling it a major aspect of constitutional government. Indeed, the other founders of the United States were as aware of this problem as was Adams and devoted much of their concern for constitutional design to dealing with it. *The Federalist* emphasizes that the American Constitution is designed so that ambition will counteract ambition, that being a basic reason for introducing checks and balances into the political system.[4]

Revolutions by their very nature stimulate ambition and offer new opportunities for its exercise, especially, but not exclusively, for people new to the political arena. Moreover, revolutions are particularly attractive to those very few who have extraordinary political ambition. Such people are likely to exist in every generation, and if they cannot capitalize upon a revolution not of their own creation, they seek to generate one for their own purposes. Abraham Lincoln was acutely aware of this problem and provided one of the most felicitous discussions of it in his well-known address before the Young Men's Lyceum of Springfield:

That our government should have been maintained in its original form from its establishment until now [1838], is not much to be wondered at. It had many props to support it through that period, which now are decayed, and crumbled away. Through that period, it was felt by all, to be an undecided experiment; now, it is understood to be a successful one. Then, all that sought celebrity and fame, and distinction, expected to find them in the success of that experiment. Their *all* was staked upon it: — their destiny was *inseparably* linked with it. Their ambition aspired to display before an admiring world, a practical demonstration of the truth of a proposition, which had hitherto been considered, at best no better than problematical; namely, *the capability of a people to govern themselves.* If they succeeded, they were to be immortalized; their names were to be transferred to counties and cities, and rivers and mountains; and to be revered and sung and toasted through all time. If they failed, they were to be called knaves and fools, and fanatics for a fleeting hour; then to sink and be forgotten. They succeeded. The experiment is successful; and thousands have won their deathless names in making it so. But the game is caught; and I believe it is true, that with the catching, end the pleasures of the chase. This field of glory is harvested, and the crop is already appropriated. But new reapers will arise, and *they*, too, will seek a field. It is to deny what the history of the world tells us is true, to suppose that men of ambition and

5

talents will not continue to spring up amongst us. And, when they do, they will as naturally seek the gratification of their ruling passion, as others have *so* done before them. The question, then, is, can that gratification be found in supporting and maintaining an edifice that has been erected by others? Most certainly it cannot. Many great and good men sufficiently qualified for any task they should undertake, may ever be found, whose ambition would aspire to nothing beyond a seat in Congress, a gubernatorial or a presidential chair; *but such belong not to the family of the lion, or the tribe of the eagle*[.] What! Think you these places would satisfy an Alexander, a Caesar, or a Napoleon? Never! Towering genius disdains a beaten path. It seeks regions hitherto unexplored. It sees *no distinction* in adding story to story, upon the monuments of fame, erected to the memory of others. It *denies* that it is glory enough to serve under any chief. It *scorns* to tread in the footsteps of *any* predecessor, however illustrious. It thirsts and burns for distinction; and, if possible, it will have it, whether at the expense of emancipating slaves, or enslaving freemen. Is it unreasonable then to expect that some man possessed of the loftiest genius, coupled with ambition sufficient to push it to its utmost stretch, will at some time, spring up among us? And when such a one does, it will require the people to be united with each other, attached to the government and laws, and generally intelligent, to successfully frustrate his designs.

Distinction will be his paramount object; and although he would as willingly, perhaps more so, acquire it by doing good as harm; yet, that opportunity being past, and nothing left to be done in the way of building up, he would set boldly to the task of pulling down.[5]

Lincoln properly suggests that the principal leaders in revolutionary times will not be people of ordinary political ambition but are likely to be of the family of the lion and the tribe of the eagle, who are potentially very dangerous to the body politic — certainly to republican institutions. Most civil societies that have undergone revolutions have been unable to control this product of revolution. Of the four great revolutions of the modern epoch, only one, the American, was able to do so.

The English Revolution (civil war), despite the great tradition of the liberties of Englishmen and the extensive institutionalization of that tradition over the previous 450 years or more, produced Oliver Cromwell, who seized power in the name of the revolution and become a despot bound only by his sense of God's expectations and his inclination to benevolence. Neither was sufficient to prevent public dissatisfaction with his rule and the ultimate restoration of the monarchy. However lacking in character the Stuarts were, the institution of the monarchy was preferable for Englishmen, even most of those of the Puritan persuasion, to a despotism, however benevolent, that seemed to be heading toward a new dynasty.

I have already suggested that the French and Russian revolutions failed even more miserably from this perspective. The traditions of English liberty rather quickly brought down Cromwell's regime and in relatively short order transformed the monarchy as well. The French Revolution produced its Robespierre as quickly as the English civil war produced Cromwell. But since Robespierre lacked all sense of restraint, neither bowing to God nor possessing a spirit of benevolence, his excesses were exacerbated just as quickly, and his downfall was more rapid and painful. His fate did not dampen the ambitions of his successors, since the situation was structurally oriented to encourage similar excesses. Only their lack of talent prevented them from achieving similar dominance until Napoleon, who was both more talented and less principled than Robespierre, came along. Although he captured the imagination of France and has held the affections of his countrymen to this day, any objective observer would have to rank him as an utter betrayer of the revolution, even though he capitalized on revolutionary ideals to bleed France on a hundred battlefields and to assert his own absolute power as ruler of that hapless country.

Napoleon's ambition knew no bounds and was further fed by his assessment that, as an upstart, he needed one success after another to stay in power. As a result he overreached himself and fell, not only bringing back the Bourbons, but starting a tradition of French military defeat that has persisted ever since. (Since the early days of his ascendancy, France has not won a war against an equal power, except on the backs of its allies.) Moreover, the struggle between those who desired Napoleonic leadership and those who feared it kept France in turmoil for the next 150 years until Charles De Gaulle, the first French leader to follow the Washingtonian model, albeit with a French style, brought the French Revolution to a successful conclusion by securing the involvement of the full political spectrum in the writing of the Constitution of the Fifth Republic. Under his leadership a regime was inaugurated that had the consent of virtually all the French people for the first time since 1789.

The Russian Revolution brought an even worse result, since Russia had even fewer institutional and cultural restraints on the excesses of leaders than did France. When the Bolsheviks seized power in an absolutist state their leader, V.I. Lenin, simply used the existing absolutist tradition to become the Russian Revolution's Robespierre without suffering the same consequences. Lenin consolidated the power of his party and regime, leaving both intact to be inherited by Joseph Stalin after a relatively mild power struggle among possible successors.

Lenin destroyed any possibility of democratic republicanism and the introduction of civil liberties through his ruthless pursuit of revolutionary goals. Stalin reinforced the results and went beyond Lenin for reasons more personal than ideological. Between the two of them they generated quantitatively the greatest bloodbath of the twentieth century and possibly of all time, utterly aborting the ideals they presumably sought to advance and imposing upon the peoples of the Soviet Union a despotism more comprehensive and penetrating in its scope than any known before.

In each of these cases, the goals of the revolutionaries were admirable enough (if in some cases too utopian to stand a chance of success). They were perverted by the leaders spawned by the revolutions themselves. To state that is not sufficient, however, to explain why these revolutions spawned such leadership and the American Revolution did not. However important, leadership is but one factor in revolutionary situations. Two other factors of equal weight are the character of popular participation and the institutionalization of the results. Every revolution could and should be assessed in terms of the action of the public that made or joined it, in the character of its revolutionary leadership, and in the way its goals were subsequently institutionalized.

It is in the nature of revolutions that there will be popular involvement. That is what distinguishes them from rebellions or palace uprisings. So it is not the existence of popular participation, but its character and quality that constitutes the crucial question.

The characteristic manifestations of popular participation in the American Revolution were the town meetings and the committees of correspondence, the state militias and the Continental Line; in other words, *self-organized* means of popular expression. Contrast that with the principal image of the French Revolution, the Parisian mob storming the Bastille or cheering on the reign of terror; or the Russian Revolution with its "masses" storming the Winter Palace and other institutions of the regime. In both cases the reality matched the image. Mobs and masses were important, and the successful leaders were those demagogues who could capture them or manipulators who learned how to turn them out. Only the English civil war, with its Puritan congregations and New Model Army, presents an image similar to that of the American Revolution.

This is not to say there were no mobs in the American Revolution. There were some. The best known were relatively light-hearted, like the highly organized "mob" that dumped the tea into Boston harbor. Others — those that attacked the Tories — were far more vicious. But such mobs as emerged were small and local; their role was very minor in the overall scheme of things and had no real political significance. Certainly they did not influence the decisions of the governing bodies — local, provincial or state, or continental.[6]

So, too, it may be added, were there occasional mobs during the English civil war, of the same relative unimportance. Cromwell seized power with an army behind him. Before that, the king was deposed, tried, and executed by Parliament.

Thus the American Revolution had a precedent for organized popular action, but the Americans carried it to new heights in scope and spread. This in turn ensured that all revolutionary leaders were, from the first, representative of organized bodies of citizens and were empowered to act through legal and orderly processes of election or appointment. Leaders did not rise to power through usurpation because they could not. There never was a stage of anarchy in the American Revolution; power was transferred in an orderly fashion; often the same bodies previously authorized to govern under the British simply disbanded within that framework and reconstituted themselves within the new one on the basis of local and statewide political compacts. Delegates to the Continental Congresses were elected by those in similar bodies, and the congresses were never rump forums.

The American revolutionaries went to great lengths to develop or sharpen a theory of popular sovereignty through political compact to ensure the legitimacy of their actions.[7] But even more than theory, they maintained regular and proper procedures throughout the Revolution. Indeed, due process became a principal means of legitimization that was carried over into post-revolutionary American constitutionalism to maintain standards of right action by governments and legitimate channels for political and social change.

Stated in so few words, no doubt the picture seems prettier than it was in reality. There were, after all, Tories who were driven out of the country. Still, the American Revolution is the only one in which no one was executed for his political stance. While there might have been excesses in one locality or another, the overall picture presented here is the most accurate one.

The initial institutionalization of popular participation continued throughout the revolutionary period, from its pre-revolutionary stages beginning in 1763 through the writing and ratification of the 1787 Constitution and the organization of the new federal government in 1789. It occurred in every arena, from the most local to the national, and moved forward as the Revolution progressed and then had to be consolidated. Moreover, there were consistent and continuous relationships between the institutions of each arena that interacted with one another to empower each other to act. To an extraordinary degree what formally became the American political system after completion of the adoption of the Articles of Confederation in March 1781 was a political system from the first, from 1763 onward. Elsewhere I have discussed and documented some of the patterns of interaction leading up to the Declaration of Independence.[8] Historians of the period have done the same in far greater depth with regard to the adoption of the Articles of Confederation and the Constitution of 1787. In the past few years there has been a spate of excellent studies on the interplay between local and state bodies with regard to the formation of the individual states and the adoption of their revolutionary era constitutions.[9] In sum, American revolutionary leaders had to function not only within the context of ordered popular control, but within an institutionalized framework that protected the Revolution and did not allow counterrevolutionary leaders even to appear.

Contrast this with the other three great revolutions. The English civil war, which did quite well in popular participation and produced good leadership in the first stages of the conflict with the king and for the war itself, failed in its efforts at institutionalization almost from the first. Although the existing institutions, both governmental and religious, prevented any serious manifestations of anarchy, they were unable to work out either the additional institutional apparatus or the inter-institutional relationships necessary to create a new overarching framework. This led to the collapse of the revolutionary movement within half a generation of the outbreak of civil war and to the restoration of the old Stuart regime. Without proper institutionalization in the countrywide arena, national leadership became a matter of usurpation, however fine its motive, and ultimately a betrayal of the revolution.

The French Revolution began with a variety of efforts to institutionalize the popular uprising, but all failed until Napoleon usurped power and imposed an institutional structure on the country. In the interim, France went through a period of virtual anarchy for nearly ten years. There is a school of American historiography that is fond of referring to the middle years of the 1780s as years of anarchy in the United States, but in fact even the occasional rebellion of debtors was localized and short and did not lead to a breakdown of the institutions of government anywhere — a great contrast to the French situation, where successive governmental experiments had virtually no staying power during the country's period of anarchy. While institutions were formally established, the struggle for their control was so violent on every level that their existence became almost meaningless.

Napoleon, like Cromwell before him and Stalin after, usurped power from within, after being chosen for a revolutionary office in a legitimate way; but it was usurpation all the same, carried further than by either Cromwell or Stalin in the sense that Napoleon finally abolished the revolutionary regime and established an empire in its place. The Napoleonic regime also was brief; in the end the old regime was restored and the revolution substantially aborted until a lesser revolution took place half a generation later. Napoleon's great legacy to France was the internal institutional structure he imposed on the country in both the governmental and the religious spheres. Apparently the French were so shaken by anarchy that they preferred to preserve Napoleon's hierarchical structure rather than try any further efforts to diffuse power broadly among the citizenry.

The Russian Revolution was even more substantially dominated by a period of anarchy than was the French Revolution, albeit for a shorter time. The Russian revolutionaries had no state or local institutions to build upon or that they could even capture and turn to their own ends. In effect, they had to build the country from the bottom up, which they claimed to do through the various levels of *soviets* serving the different arenas within the Russian empire. But the extent of the Bolshevik revolution was such that these *soviets* themselves were ultimately repressed and replaced by Bolshevik institutions bearing the same name but without the popular base.

The Russian case is almost the reverse of the English; popular participation was anarchic, and institutionalization came at the end of the revolution in the most heavy-handed manner. The prior anarchy enabled a small but very determined elite, capable of being far more ruthless than Napoleon, not only to impose on the country their own will and a regime of their design, but essentially to exterminate or expel all possible threats to that regime. In Russia, the *ancien regime* did not come back; instead there was usurpation from within, with Stalin seizing power from his revolutionary colleagues. The result was not a reactionary but reformable regime, as in England, or a slower process of consolidation of the revolution's gains, as in France, but a totalitarian police state.

The English could gain from a situation in which there was proper popular participation but insufficient institutionalization even though it took a little longer to do so and the revolution itself failed. The French could survive in a situation in which there was neither proper popular participation nor proper institutionalization; it simply took them much longer to gain the results of the revolution. The worst result was in Russia, where there was a lack of proper popular participation but rapid institutionalization by a small elite to achieve the formal goals of the revolution, yet in such a way as to produce an utterly contrary actual result.

The Varieties of American Revolutionary Leadership and Their Common Denominator

The major figures of the American Revolution can be classified into four categories: the revolutionaries, exemplified by Samuel Adams and Patrick Henry; the statesmen, exemplified by Benjamin Franklin and Thomas Jefferson; the constitutional architects, exemplified by John Adams and James Madison; and the father of his country, George Washington — in a class by himself. While each category reflected the application of somewhat different talents to different tasks, what is most interesting for our purposes is the common denominator that kept them all within the American style of revolutionary leadership. Let us look at each in turn.

Revolutionaries

Revolutions are made by people, but people are made willing to initiate or join a revolution by a very select group of individuals capable of finding reasons why a revolution is necessary and then taking the action necessary to foment it. Two of the most prominent such figures in the American Revolution were Samuel Adams and Patrick Henry.

Samuel Adams (1722-1803), who lived to be eighty-one, was a professional politician throughout the revolutionary generation. He was the chief organizer of the opposition to the Stamp Act in Massachusetts and managed the Boston Tea Party. He is generally characterized as a "born revolutionary." He was a delegate to the Continental Congress throughout the active period of the war and signed the Declaration of Independence. At the same time he helped frame the Massachusetts Constitution and was the author of its bill of rights. Although he opposed the federal Constitution, he did not retire from state politics, being elected lieutenant governor in 1789 and becoming governor in 1794, an office he held for three years.

The contrast between Samuel Adams as a revolutionary and revolutionary ideologist and similar figures from other major modern revolutions is striking in every respect. He was convinced of the rightness of his cause and the need to promote it with all the political and propaganda skills at his disposal. Adams did so because he viewed the people as capable of knowing their own interests, not as chained by habit and custom so that they had to be forcibly led to the right path even against their will, as is the view of most other revolutionaries. A clever user of mass action, he rejected mobs and carefully staged even his "mob" scenes so that those involved in them would maintain their control. He utterly rejected the notion of concentrating all power in the hands of the revolutionary elites, vigorously supporting checks and balances, federalism, and constitutionally protected rights. Adams' thought linked that of the Old Whigs or Commonwealthmen with Massachusetts Puritanism and the ideas of the Enlightenment. He and his fellow revolutionaries were as much bound by the political compact, indeed by the moral obligations of covenant, as anybody else, no matter how just their cause.[10]

Patrick Henry (1736-1800) was somewhat more incongruous as a revolutionary. Although he, like Adams, came from a modest background, early in his career he became a wealthy trial lawyer.

He too was revolutionized by the Stamp Act and soon came to be considered the most dangerous demagogue in Virginia. Like Adams, he was uncompromising toward the British. He became the first governor of the Commonwealth of Virginia and served from 1776 to 1779. Subsequently he led the opposition to Virginia's ratification of the federal Constitution, for the same reasons as Adams, namely that it concentrated too much power in the hands of a distant government. Nevertheless, he also supported checks and balances, federalism, and individual rights as key elements in his political thought. Unlike Adams, Henry was not enamored of the details of politics, nor did he enjoy the routines of office. After 1794 he rejected a number of high offices offered to him, but in the year of his death he returned to the state legislature, this time as a Federalist, to support the new federal government against the Virginia Resolves. In his case too the combination is clear: a revolutionary in the American context meant one who stimulated popular action and then took on his responsibilities within the institutionalized framework of popular government.[11]

What is characteristic of both Adams and Henry is that both men not only encouraged popular action leading to revolution but made the transition to become major officeholders, in both cases governors of their commonwealths, during the revolutionary period and after the result was already institutionalized. They were very different from the kind of "professional revolutionaries" encountered in other modern revolutions (or in the American, in the person of Thomas Paine), whose talent was fomenting revolutions. Although both opposed the federal Constitution of 1787, they did so not because they were opposed to the institutionalization of the results of the Revolution, but because they were convinced that a different mode of institutionalization was more faithful to the revolutionary goals they espoused. Both men died peacefully after illustrious careers, honored by their fellows.

What was the fate of the revolutionaries who sparked the other great revolutions? The list of those who met violent deaths in the throes of revolution is not only long but comprehensive. Who among them died in bed? Indeed, who among them even made the transition to power for other than a brief revolutionary moment before being led off to the guillotine or the firing squad?

Statesmen

Benjamin Franklin (1706-1790) is the archetypal statesman of the American Revolution in myth and in reality. He played a prominent role in both the domestic and the foreign affairs of the fledgling republic and in the governance of his adopted Commonwealth of Pennsylvania. He was also the most famous American in the world at that time. As America's premier revolutionary diplomat, he too reflected a very different model than was to be found in other revolutions. In most of the other revolutions, professional diplomats with great personal ambition but no particular loyalty to any particular regime were co-opted by the revolutionary leadership to fulfill the tasks that Franklin took upon himself. As ideologists, the revolutionary elites were not prepared to trust anyone other than those entirely without ideas or convictions, mouthpieces who would serve any master. Franklin was anything but that.

Franklin's watchword was prudence, well-tuned to a revolution of sober expectations. One of his major domestic roles was to see to it that the Revolution's expectations remained sober. There too his skills were principally diplomatic, whether in the Continental Congress and the Constitutional Convention, in the drafting of Pennsylvania's first constitution, or in daily political affairs.

Franklin was another long-lived revolutionary. Already prominent and in his sixties at the beginning of the revolutionary generation, he spent the first third of that generation in London representing Pennsylvania and other colonies, and there he became convinced that revolution was inevitable. So he returned home to serve in the Continental Congress and as a member of the committee that drafted the Declaration of Independence, where he played his usual bridging role. He was sent back to Europe for the duration of the war and the peace negotiations, where he used his considerable diplomatic skills to become the architect of the crucial alliance with France. He returned in time to serve as a member of the Constitutional Convention of 1787, helping to negotiate the acceptance of its compromises. He died in 1790 at the age of eight-four, at once distinguished and beloved.[12]

If Franklin fairly reeked of prudence, Thomas Jefferson (1743-1826) presented himself as a radical. He was perhaps the most extremely ideological figure among the top leadership of the American Revolution, the only one to suggest semi-utopian programs for restructuring society. The very use of the term sounds out of place in comparison with other revolutions — that too tells us something about the state of the American experience. Nevertheless, the two men had much in common besides their commitment to the cause of American liberty and the fact that they lived to almost the same age and died in pleasant surroundings after illustrious careers. Franklin was the prudent man who was a radical in the pursuit of liberty. Jefferson was the radical who was prudent in the pursuit of a stable republic. In today's terms, somewhat anachronistically, we can refer to both as "liberals." Both were Deists whose early training was within the framework of Calvinism or Reformed Protestantism — Franklin was a descendant of Massachusetts Puritans and Jefferson a descendant of Scots from Ulster. To use another anachronism, both were intellectuals in public affairs.

Jefferson entered political life in 1769, while the revolutionary generation was still in its formative stage, and stayed active politically until the end of his presidency forty years later. He rose to national prominence in 1774 on the very eve of the Revolution and was sent to the Continental Congress the next year, where, as we all know, he was the principal author of the Declaration of Independence. He returned to Virginia almost immediately thereafter to participate in the restructuring of his native commonwealth along republican lines, serving in the state legislature and then as governor from 1779 to 1781. He left the governorship only because of his wife's illness and death.

Jefferson returned to the Confederation Congress two years later and played a major role in shaping the legislative landmarks of the confederation era, from the plan for decimal coinage through the Northwest Ordinance of 1784. He spent the five years from 1784 to 1789 representing the United States in France and hence missed the Constitutional Convention. This experience gave him a firsthand view of prerevolutionary France and the beginnings of the French Revolution.

Jefferson came back to the United States to serve as the first secretary of state in Washington's cabinet, then resigned when Washington opted for Hamiltonian policies. In cooperation with James Madison, he founded the Democratic Republican party, today, the Democratic party, the longest-lived popular political party in the world. He became his party's candidate for the presidency against John Adams in 1796. Although he lost to Adams, under the original terms of the federal Constitution he became vice-president. Since he was in the opposition, he spent little time in Washington, working instead to organize the party for the 1800 elections that brought him to the presidency, in which he served two terms, retiring in 1809 to Monticello. He remained there as an elder statesman until his death on July 4, 1826, the fiftieth anniversary of the Declaration of Independence.[13]

Significantly, Jefferson was highly disposed to support the French Revolution, not only in its earlier stages but through the 1790s. Indeed, he was accused by the Federalists of being a Jacobin, and he did have strong sympathies in that direction, at least intellectually and from a distance. Like Franklin, he liked France, even if he was appalled by the poverty in French cities and the reactionary ways of the *ancien regime*. As an intellectual, he was attracted to French culture. His sympathies for the French Revolution, however, were manifested in most un-Jacobin ways. Thus his opposition to the Federalist administration of John Adams with regard to the undeclared sea war with France was expressed through the Virginia Resolves, which claimed that states could prevent the enforcement of federal laws they deemed unconstitutional, a position that went against the Jacobin spirit in every respect. Moreover, he was a most un-Jacobin president; the biggest "usurpation" he undertook was the Louisiana Purchase, for which he himself wanted to obtain a constitutional amendment. Fortunately his sagacity won the day, and he decided that it was too good a bargain to pass up, so he exercised the executive powers of his office to complete the purchase.

There was indeed a moment when the Federalists assumed that his election to the presidency meant a Jacobin takeover. Jefferson's victory was labeled by his supporters "the revolution of 1800." Discussion was rife in the country suggesting that the transfer of administration from the Federalist party to the Democratic Republicans would bring a Jacobin-style revolution in its train. Jefferson made deliberate efforts to disabuse people of any such notions, just as Washington had earlier rejected suggestions that he lead a military coup. In his first inaugural address he summarized his position, stating, "We are all Federalists, we are all Republicans." Thus Jefferson, supposedly the arch-revolutionary, first inaugurated the party system, which institutionalized ways to achieve change without revolution, and then presided over the transition of federal administrations from party to party with no disruption of the processes of government — two of the crucial inventions of modern democracy.

17

As was noted above, none of the other three revolutions came close to succeeding in either regard. The English civil war offered a dynastic transition that failed because of the inappropriateness of Cromwell's son and heir, Richard, and the overall rejection of the Cromwellian dictatorship. The French Revolution went from one bloody change of regime to another. It is to Napoleon's credit that once he seized power, he stopped the purges; but still, seizing power is not orderly succession, nor was the counterrevolution of the Bourbons who came after him, or the subsequent revolutions of 1830 and 1848, or the Paris Commune of 1870. It was not until the establishment of the Third Republic that peaceful transition from government to government became a reality in France, and even De Gaulle staged a kind of palace revolution 170 years later to finally bring the French Revolution to completion (or so it seems at this point). Transition in the Soviet regime started bloody, led to dictatorship, continued bloody, and now seems to be institutionalized in a less bloody but utterly undemocratic way.

Jefferson's own sense of his greatest accomplishments is reflected in the epitaph he chose for himself: "Author of the Declaration of Independence, of the Statute of Virginia for Religious Freedom, and Father of the University of Virginia." He was indeed a revolutionary, but a sober one, in the American mold, who gloried in the proclamation of human liberty and equality, the constitutionalization of individual rights, and the founding of a public university.

Constitutional Architects

For the two exemplary leaders in this category, I have chosen John Adams, the author of the Massachusetts Constitution — the model for state constitutional design — and James Madison, the principal author and expositor of the United States Constitution. John Adams (1735-1826) lived to be ninety-one, dying in bed on the same day as Jefferson, the fiftieth anniversary of the Declaration of Independence, equally venerated. He entered politics during the struggle over the Stamp Act and remained active until the end of his presidential term in 1801. He was a member of the Continental Congress from 1774 to 1778 and was one of the architects of the intersectional compromise that brought George Washington to the command of the Continental Army. With Jefferson and

Franklin, he served on the committee to draft the Declaration of Independence and led the debate on its adoption.

Adams served in three capacities as an American diplomat: as commissioner to France, as a member of the commission that negotiated the peace treaty with Great Britain, and as the first envoy to that country. In 1779/80 he was the principal author of the Massachusetts Constitution, his most enduring constitutional work. He was the country's first vice-president, serving under George Washington for both terms and then being elevated to the presidency in his own right. He served only one term, being defeated by Jefferson and the Democratic Republicans. Though he was strongly anti-Jacobin, his prudent behavior as president kept the United States from declaring war on France as most of his Federalist colleagues wished. He managed to confine hostilities to an undeclared sea war until differences between the two countries could be negotiated away.[14]

Adams' great constitutional monument, the Massachusetts Constitution, combines within it the principal dimensions of American constitutionalism — the constitution as political covenant and compact, a constitutionalized declaration of rights, and a frame of government resting upon checks and balances and separation of powers, all within a solidly republican framework. It was the first constitution to be put directly to the people for approval. That it remains the constitution of that commonwealth over two hundred years later, with only the most minimal changes, is a reflection of its enduring value.[15]

James Madison (1751-1836) can be said to have been the first political scientist to have served the American people and, in a certain sense, the founder of American political science. He lived to be eighty-five. Graduating from Princeton on the eve of the Revolution, his first major political role was participation in the drafting of the Virginia Constitution in 1776. He served in the Confederation Congress from 1780 to 1783, where he advocated strengthening the powers of the federal government. He was the author of the Virginia Plan presented to the federal Constitutional Convention in 1787, and his leadership in the convention led to his being acknowledged as the "father of the Constitution." Once the convention ended, he helped lead the battle for ratification and was the principal author of *The Federalist*. However, he accepted the popular demand for the inclusion of a bill of rights in the federal Constitution as the price of ratification and submitted the principal draft for it when the First Congress convened.

Madison served in Congress from 1789 through 1797. With Jefferson, he founded the Democratic Republican party that won the "revolution of 1800," thereby introducing the principle of orderly change in control of the federal government. He was secretary of state during both terms of Jefferson's presidency and with Albert Gallatin, the secretary of the treasury, was part of the triumvirate that headed the executive branch in those years.

Madison succeeded to the presidency after Jefferson and served two terms. Like Adams, he was not a particularly successful president, being better at designing constitutions that at operating them. Also like Adams, he was a true federalist, concerned with a properly governed nation and properly governed states, and with a proper relationship between them. Thus, despite his strong nationalist tendencies, he could join with Jefferson in authoring the Virginia and Kentucky Resolves to interpose state law against federal legislation on constitutional grounds.

Unlike Samuel Adams and Patrick Henry, who saw the states as the organic polities and the confederation as a perpetual league of quite limited powers, John Adams and James Madison saw the system as an integral whole having a number of working parts — federal and state, executive, legislative, and judicial. In that sense Madison was the first to formulate the idea of the United States as a political system, complex and intricate, but a single whole nonetheless. Subsequent students of Madison's thought who are less attuned to the theory of federalism than he have assumed that he was either a frustrated centralizer or else inconsistent, since he sometimes supported strengthening the powers of the federal government and sometimes those of the states. What they have failed to grasp is that he wanted to do both, as appropriate.[16]

It was Madison's intricate institutional design, as modified by other prudent revolutionaries of the Constitutional Convention, that provided a basis for consolidating the gains of the American Revolution and ensuring what has been, with one exception (the Civil War), an orderly yet dynamic government of a continental nation for nearly two hundred years. It is significant that we can point to no figures similar to Adams and Madison in any of the other three revolutions. None had constitutional architects, since none were even constitutionalized in the same way, if at all.

Father of His Country

If James Madison was the father of the constitution, George Washington (1732-1799) was clearly the father of his country. Although his life was shorter than that of the others discussed here, he too died peacefully in bed — in fact, soon after he had accepted a commission as lieutenant general (then the senior rank) in the United States Army to prepare it for the incipient struggle with France. Washington's great skill was to be the exemplary leader who by moral example and prudent action could both lift the spirits of those he was leading and guide them to right action. He knew how to make the most of scarce resources and hence did not build any aspect of the Revolution on exploitation of the public he was serving. His compatriots and subsequent historians have agreed that his outstanding talent was the force, even majesty, of his personality. That, coupled with his moral commitment to a republican revolution, made him what he was.

After an early military career, Washington entered politics as part of his responsibilities as a country squire. He served in Virginia's House of Burgesses from 1759 to 1774, throughout the whole period of the buildup toward revolution. There he was one of the first to resist the British policy designed to impose England's authority on the colonies and thus became an early leader of the revolutionary party. Sent as a delegate to the Continental Congress in 1774, he hoped and subtly campaigned for command of the revolutionary armies after the battle of Lexington, and he was chosen commander-in-chief of the Continental forces on June 15, 1775.

From the time he assumed command on July 3 of that year until he relinquished it in December 1783, he was the preeminent soldier of the American Revolution. Often criticized for lack of military aggressiveness, he understood the nature of the campaign he was obliged to wage, given his scarce resources and the strength of his British opponents. He waged that campaign brilliantly, wearing down the British until French reinforcements helped him defeat them in the decisive battle of Yorktown. Washington comes down to us as a grand commander, when in fact he fought a semi-guerrilla war, maintaining organized formations but after the first year rarely engaging the British in head-on combat. Between Monmouth in June 1778 and Yorktown in September 1781, he did not fight a single full-scale battle. Rather, he directed strategy for campaigns in other fields that were increasingly of a guerrilla character. Given the military tactics of the time, his thrusting and parrying were inventive and extraordinarily successful departures from the accepted modes.

It was natural for Washington to be chosen to preside at the federal Constitutional Convention. There the same personal qualities and skills that enabled him to lead the revolutionary army so successfully served him in good stead and made him the crucial figure in bringing together the different individuals with their positions so that a document emerged that was both acceptable and inspired. As in his role as commander, it was not the brilliance of his ideas but his sense of timing, his ability to conciliate people of strong views, and his sheer presence that made the difference.[17]

Unanimously elected first president of the United States, Washington proceeded to preside over the translation of the U.S. Constitution into a working government. As Leonard D. White has shown in his study *The Federalists,* in some respects this was his most brilliant achievement.[18] He gave meaning to the concept of chief magistrate as head of the executive branch of government, establishing in the process precedents that have endured to this day in a whole range of fields.

What is extraordinary about Washington is the degree to which he set the tone for the new United States of America in so many fields, from religious freedom to foreign affairs, from civil-military relations to the presidential management of the cabinet. Not the least of his contributions was teaching us and his successors what generals and presidents should not do as well as what they should. In essence, he embodied and helped shape the political culture of the United States as well as its institutions. That is what puts him in a class by himself. Canonized by the generations immediately after his own, he was then treated to a major debunking when later historians discovered that he was indeed human. Now that we have survived his humanization and indeed benefited from it, his true greatness is becoming more apparent on every level. He was indeed of the family of the lion and the tribe of the eagle.

The other great revolutions had figures of the same family and tribe but whose behavior and contributions were very different. Perhaps the most inspiring of them was Cromwell, who had many of the positive characteristics of Washington but neither his moderation nor his self-restraint. In the French Revolution, Robespierre was more like Samuel Adams gone mad, and Napoleon was Washington in reverse. In certain technical respects they had parallel careers. Both rose through the army; both presided over efforts to institutionalize the revolution, and both played major roles in the administrative organization of a new government. But those comparisons serve only to point up the differences between the two men rather than their similarities. Washington was the quintessential republican, conciliating, working within the public framework of shared powers and authority, great because he could get men to work together, not because he could impose his will by gaining control of the top of the pyramid. Napoleon was the quintessential modern dictator, inspiring to his followers and his people, but in a coercive way and only from the top.

What is one to say about the Russian Revolution? There the tasks of Washington were shared by Lenin, Trotsky, and Stalin. The first, ruthless in his ideological commitment, functioned in ways diametrically opposed to the American. The second was a commander of armies like Washington but remained an outsider otherwise. And the third consolidated like Washington but was his very antithesis in moral qualities and personal self-abnegation.

What is common to all the Americans (and many others who could have been mentioned) is that they played several roles. Though their classification as models here has not been arbitrary, it is not as though Jefferson were not a constitutional architect, John Adams not a revolutionary, Madison not a statesman, and so forth. Indeed, what is characteristic of them all is that all served in both the executive and the legislative branches of the government of their respective states or the United States or both, and in no case did they ever confuse the responsibilities of one branch with those of the other. In general it can be said that neither did they confuse the responsibilities of the state and federal governments, though there the issue is less clear-cut. In some respects this is the best indicator of the special quality of American revolutionary leaders — their sense of what was appropriate in the institutional context as well as what was necessary to achieve the revolutionary goal.

The Problem Resolved: A Different Model of Revolutionary Leadership

I have already suggested that it is the combination of proper modes of popular involvement, political institutionalization, and leaders committed to prudence that produced the different model of leadership characteristic of the American Revolution. Eric Hoffer summed up the matter: "Precisely a society that can get along without leaders is the one that's producing leaders." It is fitting to sum up by retelling Hoffer's story of his experience during the Great Depression with a work gang in the San Bernardino Mountains.[19]

During the Depression, a construction company had to build a road in the San Bernardino Mountains, and the man who was in charge, instead of calling up...an employment agency...sent out two trucks to skid row....Anybody who could climb up on that truck was hired, even if you had only one leg....They...drove us out to the San Bernardino Mountains, and...dumped us on the side of the hill. The company had only one man on the job, and he didn't even open his mouth. We found there bundles of equipment and supplies and then we started to sort ourselves out.

...it's the most glorious experience I ever had. We had so many carpenters, so many blacksmiths, so many cooks, so many foremen, so many men who could drive a bulldozer, handle a jackhammer....We put up the tents, put up the cook's shack, the toilet, the shower bath, cooked supper.

Next morning, we went out and started to build a road. If we had to write the Constitution, there would have been somebody there who knew all the "whereases" and the "wherefores." And we could...have built America. We were just a shovelful of slime scooped off the pavement of skid row, yet we could have built America on the side of the hill in the San Bernardino Mountains. Now you show me people anywhere in the world with such diffuse competence. It's fantastic. In other words, when I talk about Americans being a skilled people, I don't mean only technical skills, I mean social and political skills.

The vigor of a society should be gauged by its ability to get along without outstanding leaders. When I said that at the University of Stanford, all the young intellectuals...ran after me...and said, "Mr. Hoffer, the vigor of society should be gauged by its ability to produce great leaders." And then I stood there and I said, "Brother, this is just what happened. Precisely a society that can get along without leaders is the one that's producing leaders."

Hoffer may have exaggerated somewhat, especially since he spoke only of the first dimension: popular involvement. The founding fathers understood that with it there had to be political institutionalization as well. They devoted themselves as much to that end as to making the Revolution in the first place.

One final note: it remained for Abraham Lincoln to sense and consider the one problem that transcends both the character of popular involvement and the nature of the political institutions. Let us return to his address before the Young Men's Lyceum:

> In the great journal of things happening under the sun, we, the American People,...find ourselves in the peaceful possession, of the fairest portion of the earth, as regards extent of territory, fertility of soil, and salubrity of climate. We find ourselves under the government of a system of political institutions, conducing more essentially to the ends of civil and religious liberty, than any of which the history of former times tells us. We, when mounting the stage of existence, found ourselves the legal inheritors of these fundamental blessings. We toiled not in the acquirement or establishment of them — they are a legacy bequeathed us, by a *once* hardy, brave, and patriotic, but *now* lamented and departed race of ancestors. Theirs was the task (and nobly they performed it) to possess themselves, and through themselves, us, of this goodly land; and to uprear upon its hills and its valleys, a political edifice of liberty and equal rights; 'tis ours only, to transmit these, the former, unprofaned by the foot of an invader; the latter, undecayed by the lapse of time, and untorn by usurpation — to the latest generation that fate shall permit the world to know. This task of gratitude to our fathers, justice to ourselves, duty to posterity, and love for our species in general, all imperatively require us faithfully to perform.

Lincoln continues by raising the question:

> At what point then is the approach of danger to be expected? I answer, if it ever reach us, it must spring up amongst us. It cannot come from abroad. If destruction be our lot, we must ourselves be its author and finisher. As a nation of freemen, we must live through all time, or die by suicide.

Lincoln suggests that internal disorder is the only possible way to bring down the American polity, because sooner or later internal disorder will bring down the strongest bulwark of any Government, and particularly of those constituted like ours, may effectually be broken down and destroyed — I mean the attachment of the People....At such a time and under such circumstances, men of sufficient talent and ambition will not be wanting to seize the opportunity, strike the blow, and overturn that fair fabric, which for the last half century, has been the fondest hope of the lovers of freedom throughout the world.

Lincoln in his address focused on the question of the mob's taking the law into its own hands — in other words, improper popular involvement. His response to that was to endorse the maintenance of the political institutions bequeathed the Americans by the founders:

Let every American, every lover of liberty, every well wisher to his posterity, swear by the blood of the Revolution, never to violate in the last particular, the laws of the country; and never to tolerate their violation by others. As the patriots of seventy-six did to the support of the Declaration of Independence, so to the support of the Constitutions and Laws, let every American pledge his life, his property, and his sacred honor — let everyman remember that to violate the law is to trample on the blood of his father, and to tear the character of his own and his children's liberty. Let reverence for the laws be breathed by every American mother to the lisping babe that prattles on her lap — let it be taught in schools, in seminaries, and in colleges; — let it be written in Primers, spelling books, and Almanacs; — let it be preached from the pulpit, proclaimed in legislative halls, and enforced in courts of justice. And, in short, let it become the *political religion* of the nation.

But Lincoln knew that proper popular involvement and institutionalization are not enough, for they will not necessarily control those who belong to the family of the lion or the tribe of the eagle. His answer is perhaps less than fully satisfying, returning as he does to a reliance on a proper political religion. We are left to rely upon that, to which we can add the fostering of a proper political culture of the kind that animated George Washington and his compatriots.

Notes

1. The full story of Washington's gesture is told in John C. Fitzpatrick, ed. *The Writings of George Washington* (Washington, D.C.: Government Printing Office, 1931-44), 26:222-229.

2. Martin Diamond, *A Revolution of Sober Expectations* (Washington, D.C.: American Enterprise Institute, 1976).

3. See Peter Shaw, *The Character of John Adams* (Chapel Hill: University of North Carolina Press, 1976).

4. *The Federalist*, No. 51.

5. As cited in Abraham Lincoln, *Works* (New Brunswick, N.J.: Rutgers University Press, 1953), 1:108-115.

6. On American revolutionary mobs, see Moshe Hazani, "Samuel Adams and Saint-Just: Contrasting Examples of Professional Revolutionaries," in this volume.

7. Neil Riemer, *The Democratic Experiment: American Political Theory*, vol. I (Princeton: Van Nostrand, 1967); Clinton Rossiter, *Seed Time of the Republic: The Origin of the American Tradition of Political Liberty* (New York: Harcourt, Brace, 1953).

8. Daniel J. Elazar, "The States and the Congress Move toward Independence, 1775-1776," *Publius* 6, No. 1 (Winter 1976): 135-143 (see Appendix A).

9. Willi Paul Adams, *The First American Constitutions: Republican Ideology and the Making of the State Constitutions in the Revolutionary Era* (Chapel Hill: University of North Carolina Press, 1980); Donald S. Lutz, *Popular Consent and Popular Control: Whig Political Theory in the Early State Constitutions* (Baton Rouge: Louisiana State University Press, 1980); Ronald M. Peters, Jr., *The Massachusetts Constitution of 1780: A Social Compact* (Amherst: University of Massachusetts Press, 1978).

10. Hazani, "Samuel Adams and Saint-Just."

11. Robert D. Meade, *Patrick Henry*, 2 vols. (Philadelphia: Lippincott, 1957-59).

12. Carl Becker, *Benjamin Franklin* (Ithaca, N.Y.: Cornell University Press, 1946); Paul W. Conner, *Poor Richards Politicks: Benjamin Franklin and His New American Order* (New York: Greenwood, 1980).

13. Dumas Malone, *Jefferson in His Times*, 6 vols. (Boston: Little, Brown, 1948-82); idem, *Thomas Jefferson as Political Leader* (New York: Greenwood, 1979).

14. Catherine D. Bowen, *John Adams and the American Revolution* (Boston: Little, Brown, 1950); Page Smith, *John Adams*, 2 vols. (Garden City, N.Y.: Doubleday, 1962).

15. Peters, *Massachusetts Constitution of 1780.*

16. Irving Brant, *James Madison*, 6 vols. (Indianapolis: Bobbs-Merrill, 1941-61); Marvin Meyers, *The Mind of the Founder* (Hanover and London: Brandeis University Press and University Press of New England, 1981).

17. Forrest Macdonald, E *Pluribus Unum: The Formation of the American Republic, 1776-1790* (New York: Houghton Mifflin, 1965); James T. Flexner, *George Washington*, 3 vols. (Boston: Little, Brown, 1968-72).

18. Leonard D. White, *The Federalists: A Study in Administrative History* (New York: Greenwood, 1978); Douglass Southhall Freeman, *George Washington*, 7 vols. (New York: Scribner's, 1948-57).

19. Eric Hoffer in an interview with Eric Sevareid on CBS television (September 19, 1967).

POWER GAINED BY SURRENDER

Garry Wills

He was a virtuoso of resignation. He perfected the art of getting power by giving it away. He tried it first, unsuccessfully, as a young colonel of militia — but then only as a gesture from hurt pride. He was still learning that mere power to refuse is real, but limited. The power would later be refined, as would the gesture — when he learned the creative power of surrender.

Unlike other officers in the Revolution, he did not resign or threaten to resign when baffled of honor or advantage. He did not want to cheapen the currency; he would not anticipate his promised abdication at war's end — the surrender, not only of his commission, but of all future public office. His whole service was urged forward under the archway of two pledges — to receive no pay, and to retire from public life when independence was won. He was choreographing his departure with great care. It was an act of pedagogical theater; and the world applauded.

But adulation of the teacher displaced — for several years, at least — a willingness to learn from him. The disappointment he later expressed is the measure of his surrender's large ambition: he actually thought he could found a stronger government upon his own refusal to take part in it. Pressed to rejoin the struggle for a stronger union in 1787, he wrote to John Jay that he had retired from that "sea of troubles":

> Nor could it be expected, that my sentiments and opinion would have much weight on the minds of my Countrymen; they have been neglected, tho' given as a last legacy in the most solemn manner (GW 27.503).

Taken by itself, this passage may sound merely petulant — equivalent to: "I gave them their chance, and they would not listen; so now we're quits." Even so devout an admirer of Washington as Douglas Southall Freeman was critical of the way he hung back, in 1787, when asked to lend his crucial support and presence to the drafting convention in Philadelphia. But Freeman underestimated Washington's heavy emotional investment in the symbol of his resignation. To take up any public office would not simply be a breaking of his promise, a cheapening of his word; it would undermine the implicit argument he was making, all along, for a closer federal union — that such a union must not depend on the aggrandizement of one man, which would both make union less likely, and make it less worth having. His acts said implicitly what he expressed only rarely — that increase of power in the law could be argued for, morally, only by one who would not benefit by that increase. After his resignation he wrote to Governor Benjamin Harrison, in their continuing disagreement over Virginia's blocking of the impost, that if he was arguing for unjust powers, he would be their victim and not their beneficiary:

> For my own part, altho' I am returned to, and am now mingled with the class of private citizens, and like them must suffer all the evils of a Tyranny, or of too great an extension of federal powers, I have no fears arising from this source...(GW 27.306).

His instinct in this matter was profoundly right. Everything else he was able to achieve, even after apparent violation of his pledge, rested on the confidence inspired by his great resignation. This gave birth to the Cincinnatus legend that haloed him ever after — made King George himself, in Benjamin West's version, call Washington the greatest man alive. John Trumbull wrote his brother from England, as the news of his resignation was circulating, that it "excites the astonishment and admiration of this part of the world. 'Tis a Conduct so novel, so inconceivable to People, who, far from giving up powers they possess, are willing to convulse the Empire to acquire more" (May 10, 1784, Connecticut Historical Society). The British, who lost to him, vied with Americans in honoring Washington's act. And in the eulogies delivered at his death, no other feat was so frequently celebrated — not military victory, not constitutional establishment, not even the resignation of the presidency. Washington's contribution to the country, whatever it was to be, depended on the preservation of that symbolic moment's meaning. He resisted the abandonment of his pledge in 1787 for the same reason that he had resisted earlier attempts to involve him in state or federal office, and from the same instinct that made him seek, as soon as he had presidential power, the earliest opportunity for divesting himself of it. He planned at first to retire after setting up the government. Then he prepared his farewell address at the end of one term — to be persuaded only by the unanimous voice of his counsellors that he must stay.

Finally he arranged another didactic departure from office, one that would strengthen his policies while returning him to private station.

The requests for his participation in the Philadelphia convention came just at a time when he had resigned another office, that of president of the Society of the Cincinnati. That resignation, like his resistance to join the convention, grew in part from disappointment that his advice had not been heeded. But with the Society he was arguing for fewer institutional powers rather than more. He had moved earlier that the hereditary feature be removed from membership in the Cincinnati. Stronger power in the private organization was perceived as a threat to governmental union. His norm for the Society was the same as for himself — power to the union must grow from a pledge that private individuals would not abuse it (or, in his case, not even use it).

In fact, a contributing reason for his reluctance to go to Philadelphia in the summer of 1787 was the fact that the Cincinnati were holding their second meeting there, and he had already pleaded poor health to avoid attending. When he was at last persuaded to go, he made his presidency of the convention a ceremonial one; his only intervention, when debate had ended, was a typical concession to the side that had lost (on the ratio of representatives to the electorate). The Constitution would be stronger if the majority gave in as much as possible to the minority. Power is advanced by key retreats and personal deferrings. As president he would be accused of weakness because of his skill in holding together antithetical elements of his administration. Julian Boyd's posthumous most recent volume of Jefferson's papers offers a stunning example of the way Washington got his way by refusing to take credit for doing so (in this case, credit for the essential features in L'Enfant's plan for the federal city).

Resignation did not mean, for Washington, mere abandonment of a position, simply walking away from it. Gandhi opposed the translation of his Satyagraha as "passive resistance." It was, rather, a very active form of advocacy, but on lines conventional seekers of power find hard to understand. In the same way, Washington meant to use his resignations to advance his purpose. This can be seen in the careful preparation of his circular letter to the governors urging, in the summer of 1783, a closer union. The popular imagination fixed on the moment of surrender in Annapolis. But for Washington, what he did in December was just meant to lend urgency to what he had said in June.

What gave Washington his unorthodox view of power, what Trumbull called an ambition "inconceivable to the People"? The answer is of necessity mysterious, as genius always is. Washington was a political genius. He was not a learned man; but that has been true of other political geniuses, from Cromwell to Napoleon; and Washington differs from them only in having a surer grasp on the realities of power.

Yet some factors in his achievement seem relatively explicable. He had a great sense of theater, shown over and over, at Newburgh, at John Adams's inauguration (where he resisted Jefferson's attempt to make him precede the newly elected vice president), in the scene at Fraunces Tavern, in handsome gestures like the gift of his prize horse to Chastellux when that ally expressed admiration for it. His sense of timing and effect rested on two things — a shrewd estimate of others, and an unflinching knowledge of himself. He used power well because he feared its effects on him. He had his youthful tantrums of wounded pride, but a deeper pride made him ashamed of those, and on guard against them. He was determined not to be giddied or blinded by power, to hold it off some distance as a way of keeping his prized equilibrium. Nothing is more revealing of his attitude than his response to the semi-deification he received in the parade of triumph taking him north to the presidency. He wrote on the night of his arrival in Manhattan:

> The display of boats which attended and joined us on this occasion, some with vocal and some with instrumental music on board; the decorations of the ships, the roar of cannon, and the loud acclamations of the people which rent the skies, as I passed along the wharves, filled my mind with sensations as painful (considering the reverse of this scene, which may be the case after all my labors to do good), as they are pleasing (Diaries 5.447).

Washington would have agreed with Diderot's doctrine of theater in his day, that the actor who would control the emotions of others must first control his own.

Washington's sense of his audience did not extend merely to individuals or to American groups. He had a vision of the role the American people as a whole should play on the world's stage. The constant refrain of his writings is the need to establish "a national Character" in foreign eyes. His policy of non-alignment was strengthened by a determination not to be swallowed up by either of the "superpowers" of his day, to establish a sense of national identity. This led him, as Edmund Morgan has observed, to avoid "entanglement" with France even while taking the wartime help it offered. That theme of the Farewell Address (Paltsits 142) was at the very center of his vision. As he wrote to Patrick Henry: "I want an American character, that the powers of Europe may be convinced we act for *ourselves* and not for *others*" (GW 34.335). Or to Timothy Pickering: We "must never forget that we are Americans; the remembrances of which will convince us we ought not to be French or English" (GW 35.154). His argument for union was that, taken separately, the parts of America would drift under the influence of the contiguous great powers (English to the north, French or Spanish to the south). We must remember that he had the unusual opportunity, for any "third world" leader in his day, of serving with the military caste of both superpowers — with Braddock and others in the French and Indian War, with Rochambeau, De Grasse and others in the Revolution. He was an intense observer of men and manners — of *their* sense of theater — and he knew what he did *not* want his country to become. Dearly as he loved Lafayette and Chastellux, he wanted them to join America's effort, not for America to join them.

But when all has been granted to Washington's own gifts, which must be measured by their extraordinary effect on contemporaries, the great actor must know his audience. Without a popular willingness to accept his kind of greatness, there would have been no achievements. This does not mean that Washington knew only what would "play." The great political actor knows what people can be *brought* to accept. He can shame others above themselves, as Washington did at Newburgh. Still, no matter how he may affect an audience, the actor cannot *create* it. He finds it there; and much of Washington's achievement belongs to those who followed him. In that sense, Washington's views of power were not so unorthodox for his time. It was an age responsive to the very kind of performance Washington was equipped to give it. The proof of this is the response he elicited all over Europe, wherever men dreamed of the revived classical republic. He was the embodiment of the entire period's ideals. And those ideals, the way he played to them, gave him an advantage in coping with three of the thorniest problems of political leadership, those I shall call for convenience of reference *charisma, power*, and *myth*.

Charisma. In a time of crumbling, abandoned, or overthrown institutions, the "graced" leader must rally social energies to his person. That seems unavoidable, no matter how revolutionary doctrine may deplore elitism or the cult of personality. The most persistently personal symbols have emerged from revolutions that most appealed to mere historical process, to impersonal economic forces — witness the long reign of Stalin's icon, or Mao's. Even when there is a blurred *succession* of charismatic leaders — Lafayette, Mirabeau, Marat, Danton, Robespierre, etc. — they seem, so long as revolutionary spasms continue, to culminate in one giant image: Napoleon. Magic flits from one to the other; or is held by one man even after the crisis for which it was needed has passed; or is extended in drastically reduced form to heirs seen as unworthy. Reinhard Bendix notes the persistence of this problem in modern revolutions, those led by Nkrumah, Sihanouk, Kim, or Mao:

> The new nations provide a setting of rapid change in which charismatic leaders may achieve new forms of political integration. In his analysis of *Ghana in Transition*, David Apter has suggested that charismatic leadership helps to make way for the creation of secular legal institutions in a nation-state. He notes, however, that charismatic leadership is not easily reconciled with secular systems of authority. Perhaps a charismatic leader like Nkrumah can transfer some of the loyalty traditionally accorded to tribal chiefs to his agents and symbols of a secular government — as long as he is the leader. But the problem is: How can the loyalties of a personal following be transferred to the institutions of government? (In *Max Weber*, ed. Dennis Wrong, 1970).

Charismatic leadership seems to offer insoluble problems of legitimate succession. To the extent that it is personal, it cannot be passed on. To the extent that it is at odds with institutional rule, it disrupts all other forms of authority by assertion of its own. How did Washington escape these traps?

The ideology of his day gave him a framework within which to operate, a set of expectations both he and the nation could live up to. The classical ideal had a vision of emergency powers given only for one object, and only for the duration of a crisis. These were not extralegal powers, but extraordinary powers within the law, as Machiavelli insisted (*Discourses* 1.34). I am talking about the office of dictator. That office, like other Roman symbols (the fasces), did not have the evil resonances they have acquired since. Admittedly, Caesar had brought the office of dictator into question, but only because he violated the terms of that office. Some of the Romans most admired in the eighteenth century had been dictators, including the very two Washington was most often linked to, Cincinnatus and Fabius. Caesar held one dictatorship on legal terms (for eleven days), one on quasi-legal terms (for the fixed term of a year); but he illegally extended his third and fourth ones (the last one for life). Yet dictatorship in the pure republic meant doing what Cincinnatus had — surrendering power at once when the crisis passed. It is this legal dictatorship that Machiavelli praises.

> Three things, then, worked together: the dictatorship lasted but a short time; the dictator's power was limited [to a specific object — e.g., winning a war]; the Roman people was not corrupt. These conditions made it impossible for the dictator to go beyond bounds...(Gilbert 1.268).

The term had been sufficiently tainted by Caesar to make people chary of using it in the eighteenth century — even Napoleon was given the substance of the office under the title of "First Consul." But the ideal was still present, and it was an ideal exactly the reverse of "dictatorship" in the modern sense. We think of a dictator as assuming, by any means, all the powers of state, for so long as he can (by any means) hold onto them. The Roman concept was of a continuing republican government that delegated powers for a specific purpose and a limited time. Clearly that was the understanding by which Washington was granted extraordinary powers to recruit and manage the army. The Roman basis of the grant was implied by Congress in making it:

> Happy it is for this country that the General of their forces can be entrusted with the most unlimited power, and neither personal security, liberty or property be in the least endangered thereby (Freeman 4.338).

This charismatic role acquired its potency precisely from its presumed *sacrificial* aspect, built into the original grant. The successful dictator will not profit personally from his success. That is part of his glamour, his "grace."

Power. Washington was also helped in the performance of his task by a concept of power that was itself gaining power in his day. The idea that legitimacy of rule derived from consent of the ruled was, by then, universally accepted. But the empirical social sciences making their impact by the middle of the eighteenth century said that, in *fact*, all power comes from a suasive hold on the popular imagination. This was the power of "opinion" described in Madison's *Federalist* No. 49. It had its most influential exposition in Hume's essays. In "Whether the British Government inclines more to Absolute Monarchy, or to a Republic," we read:

> It may further be said, that, though men be much governed by interests; yet even interest itself, and all human affairs, are entirely governed by their opinion (Green-Grose 1.125).

Interest may rule, but the man who can affect the *conception* of interest rules that ruling concept. In practical terms this means getting people to think it *profits* them to obey, or they *should* obey, or both. As Hume says in "Of the First Principles of Government," "It is, therefore, on opinion only that government is founded" (*ibid.* 110) — opinion either "of right" or "of interest." So, at Newburgh, Washington had to persuade his officers that they ought to submit to Congress, and that if they did so they would strengthen his hand in bargaining for what was coming to them. He must teach them what he had learned, that one can prevail by tactical surrender.

Of itself, the idea that power is rooted in opinion might lead to demogogic leadership; but in conjunction with the Cincinnatus ideal of service to the republic, it kept Washington from a mere mechanics of power. He realized that power is a tree that grows by a constant prudent trimming; that winning the people's long-term confidence is a more solid ground for achievement than pandering to their whims or defying their expectations. This concept is far removed from the hydraulic view of power that has prevailed in much of the modern political writing — the view that power is drained away by so many vents and leaks that one should acquire the largest *amount* of it at every opportunity. Why, if you are carrying something in a sieve, pour out spoonfuls on your own?

If, as General, Washington had accepted this latter view, he would have felt the ditherings of Congress so attritive that he must seize what powers he could as soon as he could — a natural enough reaction. Instead, Washington felt that any immediate gain would be a loss in his primary assignment, to gain the trust of Congress so that it would give over a stable power in gradual increments — which is what happened. By not asking too much, he finally got enough. We have all observed the kind of people who lose their hold on us by asserting it too soon, too massively, too possessively. Washington really did live by the maxim that one must win "the hearts and minds of the people."

Myth. One of the "opinions" on which great leadership is based is that the leader ennobles his people by playing an archetypal role. This is not the same as charisma, which is personal and temporary. It is the embodiment of a timeless function the people can perceive as "larger than life." To this I assign the arbitrary word of myth. The Queen of England is mythical even when she is not charismatic. She may be both — but the myth is a more stable and lasting quality, one that does not depend on day-to-day revalidation. So, Pope Paul VI was mythical but not charismatic; Pope John Paul II is both. Charisma is ad hoc — bred out of, and addressed to, crisis; born of instability, and often perpetuating it. Myth is perduring, and forms a bridge between generations. The mythical quality tends to be inherited, the charismatic one improvised.

Washington was a charismatic leader, in time of crisis. But how could he be mythical, since he did not inherit his principal offices but inaugurated them? Once again, he was fortunate in the expectations of his time. The highest form of heroism was, for the Enlightenment, that of the founder of a government, and especially of a republic. Bacon had put the *conditores imperii* at the top of his list of human types. Plutarch's omnipresent *Lives* began with a string of founders carefully balanced and compared. Machiavelli taught that the greatest human gratitude should go to the founders of republics (*Discourses* 1.10). Montesquieu and Rousseau, among others, continued this emphasis.

There is a double paradox in the cult of a founder — it does make *inaugurators* part of a *tradition*; and, even more important for Washington's conception of power, the classical tradition made a founder give power to his laws by surrendering it himself. Plutarch says of Theseus: "Surrendering the kingship, as he had promised, he gave order to the commonwealth" (24). Lycurgus, widely held to be the greatest lawgiver, began his task by an abdication (3) and ended it by suicide, lest the state depend more on his person than his laws (29). For this same reason, Solon left Athens after his legislation was in place (25). And, when Romulus was unwilling to leave Rome, the gods took him away for the state's good (28).

We might interpret this concern with removing the founder as expressing the problem of legitimate succession to a charismatic

37

ruler; but Machiavelli is probably a subtler reader of the myths when he makes the founder a kind of scapegoat, taking on himself all the crimes or violence necessary to a revolutionary founding, and then removing them along with himself to let a new order prosper (*Discourses* 1.9). Shakespeare makes his Henry IV consciously perform this function:

> God knows, my son,
> By what by-paths and indirect crookt ways
> I met this crown, and I myself know well
> How troublesome it sate upon my head:
> To thee it shall descend with better quiet,
> Better opinion, better confirmation;
> For all the soil of the achievement goes
> With me into the earth (Part Two, 4.5).

Rousseau treats the same myths in a more secular way. For him the problem is not the guilt of overthrowing past powers. Rather, it is this: Who has the power to create a new order? Only the people's general will. But how can that will be articulated *before* the act of consent that makes law valid? By a legislator who, since his work precedes the act of consent, is himself entirely powerless:

> For a people just coming into being to favor sound views of government and act on the basic rules of political necessity, effect would have to become [its own] cause; social affection, which the institutions are supposed to shape, would have to foster *them*; men would have to *be*, without the laws, what the laws would have them become. That is why the legislator shall not use either force or [mere] argument. He must resort to another kind of authority entirely, an ability to lead without compelling, to persuade without proving....He who frames the law has no power, and should have none, to pass laws. The people cannot, if they would, rid themselves of this nontransferable power (*Contrat* 2.7).

America's constitution had a "legislator" in exactly Rousseau's sense. The drafting convention had to take on itself the onus of advocating defiance of the Articles' conditions for amendment (by unanimous action of the state legislatures). It was a body of dubious legality, and of no constitutional power at all. Washington was aware that the convention was extra-legal and perhaps illegal, as Jay had informed him early in 1787. He replied:

> In strict propriety a convention so holden may not be legal. Congress, however, may give it a colouring by recommendation, which would fit it more to the taste without proceeding to a definition [establishment] of the power. This, however constitutionally it might be done, would not, in my opinion, be expedient; for delicacy [misgivings] on the one hand, and Jealousy [suspicion] on the other would produce a mere nihil (GW 29.177).

Washington decided to attend such a dubious convention without the benefit of our retrospective glorification of it. To many at the time, its secret proceedings, its defiance of its mandate, made it a subversive engine of overthrow, urging office holders to break their oaths to state constitutions and the Articles: "Centinel," in Philadelphia, wrote:

> The evil genius of darkness presided at its birth; it came forth under the veil of mystery, its true features being carefully concealed, and every deceptive art has been and is practising to have this spurious brat received as the generous offspring of heaven-born liberty (Storing 2.164).

There would have been many more such denunciations but for the sacred presence of Washington and Franklin in what William Findley called the "dark conclave." Even Madison, in *Federalist* No. 40, could come up with no convincing defense of the convention's acts except that it offered the "informal and unauthorized propositions" of some private citizens, which were "merely advisory and recommendatory" (Cooke 265, 264). Having made the suggestion, the convention disbanded itself forever; if nine popularly elected new conventions did not act on the recommendation, it would remain simply a suggestion — exactly the status of the lawgiver's scheme in Rousseau, unless the people adopt it.

Although the drafting convention as a whole is the body that fulfills all the conditions of Rousseau's legislator, Washington was the palladium and symbol of that body — Centinel called him the Trojan Horse containing the whole dangerous plot. He would later assume power, under a different title, with authority derived from the people's action on the legislator's plan. But he remained

in spirit the lawgiver who both gives law and abdicates, who em-
powers the state by divesting himself of power. The period's mythical yearning for a founder, and his sense of power's limits,
meshed perfectly; so perfectly, indeed, that one can wonder what
lesson is derivable from so unique a set of circumstances. Later
political leaders cannot become founders in anything like Washington's sense, or draw on the symbols of classical republicanism
as he did in becoming Cincinnatus. Nonetheless, later leadership
went forward within the framework he provided. Some of the
qualities traceable to him are:

1. Leadership in America is secular and civilian. When I was
in Japan during the 1980 presidential election, students and fac-
ulty often asked me whether, if Reagan became president, the
generals of the Pentagon would take over our country. (Their
views were obviously shaped by their own national history.) With
exaggeration, but — I think — an exaggerated truth, I answered:
"No, General Washington took care of that for us." It is always
necessary to revive the ideal represented by Washington; but
when one does appeal to it, the call is strong — as when the nation
made a point of law Washington's precedent of no third term as
president (Jefferson had thought perpetual re-eligibility would be
the path toward destruction of the Constitution), or when an unpop-
ular president grew in people's eyes by toppling a popular general
(MacArthur) in the name of civilian supremacy.

2. Although the modern politician cannot, in our more egalitarian age, affect the "disinterested arbiter" role that Madison
called for in leaders of "most established and diffusive character"
(Cooke 63), our politics is one of arbitrament in the sense of compromise. Our non-ideological "Parties" are not as partisan as
those in a parliamentary system, and the president is accepted as
"president of all the people" no matter which party's platform he
ran on. There is a wide sense that it is "unpresidential" to descend
to partisan attacks while holding the office.

3. Submission to the constitution is in theory exacted and can
in fact be enforced if there is widespread perception that the president is defying it (as with Andrew Johnson or Richard Nixon).

Although the things I have mentioned may seem merely negative constraints on the presidency (and, by example, on other
kinds of political leadership in this country), I think the limits
have in fact strengthened the presidency, made it a stable and
trusted office through most of our history — perhaps too powerful

an office at times, precisely because it was so little feared. The tree did grow because of Washington's prunings.

In terms of positive qualities, we seem to have departed from Washington's concept of leadership in two ways, one domestic and one foreign. In domestic affairs, the growth of egalitarian ideals, desirable in itself, has had a spurious corollary, an opposition to all "elitism," even that of talent and public spirit. This has not really deprived us of elites — the "best and brightest" have a disproportionate say in the conduct of affairs. But it has removed the consensus on what kinds of elitism should be acceptable. Rule by crypto-elites is not a substitute for the economic use of a society's resources, including those of human talent and good will.

In foreign affairs, we have neglected the truth that power is based on opinion, defying "world opinion" as if we could strengthen ourselves by the accretion of any regime to our side, no matter what its credentials; or fearing the extent of Russian territorial claims, no matter how flimsy their tenure in the "minds and hearts of men." To be frightened by the "spread" of Russian holdings on a map, as if the color red covered a mass of uniform density, is silly. Much of Russia's power is spent trying to hold down its satellites, patrol its Chinese border, control a rebellious Afghanistan, intimidate or woo on-again off-again allies like Yugoslavia, Romania, Syria, Egypt, etc. We have neglected the central teaching of the Farewell Address (which was *not* isolationism). Our arrangement of the world into two ideological blocs, with ourselves at the head of one, violates Washington's basic insight:

> The Nation, which indulges towards another an habitual hatred, or an habitual fondness, is in some degree a slave. It is a slave to its animosity or to its affection, either which is sufficient to lead it astray from its duty and its interest (Paltsits 153).

In just this way we were, for a long time, enslaved by our animosity to China and our fondness for Taiwan, against our duty as a great nation and our interest, with tragic consequences in Korea and Vietnam.

Washington's leadership cannot be recreated, duplicated, in modern conditions. But a more enlightened leadership can be derived from the study of his.

41

Key to Brief Citations

Cooke	Jacob E. Cooke, ed. *The Federalist*. Cleveland: World Publishing, 1961.
Diaries	*The Diaries of George Washington*. Edited by Donald Jackson and Dorothy Twohig. Vols. I-VI. University of Virginia, 1976-79.
Freeman	Douglas Southall Freeman. *George Washington*. Vols. I-IV. Little, Brown, 1965-72.
Gilbert	Allan H. Gilbert, ed. and tr. *The Prince, and other works. Chicago: Packard, 1946.*
GW	*The Writings of George Washington*. Edited by John C. Fitzpatrick. 39 volumes. Washington, 1931-44.
Paltsits	Victor Hugo Paltsits. *Washington's Farewell Address*. New York, 1935.
Storing	Herbert Storing and Murray Dry. *The Complete Anti-Federalist*. Chicago: University of Chicago Press, 1981.
Max Weber	Dennis Wrong, ed. *Max Weber*. Englewood Cliffs, N.J.: Prentice-Hall, 1970.

WASHINGTON, CATO, AND HONOR: A MODEL FOR REVOLUTIONARY LEADERSHIP

Forrest McDonald

No one, I suppose, would challenge the proposition that George Washington was, as James T. Flexner called him, the "Indispensable Man" of the American Revolutionary epoch. By sheer force of character he created the Continental Army and held it together, under extremely adverse circumstances, for the eight years it took to win American independence. It is unlikely that the Philadelphia Convention of 1787 could have succeeded in drafting a constitution that the states would ratify had he not lent his awesome prestige to the undertaking; and it is almost certain that the office of president could not have been created had he not been available to fill it. Finally, and in some ways most remarkably, he never abused or sought to aggrandize the powers with which he was entrusted during the war and during his presidency, and in both instances he voluntarily surrendered those powers when the job was done, though both times he might easily have held them for life.

On the opposite hand, no scholar who has studied Washington would maintain — as schoolchildren used to be taught — that the man was flawless. As a soldier he was capable of blundering, rashness, and poor judgment. He was addicted to gambling, apparently indulged in a good deal of wenching, and was a "most horrid swearer and blasphemer." He was vain, and pompous, pretentious, and ill-tempered in the extreme; and though he was normally a perfect gentleman in his public demeanor, he was sometimes a perfect alley cat in his private behavior. Even in public he was not always entirely blameless. During the war he was quite willing to hang the innocent British prisoner, Captain Charles Asgill, in retaliation against the unauthorized misbehavior of New York Loyalists, and he was not sufficiently magnanimous to grant the request of the unfortunate Major Andre to be shot as a soldier rather than hanged as a spy. In the presidency, he more than once embarrassed the cabinet with long, almost whiningly self-pitying monologues.[1]

43

Yet he was respected, admired, even revered by his country-men, and was the most trusted man of the age. What is more, and different, he was the most trustworthy man of the age. Why he was so trusted, and how he came to be so trustworthy — in revolution-ary circumstances of a kind which almost invariably breed Cae-sars, Cromwells, Napoleons — are questions that must be exam-ined if we are to understand Washington's legacy as a leader.

In regard to his being trusted, it is easy to overlook one crucial ingredient, that Americans sorely needed someone to trust. Partly this need arose from the perilousness of the undertaking on which they embarked in 1776, but there is more to it than that. Difficult as it may be to imagine, the Americans were a monarchical people who had been conditioned to love their kings and did love their kings. George III had been especially beloved, for he had been trained as a Patriot King in the Bolingbrokean mode, and Americans had imbibed deeply of the Bolingbrokean ideology. In responding to objectionable measures emanating from London after 1763, American resistance leaders invariably placed the blame upon wicked and designing ministers, not the king; and even so ardent a revolutionary as Thomas Jefferson, as late as 1775, sincerely believed that if George could be made aware of the sinister doings of his ministers he would exert his prerogative and thwart them to protect American liberty. When they became convinced, early in 1776, that it was the king himself who was re-sponsible for the hated British policies, patriots were swept by a tremendous sense of betrayal as well as of outrage. Their response was to embrace republicanism fervently and to refuse to entrust executive power to either the Congress or the new state govern-ments. Yet the monarchical habit died hard: the craving for a symbolic embodiment of the nation remained strong. For that reason, it was not enough to have leaders, no matter how virtuous. There must be one man above all others; as Americans had ear-lier referred to George III as "The Father of His People," they needed someone now to call "The Father of His Country."[2]

Not least among the reasons that Washington could satisfy this need was that he looked the part. Tall and powerfully built, "the best horseman of his age, and the most graceful figure that could be seen on horseback," as Jefferson put it, he was readily recognized as the commander-in-chief by soldiers who had never seen him before; and it is striking how often monarchical im-agery was used in contemporary physical descriptions of him. A New England Yankee described him as "truly noble and majestic, being tall and well proportioned." An Englishman spoke of his "martial dignity" that would distinguish him as a soldier among ten thousand men, and added that "Not a king in Europe but would look like a valet de chambre by his side." A French count wrote that "His handsome and majestic while at the same time mild and open countenance, perfectly reflects his moral qualities. He looks the hero." When Abigail Adams, by then a veteran of receptions at St. James, finally met Washington in 1789, she was almost moonstruck, gushing that he moved "with a grace, dignity, and ease that leaves Royal George far behind him."[3]

His physical appearance was complemented by an aura not merely of strength but of invincibility. His apparent invulnerability to gunfire, for instance, seemed almost supernatural. Early in his career a treacherous Indian guide fired at him from point-blank range and missed; during the Braddock massacre every other mounted officer was shot but he was untouched. Once he rode between two columns of his own men who were firing at one another by mistake, and he struck up their guns with his sword while musket balls whizzed harmlessly around his head. During the Revolution he repeatedly took dangerous risks; time after time musket balls tore his clothes and killed his horses under him, but not one ever touched his body.[4] What mortal could refuse to entrust his life into the hands of a man whom the gods so obviously favored? What country could refuse to do so?

But winning the trust of Congress, the army, and the people was one thing; retaining it was quite another. That he did retain it is especially impressive in light of the fact that, between the surprise attack on Trenton on Christmas Day, 1776, and the conclusive victory over Cornwallis at Yorktown in October, 1781, Washington never won a battle. To some extent the achievement was a negative one, which is to say that Washington's behavior was unmarred by the flaws shown by many another American general — Arnold's treachery, Gates' cowardice, Conway's cabalizing, Stark's provincialism, Schuyler's bumbling, Lee's indecisiveness. It was essentially a negative achievement in another way as well: to the astonishment of many foreign observers, Washington never questioned the superiority of civil authority over the military, even though Congress was increasingly populated by knaves and fools who gratified their avarice and their egos at the army's and the country's expense. But at comparable stages of their careers Caesar and Cromwell had done the same.

45

The true test of Washington's selfless devotion to the cause would come after the fighting stopped: when the enemy had been defeated, would the army lay down its arms?

There was reason to fear that it would not. Late in 1782, as British and American diplomats were negotiating the final terms of peace, the Continental Army was encamped at Newburgh, New York, near West Point. Restlessly idle, officers and men alike grew discontented with their prospects. They had not been paid in years and though the officers had been held in check so far by the promise of a bonus of half-pay for life, Congress had established no regular revenues to fund either the bonus or the accrued arrears of pay. In November, a proposed amendment to the Articles of Confederation that would have authorized the collection of import duties was rejected. Many of the officers, having neglected their private affairs for years, faced economic ruin as their reward for winning their country its independence. In December they resolved to do something about it.[5]

They sent a deputation, headed by General Alexander McDougall, to Philadelphia to present Congress with a remonstrance. The memorial, presented on January 6, was couched as a reserved and respectful plea for "justice," that being the way demands for explanations prior to a challenge to a dual were worded; and it included the ominous suggestion, again in the language of the code duello, that "any further experiments on [the officers'] patience may have fatal effects." Most congressman were terrified by the challenge. Some saw opportunity in it: Superintendent of Finance Robert Morris and his circle of nationalist friends sought to fan the embers of discontent in the army to force Congress to enact, and the states to ratify, a comprehensive plan to make the national authority permanent and financially independent. The idea, as Gouverneur Morris wrote General Henry Knox, was that "after you have carried the post the public creditors will garrison it for you."

But the situation rapidly got out of hand: by March the mutinous Newburgh Addresses were in circulation, calling upon the officers to meet (without permission of the commander-in-chief) and to declare publicly (in defiance of orders from Washington if necessary) that they would not disband until they had obtained "justice." The gauntlet was down.

For anyone but Washington the decision might have been extremely difficult. He fully sympathized with the officers' cause, and had he chosen to lead the mutiny there can be no doubt that they would have followed him across the Rubicon. If, on the other hand, he attempted to repress them, chaos might ensue — and the British army, concentrated in New York City awaiting embarkation, was not far away. Had he followed either course, there would never have been a United States of America as we know it.

Instead, he did a grandly audacious thing. He called his own meeting, presided over it, and addressed the assembled officers. First he reminded them that he was a soldier, too. "As I was among the first who embarked in the cause of our common country," he said, "as I have never left your side...; as I have been the common companion and witness of your distresses, and not among the last to feel and acknowledge your merits; as I have ever considered my own military reputation as inseparably connected with that of the army; ...it can scarcely be supposed, at this late stage of the war, that I am indifferent to its interests." Then he played upon their shame, pointing to the ignominy they would bring upon themselves by "either deserting our country in the extremest hour of her distress or turning our arms against it," and he suggested that the author of the Newburgh Addresses must be a British emissary, "plotting the ruin of both by sowing seeds of discord and separation between the civil and military powers of the continent." Then came an appeal to patriotism: "let me conjure you, in the name of our common country, as you value your own sacred honor, as you respect the rights of humanity, and as you regard the military and national character of America, to express your utmost horror and detestation of the man who wishes, under any specious pretense, to overturn the liberties of our country." Finally, he added a master's touch. He pulled from his pocket a message from Congress that he said he wanted to read. Some moments passed in silence, then he fumbled in another pocket and extracted a pair of eyeglasses, which no one but a few intimates had seen him wear. By way of gently reminding the officers that he had endured more than any of them — and without a cent of pay — he said, "Gentlemen, you will permit me to put on my spectacles, for I have not only grown gray but almost blind in the service of my country." The officers, shamed into tears, evaporated from the room. Soon arrangements were made to provide part of their back pay, and the army was disbanded with its honor intact.[6]

Thereafter, it was unnecessary to ask why Americans so trusted Washington: the answer was obviously that they knew they could trust him. The larger question now emerges. How did a man — admittedly not an ordinary man, but one who in private

life was as far from being a saint as he was from being ordinary
— come to be so utterly trustworthy in public life?

The question is an especially slippery one for a number of
reasons. In the first place, though Washington was, as will be
seen, clearly and self-consciously trying all his adult life to live
up to a certain role model, there had been no person in his life to
provide such a model. His father died when he was eleven, his
brother Lawrence when he was in his teens. Most curiously, he
never served under anybody's command, even during his earliest
military career: he had no General Washington to pattern himself after.

Alternatively, he might have found his ideal in books, but he
was not much given to reading. John Adams could think of himself as Demosthenes or as one of the Puritan heroes of the English
Civil War, and try to act accordingly. Jefferson could regard Bacon, Newton, and Locke as the three greatest men who ever lived,
and attempt to pattern his own behavior after their example.
Hamilton could sign his polemics with a variety of pseudonyms —
Publius, Phocion, Tully, Camillus, Pericles — depending upon
which role he was playing at the time. But Washington was simply not a bookish man: one cannot imagine him picking out a hero
from a book and casting himself in that mold.

Yet, as indicated, it is abundantly evident that Washington
was ever concerned, almost obsessively, with creating and then
living up to what he called his "character" — what we would call
his reputation or public image. As early as 1753 he was showing
what Flexner called the diffidence that always marked his push
for power; lest his reputation suffer from failure, he warned Governor Dinwiddie that he was incapable of carrying out the command of the expedition to the Forks of the Ohio. More revealing is
his acceptance of command of the Continental Army. Obviously
he wanted the job: he attended the sessions of the Continental
Congress dressed in a resplendent military uniform which he had
designed himself. Yet when the position was offered him he declared solemnly that, "Lest some unlucky event should happen,
unfavorable to my reputation, I beg it be remembered, by every
gentleman in the room, that I, this day, declare with utmost sincerity, I do not think myself equal to the command I am honored
with." To his brother-in-law Washington wrote, "I can answer but
for three things: a firm belief in the justice of our cause, close attention in the prosecution of it, and the strictest integrity. If these

cannot supply the place of ability and experience, the cause will suffer, and more than probable my character along with it."[7]

After his "character" was firmly established in the hearts of his countrymen, Washington was reluctant to hazard it by further participation in public life. It was with something bordering on dread that he consented to attend the Constitutional Convention of 1787. When the convention worked out satisfactorily, the prospect of the presidency put him in an extremely awkward position. Upon surrendering his command in 1783 he had declared that he was unequivocally and unalterably retiring from public life, and in 1789 he feared that if he accepted the office of president he would be regarded as having broken his word. Hamilton, sensing that his former chief would feel that way, wrote him a circumspect letter urging him to heed the call when it came. Washington was grateful to Hamilton for raising the problem, which no one else had had the wits to do. He had wanted to discuss the problem with someone, Washington wrote Hamilton, but, "situated as I am, I could hardly bring the question into the slightest discussion, or ask an opinion even in the most confidential manner; without betraying, in my judgment, some impropriety of conduct, or without feeling an apprehension that a premature display of anxiety might be construed into a vain-glorious desire of pushing myself into notice as a Candidate." After a further exchange of letters, Hamilton was able to overcome his former chief's scruples, partly by insisting that it would be inglorious and damaging to his reputation if he refused to risk the glory he had already won, partly by appealing to his sense of duty to give unqualified support to the Constitution he had signed.[8]

Even after he became president his first concern, regularly, was his public image. His inauguration was characteristic. He and everyone else knew he would be elected, and the newspapers announced the results early in 1789, but he did not go to the temporary capital of New York until Congress officially tallied the votes and gave him formal notice. His concern lest unseemly haste suggest that he was improperly eager for the office thus delayed the organization of the government more than a month. While others in government concerned themselves with such matters as setting up revenues, establishing the federal judiciary, and passing the Bill of Rights, Washington was preoccupied almost to the exclusion of all else with working out rules for meeting the public. It was crucial, he insisted, that a balance be struck between "too free an intercourse and too much familiarity" (which would reduce the dignity of the office) and "an ostentatious show" of monarchical aloofness (which would be improper in a republic).[9]

Indeed, what was arguably the most important domestic policy decision of his presidency, and certainly the most important constitutional decision — to sign the bill chartering the Bank of the United States — stemmed from considerations neither of policy nor of constitutionality, but from concern with public image. In the 1790 statute to locate the permanent capital on the Potomac, Congress authorized a three-man executive commission to choose a site at any point along the river between the Eastern Branch (Anacostia River), a few miles below the fall line, and Conococheague Creek, sixty miles above the fall line. Instead, Washington chose the site himself, and picked one three miles downstream of the authorized southeasternmost location — and that much closer to Mount Vernon. Only afterward did he tour the prospective upstream sites so as to give the impression that he was considering them as the Act of Congress required. This made it necessary to invite proposals from the upstream inhabitants and to go through the motions of appearing to weigh them in arriving at a decision. There was nothing unreasonable or unethical in what Washington had done; and after all, he knew the area far better than the Congressmen did. But it was beginning to look as if his actions had stemmed from unworthy motives — the choice of location increased the value of Washington's property by a handsome amount, as he admitted — and he groped for a means of putting a proper face on the whole affair. He asked Congress to amend the Federal District Act so as to cast, retroactively, its mantle of approval over his actions. The House readily enacted the requested legislation, but friends of the bank charter held up approval in the Senate until Washington should sign the bank bill; in effect, they held his character hostage to his signature. After a ten-day war of nerves, Washington capitulated: he signed the bank bill into law, and only then did the Senate approve the amendatory legislation.[10]

Because Washington was self-consciously playing a role — was living his life in such a way as to create and maintain a certain public image — the question as to the source of his model becomes tantalizing. Two such models which were in the contemporary atmosphere — and which demonstrably governed many of the Founding Fathers — suggest themselves, though neither, on close observation, turns out to be suitable to Washington. One was the eighteenth century military conception of the officer and gentleman. The ruling passion, to the military man, was the love of glory, which could be won only on the battlefield; but it must be protected by proper behavior in one's relations with other officers and gentlemen. Proper behavior was governed by sense of duty, deference, responsibility, courage, graciousness, gallantry, candor, magnanimity, and above all, honor. Superficially the military model might seem to fit Washington, for he had most of the appropriate attributes and he did, in his youth, ardently aspire to a military career.[11]

But there were parts of the military ideal that were utterly alien to him, quite in addition to the fact that the Fabian strategy by which he conducted the war was inconsistent with the pursuit of glory. The ideal included, for instance, the code duello: if one was insulted by someone with pretensions to being a gentleman, one was obliged to obtain satisfaction on the field of honor. The case of Alexander Hamilton springs readily to mind; but, though Hamilton and Washington were much alike in many ways, Washington could no more have felt the need to respond to a challenge to a duel than Hamilton could have declined to do so. More importantly, the military ideal left open the possibility, under certain circumstances — say, of corruption and incompetence in the civil authority, with which both Caesar and Cromwell had had to deal — that the successful soldier take over the power of government. Clearly then, though Washington understood and respected the military ideal, he did not embrace it.

Another common contemporary model was afforded by the ideal of republican virtue. Again, the model would seem at first glance to fit, for the most important requirement of the ideal was that one put the good of the republic ahead of self-interest, and Washington obviously qualified in that regard. Moreover, despite the personal shortcomings mentioned earlier, he was clearly a man of virtue in the twentieth century sense of the term. But as republican principles of political theory had evolved in the eighteenth century, virtue had taken on a special signification that was quite foreign to Washington's way of thinking.

That body of theory held that inequality of wealth, and even the free transfer of property, was fatal to republican government. As Montesquieu put it, frugality, simplicity, and a "mediocrity" of "abilities and fortunes" were indispensably necessary to sustain republican virtue. Indeed, he said that if equality broke down, "the republic will be utterly undone," and thus it was "absolutely necessary there should be some regulation in respect to...all...forms of contracting. For were we once allowed to dispose of our property to whom and how we pleased, the will of each individual would disturb the order of the fundamental law." Other versions of the theory called for periodic redistribution of wealth, sumptuary legislation to prevent the development of a taste for luxury, and measures to prevent economic growth on the ground that it led to a love of material possessions and bred effeminacy, vice, and corruption. Washington was not long on political philosophy, but the way he lived abundantly testified that frugality, simplicity, and a mediocrity of fortune scarcely accorded with his notion of the good life.[12]

There was one more thing about the idea of republican virtue that was anathema to him: it had become a dogma, a secular millennialist ideology. Such an ideology leads not to Caesar but to Robespierre, and Washington simply had too much common sense to have any part of it. Washington's conception of the way he should lead his life, then, derived from neither of the most common sources from which other idealists among the Founding Fathers drew their inspiration.

But there is another prospective source, namely the theater. Eighteenth century dramatists, in addition to amusing and entertaining, sometimes sought to ennoble, especially with dramas about heroes of the ancient world; and the ennobling dramas could be powerfully effective in that sentimental and lachrymose age. Washington, we know, was an ardent theater-goer; and we also know a great deal about which plays he saw.[13]

Among those, it seems that the prime candidate for the source of Washington's "character" is Joseph Addison's *Cato*. That *Cato* was, with the possible exception of Sheridan's *School for Scandal*, Washington's favorite play, and that he saw it a number of times from early manhood into maturity, are documented facts; indeed, at Valley Forge he permitted it to be performed for his troops to raise their morale, and he attended along with them, despite a congressional resolution that plays were inimical to republican virtue. That he identified himself with one of its characters at least once in a letter is also a matter of record. Moreover, in many letters he wrote during the darker hours of the Revolution, there was one quotation that he repeatedly employed — "'Tis not in mortals to command success" — and that came from *Cato*, as did the line he quoted when he retired from the presidency in 1797,

"The post of honor is a private station." That *Cato* provided the source of Patrick Henry's famous line, "give me liberty or give me death," and of Nathan Hale's equally famous "My only regret is that I have but one life to give for my country," was pointed out some years ago by Douglass Adair. That it offered a role model — or, actually, two role models — that are strikingly similar to the way Washington patterned his life is indicated by careful reading of the play.[14]

The drama is set in Utica, where Cato the Younger holds together the remnants of the Roman republican Senate against the usurping arms of the all-conquering Caesar. Already Caesar, "who owes his greatness to his country's ruin," has "ravaged more than half the globe"; Cato, with "a feeble army, and an empty senate," has vainly fought "the cause of honour, virtue, liberty, and Rome." There are ten characters: Cato, his sons Portius and Marcus, Senators Lucius and Sempronius, Prince Juba of Numidia, the Numidian General Styphax, an ambassador from Caesar, and Cato's daughter Marcia and Lucius' daughter Lucia. Against the backdrop of the larger drama of Cato's refusal to bow to Caesar's yoke, there are three subplots, one involving the treachery of Sempronius and Styphax, the other two involving the love of Prince Juba for Cato's daughter and the love of Cato's sons for Lucia. The mutinies of Sempronius and Styphax are suppressed, Marcus dies heroically, and Cato spurns Caesar's overtures, sees to the safe evacuation of his followers, gives the lovers his blessings, and commits suicide.[15]

Two scenes are especially relevant for present purposes. One of these is Cato's confrontation with the mutineers (Act III, Scene V). Contemptuously, Cato faces them saying:

> Where are these bold intrepid sons of war,
> That greatly turn their backs upon the foe,
> And to their general send a brave defiance?

In an aside, the treacherous Sempronius says "Curse on their dastard souls, they stand astonished," then Cato goes on:

> Perfidious men! and will you thus dishonor
> Your past exploits, and sully all your wars?
> Do you confess 'twas not a zeal for Rome,
> Nor love of liberty, nor thirst of honour,
> Drew you thus far; but hopes to share the spoil
> Of conquered towns and plundered provinces?
> Fired with such motives you do well to join

With Cato's foes, and follow Caesar's banners.
Bemoaning that he has lived to see the day, he goes on:

> ...why could not Cato fall
> Without your guilt? Behold, ungrateful men,
> Behold my bosom naked to your swords,
> And let the man that's injured strike the blow.

The hero then recalls the campaigns they have endured together and, without boasting, reminds the soldiers that it was always he "who was the first to explore the untrodden path, when life was hazarded at every step." Swept with remorse and shame, the mutineers break into tears and lay down their weapons.[16]

Washington's confrontation with the mutinous officers at Newburgh was a muted variation of that scene: Addison might have written the lines for the occasion.

The other scene (Act II, Scene 5) involves Prince Juba — who, interestingly, is the character with whom Washington identified himself in a youthful letter. Juba, as a Numidian, not a Roman, is self-consciously an outsider, though he has in fact absorbed the best of what was Roman. In the scene he is much concerned that he may have earned Cato's disfavor by being preoccupied with his love for Marcia at such an inappropriate time, and says, "I'd rather have that man approve my deeds, than worlds for my admirers." Just before, he had uttered what were once famous lines:

> Honour's a sacred tie, the law of kings,
> The noble mind's distinguishing perfection,
> That aids and strengthens virtue where it meets her,
> And imitates her actions, where she is not.[17]

Juba's words, properly understood, provide the clue to understanding Washington. Interpreting passages in dramatic and poetic literature can be a problematical affair, but it is not in the present instance. As it happens, Addison subsequently wrote a little essay in *The Guardian* explaining what Juba meant. Addison begins by distinguishing between two kinds of motives to good actions: "What some men are prompted to by conscience, duty, or religion, which are only different names for the same thing, others are prompted to by honour." He is not talking about the kind of honor which attended the military ideal; he calls that "false honour." True honor, he says, "though it be a different principle from religion, is that which produces the same effects....Religion embraces virtue, as it is enjoined by the laws of God; honour, as it is graceful and ornamental to human nature. The religious man *fears*, the man of honour *scorns* to do an ill action." The one considers vice as offensive to the Divine Being, the other considers it as something beneath him; the one as something forbidden, the other as what is unbecoming.[18]

Honor, in these verses, is that principle of human action which operates out of regard for "*the esteem of wise and good men.*" Virtue, by contrast, is stoical virtue, "which regulates itself by the sense of the *honestum* simply, or, in other words, by *self-esteem.*" The principles may exist in the same person, and when they do, honor "aids and strengthens virtue where he finds her." But the combination is rare, and where genuine virtue is absent, honor "prompts to the same conduct which virtue prescribes."

The line about kings is crucial: it means that public persons are and should be governed mainly "by the law of *honour* or *outward esteem*," which is "a more obvious, and, generally, more binding law, to men so employed, than that of *virtue* or *self-esteem.*" To put it another way, Addison is advising young Washington, through young Juba, to follow precisely the opposite course from that recommended by Shakespeare's Polonius. Polonius says to Laertes, in a much quoted passage, "This above all: to thine own self be true, and it must follow, as the night the day, thou canst not then be false to any man." Shakespeare put the words in the mouth of a prattling fool, and Addison's message is that, for public men, they are foolish words. Rather, he says, To others be true; seek the esteem of the wise and the virtuous, and it follows that thou canst not then be false to thyself.

Washington, then, was no superman or demigod. He was a man with ordinary human failings, but one who made the polestar of his conduct an unceasing effort to win the esteem of the wise and the virtuous — but only the wise and the virtuous. As he said in regard to the Constitutional Convention, "If, to please the people, we offer what we ourselves disapprove, how can we afterwards defend our work? Let us raise a standard to which the wise and the honest can repair." In the circumstances, nothing else would have done, for few individuals and no societies can long maintain the kind of virtue that classical republican theory required.

His was not, however, a model for all seasons. As time went by, American society grew progressively more democratic, and along the way it became necessary for the nation's leaders to depart from Washington's standard — to seek the esteem not of the wise and virtuous but of the vulgar multitude. And, as

Washington's quest for outward esteem shaped him to greatness, theirs shaped them to pettiness: throughout the nineteenth century, with the sole exception of Lincoln, the quality of American presidential leadership inexorably declined.

America had the singularly good fortune of becoming a republic before it became a democracy. Had things been the other way around, the United States could have had a Caesar, a Cromwell, a Napoleon. Instead, it had a Washington.

Notes

1. The biography that catalogues Washington's shortcomings in the most balanced way is James T. Flexner's *George Washington* (4 vols.; Boston: Little, Brown, 1965-1972); see also Flexner's one volume version, *Washington: The Indispensable Man* (Boston: Little, Brown, 1974).

2. Robert Dennis Fiala, "George III in the Pennsylvania Press: A Study in Changing Opinions, 1760-1776." (Ph.D. Diss.; Wayne State University, 1967); William David Liddle, "A Patriot King, or None: American Public Attitudes towards George III and the British Monarchy, 1754-1776." (Ph.D. Diss.; Claremont Graduate School, 1970).

3. Quoted in Paul Leicester Ford, *Washington and the Theatre* (New York: The Dunlop Society, 1899), p. 50; Flexner, *George Washington*, vol. 2, pp. 40, 372; Forrest McDonald, *The Presidency of George Washington* (Lawrence, Kansas: University Press of Kansas, 1974), p. 26.

4. Flexner, *Washington: The Indispensable Man*, pp. 14, 26-27, 34, 36, 84, 97-98, 106, 152.

5. Accounts of the episode at Newburgh are numerous. The following is drawn largely from Forrest McDonald, *E Pluribus Unum: The Formation of the American Republic, 1776-1790* (Cambridge: Houghton, Mifflin, 1965), pp. 22-32, and the numerous sources cited therein. See also E. James Ferguson, *The Power of the Purse* (Chapel Hill: University of North Carolina Press, 1961), pp. 154-171, and Richard H. Kohn, *Eagle and Sword: The Federalists and the Creation of the Military Establishment in America, 1783-1802* (New York: Free Press, 1975), pp. 17-39.

6. Washington's full statement is in John C. Fitzpatrick, ed., *The Writings of George Washington* (39 vols.; Washington: Government Printing Office, 1931-1944), vol. 26, pp. 222-229.

7. Flexner, *Washington: The Indispensable Man*, p. 15; Flexner, *George Washington*, vol. 2, p. 16; John Adams to Mrs. Adams, May 29, 1775, One of the Virginia Delegates to ____, June 14, 1775, Eliphalet Dyer to Joseph Trumbull, June 17, 1775, John Adams to Mrs. Adams, June 17, 1775, in Edmund C. Burnett, ed., *Letters of Members of the Continental Congress* (8 vols.; Washington: Carnegie Institution, 1921-1936), vol. 1, pp. 102, 124, 128, 130; Worthington C. Ford and others, *Journals of the Continental Congress, 1774-1789* (34 vols.; Washington: Government Printing Office, 1904-1937), vol. 2, p. 92; Washington to Burwell Bassett, June, 1775, in Fitzpatrick, ed., *Writings of Washington*, vol. 3, p. 297.

8. Washington to Thomas Jefferson, May 30, 1787, to Lafayette, June 6, 1787, Madison to Edward Everett, June 3, 1827, in Max Farrand, ed., *Records of the Federal Convention of 1787* (4 vols.; New Haven: Yale University Press, 1937), vol. 3, pp. 31, 34, 476; Flexner, *George Washington*, vol. 3, pp. 85-111; Alexander Hamilton to Washington, August 13, September, November 18, 1788, in Harold C. Syrett, ed., *The Papers of Alexander Hamilton* (26 vols.; New York: Columbia University Press, 1961-1979), vol. 5, pp. 201-202, 206-208, 220, 222-224, 230, 233.

9. Flexner, *George Washington*, vol. 3, pp. 195-196; Fitzpatrick, ed., *Writings of Washington*, vol. 30, pp. 319-321; Hamilton to Washington, May 5, 1789, in Syrett, ed., *Papers of Hamilton*, vol. 5, pp. 335-337 and 335 note; McDonald, *Presidency of Washington*, pp. 25-26, 29-30.

10. This episode is described at some length in Forrest McDonald, *Alexander Hamilton: A Biography* (New York: W.W. Norton, 1979), pp. 202-210. See also Kenneth Bowling, "The Bank Bill, the Capital City, and President Washington," *Capital Studies* 1 (1972); Washington to Arthur Young, December 5, 1791, December 12, 1793, in Fitzpatrick, ed., *Writings of Washington*, vol. 31, p. 438, vol. 33, pp. 175-176; Julian Boyd, ed., *The Papers of Thomas Jefferson* (21 vols. to date; Princeton: Princeton University Press, 1950-), editorial notes vol. 19, pp. 26, 30, 47-49, 281.

11. Most Americans, having a tradition of opposition to and fear of standing armies, shunned the military ideal; but a large number of officers in the Continental Army embraced it nonetheless. They could acquire it from Plutarch, military history, Vattel, and other writings, but most probably picked it up from association with Europeans in American service. To sample its flavor, see the personal correspondence in Syrett, ed., *Papers of Hamilton*, vols. 1 and 2.

12. The quotations are from Baron de Montesquieu, *The Spirit of the Laws* (Thomas Nugent translation; New York: Hafner, 1949), pp. 40-46. See also J.G.A. Pocock, *The Machiavellian Moment: Florentine Political Thought and the Atlantic Republican Tradition* (Princeton: Princeton University Press, 1975), pp. 387-390, 443, 534, and passim; and Drew R. McCoy, *The Elusive Republic* (Chapel Hill: University of North Carolina Press, 1980). This subject is developed at greater length and set in the context of the framing of the Constitution in Forrest McDonald, *Novus Ordo Seclorum: The Intellectual Origins of the Constitution* (Lawrence, Kansas: University Press of Kansas, 1985).

13. Ford, *Washington and the Theatre*; Oral Sumner Coad and Edwin Mims, Jr., *The American Stage* (New Haven: Yale University Press, 1929), pp. 9-44.

14. Ford, *Washington and the Theatre*, pp. 1-2, 18, 24-26; Russel B. Nye, *The Cultural Life of the New Nation, 1776-1830* (New York: Harper, Row, 1960), p. 264; Coad and Mims, *American Stage*, pp. 16, 27-28, 32-33; Flexner, *George Washington*, vol. 2, p. 30; Trevor Colbourn, ed., *Fame and the Founding Fathers: Essays by Douglass Adair* (New York: W.W. Norton, 1974), pp. 284n-285n; Samuel Eliot Morison, *The Young Man Washington* (Cambridge, Mass.: Harvard University Press, 1932), pp. 19-21, 41; Frederic M. Litto, "Addison's Cato in the Colonies," *William and Mary Quarterly*, 23:431-449 (1966).

15. The play is in Richard Hurd, ed., *The Works of Joseph Addison* (6 vols.; London: George Bell, 1881), vol. 1, pp. 172-226.

16. *Ibid.*, vol. 1, pp. 207-209.

17. *Ibid.*, vol. 1, p. 198.

18. *Ibid.*, vol. 4, p. 308.

GEORGE WASHINGTON AND THE WHIG CONCEPTION OF HEROIC LEADERSHIP

Barry Schwartz

No figure in American history has been esteemed more highly during his own lifetime than George Washington, Commander-in-Chief of the Continental Army and first President of the United States. Since Washington's death, every generation of Americans has found it necessary to reassess his personal character and the events of his public career.

This effort has produced a literature that is positively overwhelming. But while the facts of Washington's life have been documented in excruciating detail, little is explicitly known about why that life was the object of such intense veneration.

Existing statements relating to Washington's prestige fall into two categories. Authoritative biographical accounts, from Washington Irving and Jared Sparks to Douglas Freeman and James Flexner, supply abundant description of Washington's personal qualities and achievements.[1] The accounts never tell us, however, why these qualities and achievements were invested with such significance. A second group of writings portrays Washington as a monument or symbol of his age (see, for example, Cunliffe, 1958; Boorstin, 1965; Fishwick, 1954; Wright, 1955). Unfortunately, the writers never get around to providing us with convincing evidence of precisely what he symbolized during the different phases of his public career. After almost 200 years of biography and commentary, then, we remain uncertain about the bases of the enormous prestige accorded to Washington by his contemporaries.

This paper adds nothing to what is already known about the life of Washington but rather takes the fact of his veneration and examines its changing qualities in the context of late eighteenth century American society. The main premise of the paper is that Washington's great prestige is not constituted by its existence at any one moment in time, but is the unsettled result of constantly

* This chapter first appeared in the *American Sociological Review*, Vol. 48 (February 1983):18-33.

shifting social concerns and definitions. As will be shown, the initial expression of praise for Washington took place in the context of great political resentment and military fervor. Washington symbolized these sentiments in his role as military commander. By the end of the war, however, the public's attention shifted from military to political concerns, and it was against this new background that Washington was transformed from a military hero into the nation's great moral symbol. To show how and why this transformation occurred is to throw better light on one neglected variety of heroic leadership.

Varieties of Heroic Leadership

Heroic leadership is a form of domination which evokes strong reverential sentiment in the context of fateful enterprises, campaigns, and movements. The heroic leader, then, is not any leader who is revered because of the authority or the personal qualities he possesses, but one who uses these attributes to mobilize people for strenuous efforts to change or maintain existing cultural values and institutional structures.

Max Weber's conception of charismatic leadership deals with only one type of heroic leadership — the great men whom Weber considers are dedicated exclusively to radical change: "In a revolutionary and sovereign manner," he says, "charismatic domination transforms all values and breaks all traditional and rational norms" (Weber, 1968b:1115). Weber's charismatic leader is also an authoritarian leader. His influence "knows of no abstract legal codes" but rather stems from his godlike personal strength, to which his followers are duty-bound to submit (Weber, 1968b:1113, 1115). When charisma does take a democratic course, it usually leads to "Caesarism," or charismatic dictatorship (Weber, 1968a:266-271). Indeed, Dorothy Emmett (1958:233) goes so far as to suggest "that there is something rather Teutonic, suggesting the *Fuhrer-Prinzip,* about Weber's description." (See also Schlesinger, 1963:10.)

Closely related to Emmett's observation are the extraordinary talents of the charismatic leader: those qualities of his "individual personality by virtue of which he is considered extraordinary and treated as endowed with supernatural, superhuman, or at least specifically exceptional powers or qualities" (Weber, 1968a:241). Of course, Max Weber did not ignore the social context inside of which these powers are exercised. He was explicit about the followers' perception of the leader's "gift of grace" as being decisive for the validity of charisma. He was aware of the part played by social crises — particularly those which result in a political and/or normative vacuum — in the inducement of such a perception. On the other hand, the personal virtuosity of the leader is the central and prior element in Weber's formulation. Emerging in the midst of structural conflict and psychological ambiguity, the charismatic leader satisfies the need for a new order by exercising extraordinary personal power (Weber, 1968a:242, 1968b:1111-1112, 1114).

Charismatic leadership is an historically important form of domination;[2] however, it contributed nothing to the American struggle for independence. The American revolution, as has been frequently noted, was a conservative uprising which aspired not to the creation of a new order but to the restoration of previously held rights and liberties. It was to this objective that George Washington committed himself. Washington, therefore, did not employ his talents (which were somewhat less than extraordinary) in a situation of chaotic disorder, nor did he advocate alternatives to the prevailing political ideology. As a staunch conservative (Padover, 1955), he was devoted to the preservation rather than the radical change of his society's political culture. Moreover, Washington's leadership contained no authoritarian elements; he distinguished himself not by feats performed to acquire power but by the length he went to avoid power, and by the enthusiasm with which he relinquished the power vested in him by his countrymen.

Although George Washington was not a charismatic leader, he was the object of the most intense display of hero worship this nation has ever seen (Wector, 1941:99-147). By understanding the basis of his great attraction, we learn something about a form of heroic leadership which is quite different from that described by Weber. What is ultimately at stake in such an understanding is the resolution of an enduring structural dilemma: the contradiction between reverence for individual leaders and the ideas of democracy (Hook, 1943:229-245). Let me restate this broader aspect of the problem in the appropriate historical context.

Heroic Leadership and Democracy

The model of government to which the revolutionary American was committed, says Gordon Wood (1969:18), "possessed a compelling simplicity: politics was nothing more than a perpetual battle between the passions of the rulers, whether one or a few, and the united interest of the people — an opposition that was both inevitable and proportional." Of the words used to express this attitude in the late colonial period, those of the early eighteenth century ideologist, Thomas Gordon, were among the most widely read. "Without giving his People Liberty," wrote Gordon, "[the Governor] cannot make them happy; and by giving them Liberty, he gives up his own Power. So that...whatever is good for the People is bad for their Governors, and what is good for the Governors, is pernicious to the People" (Trenchard and Gordon, [1733] 1969:256). Assuming that hero worship cannot be generated in a society whose definition of power relations precludes strong personal authority and impassioned loyalties to a leader (Willner, 1968:4), we find ourselves faced with two problems. Not only must we ascertain the nature of the heroic leadership which emerged during the American Revolution; we must also determine how any notion of heroic leadership could have been conceived, let alone realized, at that time. Specifically, we will be concerned to know how, and why, a cult of veneration formed around one man in a culture that was explicitly disdainful of the glorification of personality, a culture in which complete deference to higher authority was ridiculed and every form of power deliberately and systematically scrutinized. We want to know how this barrier to hero worship was overcome.

An Uncharismatic Hero

That George Washington was virtually deified by his generation is certain; but there is no apparent reason why he should have been. Although Washington was, by any standard, intelligent and accomplished, he was neither a brilliant nor a self-confident man, nor was his experience (which did not include leadership of large armies) precisely suited to the needs of his time. Upon his appointment as commander of the Continental Army, therefore, Washington did not promise victory. He did not seek to embolden his followers by rattling his saber or by otherwise affirming the strength of his leadership. "Lest some unlucky event should happen," he warned, "I beg it may be remembered, by every gentleman in this room, that I, this day, declare with the utmost sincerity, I do not think myself equal to the command I am honored with" (Washington, 1931a:292). Washington's expression of modesty was not just meant for public consumption. To Patrick Henry, he privately expressed the fear that his appointment would "date my fall, and the ruin of my reputation" (Freeman, 1968:220).

Washington's diffidence proved not to be unfounded. His own eulogists admit that his armies suffered "a succession of disasters and retreats," partly through his own mistakes, and that "it may not be said of him as of Marlborough, that 'he never formed the plan of a campaign that he did not execute; never beseiged a city that he did not take; never fought a battle that he did not gain'" (Daniel, [1876] 1903:274).

Unlike some of his "self-made" contemporaries, Washington's native capacities could not overcome his limited military and political experience. "His mind was great and powerful," says Thomas Jefferson ([1814] 1926:188-189); but that mind, he adds, was not "of the very first order....It was slow in operation, being little aided by invention or imagination but sure in conclusion," In peace as well as war, therefore, Washington depended heavily on his advisors (Winthrop, [1876] 1903:251). During his first term as President, he confessed to James Madison that "he had from the beginning found himself deficient in many of the essential qualifications" for office (cited in Charles, 1956:40). The great man was also aware of his own intellectual shortcomings, making reference on more than one occasion to his "inferior endowments from nature."

Not even personal magnetism, which is often an important basis of public veneration, could be claimed by Washington. As a writer, he was fluent but lacked elegance; as a speaker, he "never outgrew a heavy, somewhat clumsy manner" (Wector, 1941:102). In addition, he was not magnanimous toward the shortcomings in others. His was a heart, in Jefferson's ([1814] 1926:189) words, "not warm in its affections." As a general, for instance, Washington commanded more respect than devotion. He believed in discipline and used the whip, gallows, and his own pistol (Flexner, 1967:46-47, 110) to enforce it. "His deeds of severity," pleads one of his eulogists (Mason, 1800:12), "were his sad tribute to justice." To social equals as well as his soldiers Washington was "the archetypal stranger" (Albanese, 1976:145): stern, distant, and glacial. "Today I dined with the President," wrote Sedgwick, "and as usual the company was as grave as at a funeral" (Charles, 1956:38).

I will discuss later the more appealing of Washington's

personal traits. His less attractive sides have been stressed now only to make the point that he was a man not unlike other men, and that other leaders of the Revolution were at least as well endowed with talent and charm as he. But to argue thus is only to affirm what hero worship entails: not the *recognition* of greatness but the *transformation*, by social definition, of the ordinary into the heroic. If we are to understand this transformation, we must place it in proper context. Statements about Washington must be matched by statements about the central needs and concerns of his society.[3]

How the Cult Emerged

In May 1775, shortly after fighting broke out at Lexington and Concord, the Second Continental Congress assembled. The public was in an excited mood. That same road on which Washington and the Virginia delegation had passed unnoticed six months earlier was now thick with onlookers. When he arrived in Philadelphia, Washington learned that he had been assigned as military advisor to New York. Several weeks later, word leaked out that he was under consideration for the general command. If that were actually to fall upon him, however, it would be through "no desire or insinuation" of his own. He even induced his friend and fellow delegate, Pendleton, to argue publicly against him. Nevertheless, the conditions of the day made Washington's appointment almost inevitable.

In its Declaration of the Causes of Taking Up Arms, Congress emphasized "We mean not to dissolve the union which has so long and so happily subsisted between us." Combining a plea for reconciliation with a threat of armed resistance, this document embodied, if it did not precisely state, the ambivalence of Congress toward its relationship with Great Britain. On the horns of this dilemma hung the choice of Washington as military commander. Proponents of reconciliation could support Washington because they knew his political position was compatible with (if not as optimistic as) their own. Proponents of separation could support him because he was a Southerner and his appointment would lend more favor to the military option, which was central to their policy.

The quality of the command given to Washington was strongly affected by uncertainty within Congress. No decision had been made by Congress that directly brought the thirteen colonies into the war being fought in New England. No continental army had been raised. There was not even a nation to fight for (the Declaration of Independence came a year later). There was only Washington, and it was to Washington, personally, that Congress pledged itself: "[T]his Congress doth now declare that they will maintain and assist him and adhere to him, the said George Washington, Esq., with their lives and fortunes...." And so from the moment he took command, says Flexner (in an unmistakably Durkheimian tone), "Washington was more than a military leader: he was an eagle, the standard, the flag, the living symbol of the cause" (1965:339).

Washington's ascension to national honor was abrupt. On his way to Boston, where the Massachusetts militia had already begun to hem in the British occupying force, he was repeatedly delayed by enthusiastic crowds. Symbols of his adoration emerged before he even did anything. While Washington was still encamped in Boston, and before even a shot was fired on his command, books were dedicated to him, children were named after him, and ships were named after both him and his wife (*Massachusetts Gazette*, October 30, 1775, March 4, 18, 1776, April 1, 1776, January 29, 1777; *Virginia Gazette*, October 1775; *Pennsylvania Gazette*, August 7, 14, 1776). In March 1776, the British (outgunned but not defeated) withdrew their troops from Boston. Before seeing a demonstration of Washington's military skill in pitched battle, Congress voted him a gold medal (Washington, 1931b:488-490) and his praises were sung throughout the land. The local homage was especially keen. The Massachusetts Assembly presented to Washington an address which praised his achievements. Harvard, in its turn, voted him the honorary degree of Doctor of Laws (*Boston Gazette*, April 8, 15, 1776).

There was no letup in veneration when the real battles sent the now "godlike Washington" and his men reeling southward in defeat. "Celebrations of his birthday [were held] while he was still the harassed commander of a lank, losing army" (Fishwick, 1954:40).

Washington as Symbolic Leader

In the introduction to one of his six volumes on the life of Washington, Douglas Southall Freeman concedes that "the transformation of the quiet Virginia planter into the revered continental commander is beyond documentary explanation" (1951:xiii). Freeman's statement points to the need for a theory that seeks to account for the onset of Washington's virtual deification. To this end, Emile Durkheim ([1912] 1965:243-244) supplies a point of departure:

> [I]n the present day just as much as in the past, we see society constantly creating sacred things out of ordinary ones. If it happens to fall in love with a man and if it thinks it has found in him the principal aspirations that move it, as well as the means of satisfying them, this man will be raised above the others and, as it were, deified....And the fact that it is society alone which is the author of these varieties of apotheosis, is evident since it frequently chances to consecrate men thus who have no right to it from their own merit.

As a prototype of the "symbolic leader" which Durkheim describes, Washington offered not "representation without mastery" (as Martin Spencer [1973:350-351] would put it), but rather more representation than mastery (for a more contemporary example, see Dow, 1968.) But what, precisely, did Washington represent during the initial phase of his career? What were the "principal aspirations" that Washington, despite his setbacks, seemed so well to satisfy?

The Rage Militaire

The abruptness and intensity of Washington's veneration after his appointment as military commander must be understood in the context of American attitudes toward the war itself. Although Washington doubted his own capacities to lead the colonies to victory, the prevalent opinion among those who favored armed resistance was not so pessimistic. Past experience had already shown the great logistical problems of European armies fighting on American soil and the dissenters felt that they could exploit this disadvantage (Buel, 1980:38). But what really motivated the Americans were religious sentiments, not technical considerations. Before Washington's appointment there had already been several skirmishes with the British, and in most of these (at Great Bridge, Nantucket, Hog Island, Gloucester, Ticonderoga, Lexington, and Boston), the Americans gave a good account of themselves. These small victories inspired confidence largely because the press and pulpit ascribed to them a religious significance. In Charles Royster's (1979:13) words, "One source of the revolutionaries' confidence lay in their obedience to God. A religious vocabulary voiced many of the calls to serve in the Continental Army and to promote its cause....God intended His punishment of warmakers only for Britons, and He entrusted its execution to Americans....This explanation obviously allowed only one outcome — American victory." While Royster exaggerates the optimism of the Americans, his statement has the merit of not underestimating it. Royster also succeeds in capturing the prevailing belief in providential intervention, well expressed in Elbridge Gerry's (1775) declaration that history could "hardly produce such a series of events as has taken place in favor of American opposition. The hand of Heaven seems to have directed every occurrence" (Albanese, 1976:83; for detail on the American "legend of providential intervention," including its use in the Revolution, see Hay, 1969a).

Associated with this religious conviction was a political climate of "hysterical and emotional ideas...inflammatory phrases...fear and frenzy, exaggeration and enthusiasm" (Wood, 1968:70, 73), all related to a strong belief in the existence of a Ministerial conspiracy to enslave the colonies (Bailyn, 1965:86-89) and a conviction that British forces were bent on a campaign of plunder and rape (Davidson, [1941] 1973; Kerr, 1962:106-107). In this context, the Americans indulged themselves in a *rage militaire* which, according to one correspondent, "took possession of the whole continent" by Spring, 1775 — the time of Washington's appointment. At this time, reports from Philadelphia indicated that "the city has turned out 4,000 men, 300 of whom are Quakers. Every County in our Province is awakened and several thousand Riflemen on our frontiers are in readiness to march down to our assistance...." Scholarly John Adams estimated that Philadelphia turned out "two thousand every day" and, after indicating that he himself was reading military books, announced "Everyone must, and will, and shall be a soldier." Abigail Adams concurred, describing the sound of cannon as "one of the grandest in nature, and is of the true species of the sublime." Another observer reports: "By accounts from all parts of the country, we find, that they are everywhere learning the use of arms, and seem determined on Liberty or Death....It is impossible to describe the military ardor which now prevails." Given the divine sponsorship of the resistance, America's newfound military fervor was amplified by pronouncements from the pulpit. As one minister warned, "When God, in his providence, calls to take the sword, if any refuse to obey, Heaven's dread artillery is levelled against him....Cursed be he that keepeth back his sword from blood." Other clergymen appeared before their congregations in full military uniform to sign recruits, before taking the field themselves. (See Royster, 1979:25; Albanese, 1976:101; Davidson, [1941] 1973:206; *Georgia Gazette*, May 31, 1775. For additional descriptions of the 1775 "war psychosis," see Buel, 1980:36-38; Scheer and Rankin, 1957:65-66.)

By the end of the first year of the war, the *rage militaire* had dissipated. Still, the early craze was repeatedly invoked as a moral standard, part of the golden age when martial enthusiasm was everywhere joined to a zealous commitment to self-sacrifice (Royster, 1979:31). But if Americans were to feel initially and later fondly recall this intangible sense of "collective efferves-cence," they would need to connect that sentiment and that recol-lection to something hard and visible. In Durkheim's ([1912] 1965:251) words:

> [We] are unable to consider an abstract entity. For we can represent only laboriously and confusedly the source of the strong sentiments which we feel. We cannot explain them to ourselves except by connecting them to some concrete object of whose reality we are vividly aware.

In essence, this is what Marshall Fishwick (1954:40) meant when, of the situation in 1775, he said, "Most Americans were hungry for a living symbol of their revolt."

The hunger, of course, explained neither the choice nor the le-gitimacy of the symbol. The symbol was in fact chosen and legit-imated by Congress. Washington (along with all general officers selected by Congress) acquired instant legitimacy because his ap-pointment came out of an honored process of reconciling regional interests and opinions. While the contemporary mind does not see this as a very good way to choose a commanding general, Ameri-cans of the revolutionary period saw things differently.

The Meaning of Republican Military Leadership

A few months after Washington received his commission, there appeared the immensely popular "New Song," whose very first stanza makes use of the new military commander as a symbol for the colonies' martial sentiments: "Since WE your brave sons, insens'd, our swords have goaded on,/Huzza, huzza, huzza, huzza for WAR and WASHINGTON" (*Virginia Gazette*, February 24, 1776). Likewise, comments on Washington's "vast military experience" and "genius" were scattered throughout the major newspapers of the day. But these kinds of statements, both poetical and prosaic, derived from an overheated emotional climate and did not capture the full complexity of what Washington meant to his contemporaries at the beginning of the war.

Washington, of course, meant different things to different people. For some of his contemporaries, experience and genius were the most important qualifications for the command, and on this basis those who disdained Washington's military competence tried to justify themselves. The most important element of this criticism, however, was its secrecy. Washington's detractors expressed themselves mainly through private correspondence rather than through formal petition to Congress (see Freeman, 1968:366-383). The critics felt they were in a minority, and they were right. For most Americans, the radically instrumental reasoning of Washington's antagonists would have made little sense.

The Americans' intuitive distrust of all political authority, especially standing armies, led them to see military genius as a particularly dangerous quality. To be sure, they wanted a soldier to help express their defiance of "the Ministry," but they wanted no part of a professional soldier. Just a few weeks after his appointment, Washington was personally addressed by the New York Congress: "[We] have the fullest assurances that whenever this important contest shall be decided...you will cheerfully resign the important deposit committed into your hands, and re-assume the character of our worthy citizen" (*Virginia Gazette*, July 14, 1775). Lacking tested institutional constraints on the ambitions of strong leaders,[4] and with the everpresent examples of Caesar and Cromwell to justify anxieties about the imposition of dictatorship, Americans at war looked not to their best military man for direction but to the military man in whom they had the most trust. One commentator thus justifies his preference for a native-born commander over the superbly trained and experienced Charles Lee, declaring that "the colonies are not so wrapped up in General Lee's military accomplishments as to give him preference..." (*Virginia Gazette*, May 1775). Acutely suspicious of the aspirations of men in power, the colonials were unwilling to base their main judgment of any leader on "mere" technical skill.

American attitudes toward Washington were shaped by another, more positive, conception regarding military leadership. Believing firmly in their divine covenant and in their own "native courage," Americans looked to the military commander (and to "rulers" in general (McKeen, 1800:7, 18) mainly for exemplary leadership and inspiration. Ironically, the tremendous prestige accorded Washington was initially based on the conviction that the war would be won (indeed, could only be won) by the righteous willfulness of the republican soldier. The great general was seen as one who, by firmness rather than brilliance of mind, harnesses and directs the citizen-soldier's supposed virtue (for detail, see Royster, 1979). This attitude was such as to lift from Washington's shoulders some of the responsibility for the outcome of his military encounters. If the victories of war result from the character of the men who fight, defeats (of which there were many) cannot be attributed to the leader alone.[5] What mattered in the leader was motivation, and the Americans hastened to acknowledge its priority. "[Concerning] the affairs of Long Island and Fort Washington," explains one commentator, "I intend no reflection on the judgement of the general officers whose opinions may have been the foundation of those disasters, for their opinions certainly proceeded from a spirit of enterprise and true intrepidity, a spirit which, I trust, will never be severely condemned by us, however it may fail of success" (*Virginia Gazette*, January 17, 1777).

Prevailing religious ideas complement this attitude. From covenant theology were drawn images of the Exodus and these furnished a "conceptual archetype" by which many Americans understood the significance of the war. Citizens of the "New Israel" knew that Moses, the leader of their spiritual predecessors, overcame his enemies not by destroying them but by preserving his followers from annihilation. Not by his own powers did he do so, but by the force of the Covenant. Correspondingly, the military retreats of the "American Moses" (for detail, see Hay, 1969b) were defined by many as either disasters occasioned by the displeasure of God and followed by public penance, or great acts of deliverance, followed by prayers of gratitude. (For detail on these religious practices, which customarily followed crises of any kind, see Kerr, 1962:59-89.)

In brief, the earliest manifestation of worship of "godlike Washington" did not depend — could not have depended — on technical genius. It emerged in the context of society's need to articulate and make concrete the fervent emotions of its citizens and the intangible virtues of its cause. And it was in the context of this need that Washington became the living symbol of the Revolution.[6]

Washington as a Symbol of Whig Values

The meaning of the Washington symbol eventually connected itself with stable cultural forms already established in the American mind. If the war effectively disposed of the substance of monarchy, the cult of the monarchy could be preserved and exploited by a new republic. The last stanza of the previously mentioned "New Song," written at the beginning of the war, concludes: "And George, his minions trembling round, dismounted from his throne/ Pay homage to America and glorious WASHINGTON." Throughout the war itself, the King's statutes and portraits were torn down; Washington's were immediately put up in their place (Cunliffe, 1958:13). The tune of the traditional anthem "God Save the King" remained the same; however, its lyrics were changed to "God Save Great Washington." By the end of the war (1783), Washington had replaced the monarch as America's base of symbolic orientation.

The prestige conferred upon Washington during the Revolutionary War was more than just a form of "expressive symbolism"; it was an interest-gathering deposit later drawn upon to sanctify the presidency (for detail see Freeman, 1968:549-550; Rossiter, 1956:76; Main, [1961] 1974:141; Charles, 1956:37-38). On the other hand, the social context and basis for Washington's election to the presidency in 1789 were not the same as for his military appointment in 1775. During this interval, the public perception of Washington underwent a profound change. As newly appointed military commander, Washington supplied the nation with a focal point for its military fervor. By the end of the war, however, Washington was the nation's central moral symbol. To understand this transformation, and to learn precisely what moral values he symbolized to those who elected him president and to those who supported that election, we need to know something about the political culture of the Revolution.

Whiggery and the Revolution

The ideology of the American Revolution drew from many sources, including Enlightenment rationalism, English Common Law, New England Puritanism, and classical antiquity. These last two sources provide many of the metaphors or "model types" through which the veneration of George Washington was expressed. From Puritanism derives the notion of Washington as the "American Moses"; from the classics comes the notion of Washington as *Pater Patriae*, "Cincinnatus of the West," and so forth. However, neither Puritanism nor classicism (nor rationalism or common law) contribute directly to the veneration of Washington, or even to the ideology of the Revolution itself. As Bailyn (1965:23) puts it, "they are everywhere illustrative, not determinative, of thought." The concepts and "root metaphors" supplied by these traditions were used to express the ideals of one branch of late seventeenth and eighteenth century whiggery.[7] Whether we document this connection through Colbourn's (1965) inventory of the libraries of the American colonies and founding fathers, or Bailyn's (1965) study of the political pamphlets distributed in the colonies during the eighteenth century, the influence of the radical social and political thought of the "Real Whigs" (John Trenchard, Thomas Gordon, Benjamin Hoadly, Robert Molesworth, Viscount Bolingbroke, and other interpreters and populizers of Locke) is beyond dispute. "More than any other single group of writers" says Bailyn (1965:19), these Englishmen "shaped the mind of the American Revolutionary generation."

Developed further by a new generation of writers, the ideals of the Real Whigs (which never evoked much interest in England) were embraced by most Americans before and after the Revolutionary War. "Before the revolution," said Jefferson, "we were all good Whigs, cordial in free principles...jealous of the executive Magistrate." During the revolution, the consensus was less perfect. Many colonists of whig persuasion were indifferent to the American cause and some remained loyal to the crown (Benton, 1969).[8] John Adams' statement, therefore, is the more precise: "In political theory, if not devotion to the patriot cause, nine tenths of the people are high Whigs" (Rossiter, 1953:143, 353). To explain which of George Washington's personal characteristics and achievements had the most significance for his countrymen, and to show why the veneration of these qualities eventually became so intense, persistent, and widespread, an understanding of whig theory, especially the doctrines of "power" and "virtue," is necessary.

The Bane of Power

The disposition of power was central to every political controversy before, during, and after the Revolutionary War. Whatever his attitude toward independence, power was dwelt upon by the eighteenth century American "endlessly, almost compulsively" (Bailyn, 1965:38), for its natural prey was individual liberty. The issue was discussed with passion and metaphoric elegance. Power has "an encroaching nature"; it "creeps by degrees and quickly subdues the whole." Power is "elastic," ever extending itself. The hand of power is "grasping" and "tenacious"; what it seizes it retains. Power is gluttonous: "restless, aspiring, insatiable," a jaw "always open to devour," an appetite "whetted, not cloyed, by possession." These concerns, as Main ([1961] 1974:127) and Kenyon (1955) make clear, became more acute as the years passed, and they preoccupied political and public discourse during the Constitutional Convention (of which Washington himself was president).

What makes power so malignant is not its intrinsic force, the prudent use of which was considered quite necessary for social order, but rather the nature of man himself. On this assumption there was strong agreement. Neo-Calvinists and freethinkers alike were convinced that man is incapable of withstanding his own temptations of power. Corruption (defined as lust for self-aggrandizement) is inherent in the species. "Such is the depravity of mankind," explains Samuel Adams, "that the ambition and lust of power above the law are predominant passions in the breasts of most men." Thus "Every man," says Thomas Allen, "by nature has the seeds of tyranny deeply implanted within him." From these premises flows "the strongest suspicion of men in authority" and a fear of the institutional weapons they control (Bailyn, 1965:41; Rossiter, 1953:372).

The Glory of Virtue

Beside the whigs' melancholy doctrine of power stands their cult of virtue. The Americans, whigs to the core, never tired of

73

celebrating the noble "private virtues," such as justice, temperance, courage, honesty, sincerity, modesty, integrity, calmness, benevolence, sobriety, piety, rationality; nor did they let up in extolling the great "public virtues," e.g., love of liberty, disinterested attachment to the public good, self-sacrifice, moral action without external coercion. What is important about this list is its function, which, unlike its content, is historically unique. Early Americans politicized the traditional Roman and Christian virtues by defining them as the counterweight to man's lust for power. As Samuel Adams (1968:Vol. 4, 124-125) put it, "Virtue and Knowledge will forever be an even Balance for Power and Riches." Thus is man saved from his own innate depravity.

Given the expansive quality of power, its division and balance was assumed to be the best structural guarantee of liberty. At the same time, whig theory taught that structures do not maintain themselves but rest ultimately on the qualities of the people who occupy positions within them. As one commentator explains, "He is the truest Friend to the Liberty of his Country, who tries most to promote its Virtue — And who so far as his Power and Influence extends, will not suffer a man to be chosen into any Office of Power and Trust, who is not a wise and virtuous Man" (*Boston Independent Advertiser*, May 29, 1749). Later, in the debate over the ratification of the Constitution in Virginia, James Madison declared, "No theoretical checks, no form of government can render us secure. To suppose that any form of government will secure liberty or happiness without any virtue in a people, is a chimerical idea" (cited in Rheinhold, 1977:8).

At a time when most Americans take for granted their government's ability to outlive its unscrupulous leaders and protect individual liberties, it is difficult to appreciate the whiggish obsession about abuse of power, or to take seriously the conviction that government stands or falls on the virtues of its leaders. But in Washington's time these fears and these beliefs were felt with special poignancy. In particular, "'the incantation of virtue,'" Meyer Rheinhold (1977:7) observes, "was most fervent during the uncertainties of the war and ensuing polemics over the Constitution." Against this background, we can better understand both the significance of Washington's veneration during the late-war and postwar period and the anxieties to which that veneration gave rise.

The Whig Hero

During the war, Washington was the most prestigious figure in the United States. However, the praise accorded him was not unambivalent. If the overwhelming and seemingly unconditional praise of Washington helped to mobilize the aspirations and sentiments of the rebelling colonists, it might also allow Washington to assume power outside the law and to use that power to impose his will upon others, with the help of the army. William Tudor expressed the concerns of many Americans when, in 1779, while speaking of Washington, he warned that "bondage is ever to be apprehended at the close of a successful struggle for liberty, when a triumphant army, elated with victories, and headed by a popular general may become more formidable than the tyrant that has been expelled....Witness the aspiring CROMWELL!....A free and wise people will never suffer any citizen to become too popular — much less too powerful. A man may be formidable to the constitution even by his virtues" (Tudor, 1779:8, 11).

In view of the political anxieties of the time, what Washington did not do during the final phase of his military career was more important than his positive accomplishments. As Daniel ([1876] 1903:274) later put it, "he left mankind bewildered with the splendid problem of whether to admire him most for what he was or what he would not be." Indeed, what Washington was derived from what he would not be. The facts of the matter are many and well known. The main point was recognized by Chastellux during his 1781 travels: "This is the seventh year that [Washington] has commanded the army, and that he has obeyed the Congress; more need not be said, especially in America, where they know how to appreciate all the merit contained in this simple fact" (Chinard, 1940:56). This observation was a sound one. Despite many wartime disagreements with Congress, Washington faithfully deferred to its policies and so affirmed the then cherished but not yet established principle of civilian control of the military. Despite his great popularity, which could have been used as a cushion against military setbacks and a weapon against Congress, Washington made it known to Congress that he was ready to resign his command at any time. Even more, he showed himself to be a great ally when Congress was itself in need. During the post-Yorktown crisis, when Washington could have easily taken over the government by military coup, he dissuaded his unpaid officers and men from taking action against a vulnerable and financially bankrupt government. And not only did Washington sternly rebuke those who wished to restore the monarchy around him; he hastened to surrender his military power at war's end and return to private life. Only the most persistent appeals of his countrymen could induce him later to renounce that life and accept the presidency. Ironically, it was this repeatedly demonstrated indifference to personal power which allowed Washington to become a stronger president than a more avaricious incumbent could have hoped to become. Given deep public distrust in the office, the presidential prerogatives on which he insisted, though they were all well within the Constitution, would probably not have been granted to a less trusted incumbent (Rossiter, 1956:85-87, 1959).

Against a background of almost paranoiac concern over the use and usurpation of power, and an ideology which attributed to man an inherent "corruption" or lust for power, it is no wonder that Washington was looked upon as the most extraordinary moral hero of his time. In those authoritarian contexts which give rise to the Weberian model of heroic leadership, it is the successful taking and exercise of power that evokes admiration; in late eighteenth century America, it was just the opposite: refusal to assume power, and haste in giving it up, were the ingredients that went into political spectacles. (The extraordinary Annapolis ceremony, wherein Washington surrenders his commission to Congress, is the signal illustration of this point. [For eyewitness detail, see Burnett, 1934:Vol. 7, 394-395, 398-399].) Refusing under every condition to convert his prestige into political gain, Washington personified the heroic archetype implied by the Anglo-American whig tradition. Thus did he allay the public's intense suspicion of power, a suspicion which might have otherwise handcuffed his and many subsequent governments.

Taking Stock of a Hero

The correspondence between the public's whiggish values and Washington's own conduct and beliefs[9] does not in itself account for his enormous prestige during the postwar period. Proof of this connection can only be obtained by looking at Washington directly through the eyes of his contemporaries. The problem is to find the data that would enable us to do so.

While expression of praise for Washington was effusive during the postwar years, few documents actually described the ultimate grounds of this praise. Letters sent back and forth among delegates to the Constitutional Convention and among other influential citizens say much about the desirability of Washington as president but little about precisely *why* he should be elected. And while Washington's prestige grew during his first term as president, little was said to help us understand its source.[10] Perhaps the first serious effort to make explicit the moral values personified in Washington was that of Parson Mason Locke Weems (1962). Weems' immensely popular biography, already completed in first edition form by 1799, was "sufficiently minute" on the military and political aspects of Washington's life and very expansive on "his Great Virtues." However, this production represents the perceptions of but one man. Not until Washington's death do we find a collective effort to articulate systematically the basis of his greatness. This effort is condensed in the funeral orations delivered during the last days of 1799 and the early months of 1800. Better than any single writing, this set of orations makes explicit what Washington meant to his contemporaries.

The 1799-1800 funeral eulogies did much to crystallize popular conceptions of Washington (Bryan, 1952:55). Authority of source is one reason why the eulogies were so influential. Among the men who delivered orations immediately after Washington's death were many ministers addressing religious congregations. These men were political as well as spiritual leaders and in their sermons we find every nuance of the dominant political faith (Rossiter, 1953:55; Kerr, 1962; for a summary of the political activities of many of these clergymen, see the *Dictionary of American Biography*). Political convictions are reflected in the whiggish vocabulary with which the clergy eulogized the fallen leader and in the clergy's whiggish preoccupation with the tension between ambition and virtue. This vocabulary, and the resolution of this tension, is expressed through reference to Washington's activities during and after the war.

Eulogists hastened to point out that the civic virtue that Washington displayed during the war was motivated by his devotion to Providence, which had made him the instrument of Its plan, and not by his desire for gain after the war. Of the many proofs of his "disinterest," the most dramatic is the occasion on which he voluntarily resigned his commission to Congress. Whig ideologist and poet Jonathan Sewall (1799:12) declares:

> Did he, like Caesar, after vanquishing his countrymen's foes, turn his conquering armies against that country? Far,

far otherwise. Before the great Council of our Nation, the PA-TRIOT-HERO appeared, and in the presence of numerous, admiring spectators, resigned his victorious sword into the hands of those who gave it.

AUGUST Spectacle! Glorious Example! For my own part, I never contemplate it but each fibre vibrates with rapture, and the vital current trembles through every artery of my frame!

In minds haunted by the dangerous specter of power, such ecstacies could be, and were, induced by any form of political diffidence. Central to the Washington cult's stock of knowledge, therefore, was not only the spectacle of his relinquishment of military power but also the certainty of his reluctance to assume political power.

From the presidency of the Constitutional Convention to the presidency of the United States, Washington is known to have assumed power with noble intention but little enthusiasm. Once established in high office, his main problem was not how to retain the position but how to relinquish it. Thus, having allowed himself to be twice elected to the presidency, only "the promulgation of his fixed resolution stopped the anxious wishes of an affectionate people from adding a third unanimous testimony of their unabated confidence" (Lee, 1800:13). This voluntary retirement from the presidency, says the Reverend Bancroft (a former Minute Man) "is the consummation of character; the last evidence of the greatness of the man" (1800:12). There is in all of this a certain contradiction: sacrifice is made, and temptation resisted, by both taking power and by giving it up. But such a violation of logic underscores the main point of the eulogy: that the ultimate grounds of Washington's veneration is not prowess, but morality; not achievement, but virtue. No better summation (or more effective continuation) of a century of whig political discourse could be conceived.

Conceptions of heroic leadership which emphasize talent and deed have little affinity with that which emerges from the Washington eulogies. These are not centrally concerned with great exploits. If Washington's achievements are celebrated, it is mainly because they allow us to gauge his character, and it is this inner merit which defines his greatness. In the words of Henry Holcombe, a minister and former officer in the Revolutionary Army (1800:11), "He would have been equalled by several, if he had not shone in the mild majesty of morals." On this point most of the eulogies are emphatic. Fisher Ames (1800:130), a political leader and biblical scholar, explains:

> [It] requires thought and study to understand the true ground of the superiority of his character over many others, whom he resembled in the principles of action, and even in the manner of acting. But perhaps he excels all the greatness that ever lived, in the steadiness of his adherence to his maxims of life, and in the uniformity of all his conduct to these same maxims....[If] there were any errors in his judgment, we know of no blemishes in his virtue....He changed mankind's ideas of political greatness.

Considering the uniqueness of the republican ideals made animate by Washington, Samuel West, one of the most ardent of revolutionary whigs, agrees with Ames. "How widely different," West (1800:12) declares, "is this from what the world has been used to estimate as greatness."

To dramatize the nature of this contrast, Washington's eulogists looked for counterparts among history's great leaders and founders of states. (This tactic also served nationalistic interests by demonstrating the superiority of America's founding hero over the heroes of other states, present and past.) Since many Americans saw their new republic as a religious as well as a political entity (Albanese, 1976), eulogists sought and found positive counterparts to Washington in the sacred history of the Old Testament. Joshua, Gideon, Elijah, David, and, above all, Moses, were moral prototypes of the leader of the New Israel. Discussed in much more detail are the negative prototypes supplied by the whig interpretation of political history. The more recurrent comparisons are drawn between Washington and Alexander, Julius Caesar, Cromwell, Peter the Great, Frederick the Great, Marlborough and Napoleon. To each of these figures Washington compares favorably. This is not because of his genius, which is in fact no match for theirs, but because every one of his counterparts is blemished by a fatal moral weakness: for Alexander, it is self-indulgence and intemperance; for Caesar and Cromwell, a willingness to compromise the liberties of their countrymen; for Peter the Great, fiendishness and criminality; for Frederick the Great, ostentation and perversion; for Marlborough, shameless fraudulence; for Napoleon, a thirst for domestic dictatorship and foreign conquest. These men and their assembled exploits embody the established formula for heroism "to which the aspiring son of pride has waded" (West, 1800:12-13). Among such men "greatness and guilt have too often been allied," says the Reverend (and former Connecticut legislator) Thomas Baldwin (1800:23). In distinct contrast, Washington's achievements were "not erected upon the agonies of the human heart" (Bancroft, 1800:16). He could "lead without dazzling mankind" (Ames, 1800:3), and so achieve a fame that is "whiter than it is brilliant" (Baldwin, 1800:23).

This conclusion, along with the reasoning which supports it, represents the most conspicuous and elaborate theme — and the most common denominator — of the eulogies delivered during the months following Washington's death. For every succeeding generation this message has been repeated and amplified (Schwartz, 1982).

Conclusion

Grounded in a different set of social circumstances, the perception of Washington at the time of his death was not something that could be read from the way he was perceived during the early part of his career. The instant veneration that Washington enjoyed upon his military appointment was generated in a context of great emotional fervor. Since the excited expressions of praise for Washington preceded any concrete achievements on his part, it is fair to assume that any man filling the role of commander-in-chief would have been as much esteemed as he was. In this sense, the initial phase of Washington's career as a national symbol was "role-based" and the result of "affective induction." In contrast, the postwar praise of Washington invariably made references to what he did and did not do as commanding general, and those aspects of his performance expressly singled out for acclaim had, as we have seen, a distinct affinity for the tenets of the Anglo-American whig tradition. The tradition itself played a different part in society's reaction to Washington in the early and later phases of his career. While the ideals of whiggery had nothing directly to do with his abrupt deification in 1775, these ideals did generate assumptions about Washington's "disinterested" motives, his respect for the role of citizen-soldier, the minimal contribution of genius to his military greatness, and so forth. Only at war's end were these assumptions verified by actual performance, and, in the context of public preoccupation over the redistribution of institutional power, it was this verification which transformed

Washington into an absolutely credible symbol of the nation's political morality. In this sense, the second phase of Washington's veneration was "performance-based" and the result of "moral induction."

In both phases of Washington's career, the correspondence between his veneration and the concerns of his countrymen is mediated by a kind of "venerational reason," a form of encoding based on metaphoric appreciation. Commitment to a political culture thus shows up in the form of devotion to a man. To see Washington in this way is to see him as a "collective representation," a visible *symbol* of the values and tendencies of his society rather than a *source* of these values and tendencies. Representing the conservative tone first emitted by Durkheim,[11] this formulation cannot be applied to the more innovative types of heroic leadership. Of these types Max Weber speaks with the greatest force and clarity. On the other hand, to see Washington as the symbol of a deeply entrenched whig tradition is important because it permits us to see the charismatic hero from a different point of view. Personified by Washington, the republican ideal does not merely deviate from Weber's conception of charisma; it is its very antithesis. The republican leader and the charismatic leader represent the two polar forms of heroic leadership.

While the great charismatic leader exudes confidence in his extraordinary abilities, thrives on power and glorification and, lacking ties to the established social order, seeks to effect its radical change, the great republican leader, as exemplified by Washington, affirms the traditional values and structures of his society by repudiating personal power. Thus if the American Revolution was an essentially conservative uprising — a struggle not to create but to maintain freedoms and rights — then the image of Washington may be its perfect symbolic expression. The respects in which this expression opposes Weber's image of heroic leadership are summarized in Table 1.

Stressing change over tradition, assigning priority of action over structure, and focusing on the possibility of sudden social transformation by extraordinary men, the elements in the left-hand column of this table celebrate the decisive deed and the historical significance of a leading figure's initiative. By contrast, the traits listed in the right-hand column of Table 1 reflect a political ideology more respectful of institutional restraints and procedures, one which conceives of power not as a prize to be seized from the community but as an obligation imposed by it.

Accordingly, whoever personifies this ideology must be the model public servant who overcomes the authoritarian potential inherent in his own glorification; he must distinguish himself from the Caesaristic leader who exploits mass support for the purpose of establishing charismatic dictatorship.

According to the German scholar Johannes Kuhn (1932:142), "It is not easy for Europeans to comprehend the significance of a man like Washington. We are too accustomed to seek human greatness in unusual talents and gifts of an individual nature." Drawing from this same intellectual tradition, a tradition which informed the leadership theories of Nietzsche, Freud, and Michels (Bell, 1965), Weber could find in the leader's "specific gifts of the body and mind" the basis of his followers' "duty" to submit to his commands (1968b:1112). Against this conception, with its emphasis on entitlement, privilege, and strength, the ideal of heroic leadership that took root in eighteenth century America stressed the republican virtues of obligation, sacrifice, and disinterestedness. This ideal is important not only for its practical political significance but also because it embodies a solution to one of political philosophy's most enduring dilemmas: the reconciliation of democratic structures to the veneration of the individual hero. The great historical significance of Washington is that he gave this ideal its first and most dramatic personification. By worshipping Washington, then, Americans could worship themselves.

Table 1

Washington and the Weberian Hero

The Charismatic Leader	*Washington*
Leader is self-appointed. He is "called" to a social mission and exudes self-confidence in his ability to carry it out.	Believes in mission but expresses no confidence in his ability to lead it. Seeks to avoid the leadership role to which he is appointed by others.
Leader is unattached to established social institutions and plays no part in their activities.	Washington is a member of the elite establishment, an incumbent representative and protector of the central institutions of his society.
Leader is a radical who seeks to destroy existing traditions.	Washington is a conservative who is totally committed to existing traditions.
Leader achieves and maintains authority by putting extraordinary talents to use in the performance of miraculous feats and/or the formulation of a new ideology.	Washington's talents are not extraordinary. He performs no unusual military or political feats and propounds nothing new in the way of ideology.
Leader rejects rational administrative conduct. He dispenses power and justice in a "particularistic" manner, consistent with his personal interests and missions.	Washington is an incumbent in military and political bureaucracies. Administers power and justice according to impersonal "universalistic" standards.
Leader takes no part in institution building. His ideals and authority are routinized by disciples and successors.	Washington plays a direct role in both the creation and administration of new institutional structures.
Leader derives his prestige by the seizing and effective use of power, thus demonstrating "strength in life."	Washington derives his prestige by the avoidance and relinquishment of power, thus demonstrating "virtue."

Notes

* Useful comments on earlier versions of this paper were made by Robert Ellis, Barry Glassner, Eugene Miller, Martha Myers, Michael Schudson, Terence Thornberry, and Eviatar Zerubavel. Criticism and recommendations of three anonymous reviewers were especially helpful. The project was supported by the Institute for Behavioral Research, University of Georgia.

1. Sparks' life of Washington was published in 1835; the first of Irving's volumes appeared in 1855. For a survey of earlier and later biographical works, up to 1935, see O'Neill (1935:155-176). Of the many lives of Washington published since 1935, Freeman's and Flexner's are the most comprehensive. The initial volumes of these works appeared in 1948 and 1965 respectively.

2. For inquiries into the part played by charismatic leadership in the recent emergence of new states in the Third World, see Apter, 1963; Dow, 1968; Fagan, 1965; Friedland, 1964; Runciman, 1963.

3. There were central or modal tendencies in the veneration of Washington and the concerns of his society. The correspondence between these tendencies, as they evolved over time, is the main topic of this paper. A proper treatment of the variability in attitudes toward Washington, and of the social needs and concerns unique to different parts of his society, must be given elsewhere.

4. Although Congress was empowered to appoint and dismiss officers, many doubted its ability to use that power to dismiss a popular officer — especially one whose prestige would eventually become, in Fishwick's (1954:40) words, "greater than the prestige of the United States government." As a matter of fact, Congress's power over any officer was called into question by the Newburgh revolt, which was checked not by Congress itself but through the personal influence that Washington exerted on its behalf. In this respect, it may be said that the Articles of Confederation, designed to limit the authority and dignity of Congress, worked too well.

5. In hindsight, Washington could be attributed with more responsibility for the outcome of the war. Although confidence in the civic virtue of the republican citizen and soldier was strong during the war's initial phase, it petered out as the war dragged on. Enlistment and discipline problems, mass desertions, outright disloyalty, as well as civilian unwillingness to lend all-out support for the war, gradually eroded the Americans' belief that they were "republicans by nature." Against this background of apathy, treachery, and half-hearted gestures, examples of genuine devotion to the cause stood out in bold relief. By war's end, this

84

devotion was nowhere better exemplified than in Washington's conduct.

6. The contest was of course not exhausted by this one need. There were others. During the Revolutionary War, the integration of competing regional, political, and economic interests under a single government was high on the list of American concerns. The war itself raised this colonial society to a higher level of integration, which was eventually formalized by federal charter; however, the solidarity thus achieved was fragmentary and tentative. It was this condition — the still precarious state of political union — which intensified America's search for symbols of nationality and tradition. In a separate paper, I am considering these two quests in relation to Washington's veneration and exploring the respects in which he helped satisfy his society's need for symbols of union and nationhood. But this need does not explain why Washington was initially embraced as a national hero; nor does it explain what values he eventually came to symbolize, or why he came to symbolize them.

7. The word whig derives from *Whiggamore*, which was originally applied to the poorer rural peasant of western Scotland. In 1648, the Presbyterians who marched on Edinburgh to seize control of the government from the Royalist Party were designated as whigs, as were both the "exclusioners" who opposed the succession of the Catholic James II to the throne and those who overthrew him in the Glorious Revolution of 1689. However, William of Orange, whom the whigs placed in power, was indifferent to their support, and his successor, Anne, relied on Tory ministers. Not until the accession of the Hanoverian line in 1714 did the 46-year whig oligarchy begin. Distinguishing themselves from their nominal counterparts in Parliament (by whom they were vastly outnumbered), the Real Whigs denounced the shortcomings of the Glorious Revolution and the Hanoverian monarchs. Limitations on the crown were proposed and justified by asserting the values of (pre-Norman) Saxon democracy. The old Gothic limits on power were construed to be the institutional ancestor of Parliament itself. Real Whigs believed that the viability of this "constitution" depended on the virtues and self-restraint of rulers as well as common citizens. From their perception of ambition and venality in high places, the whigs concluded that this constitution had been betrayed (Robbins, 1959; Colbourn, 1965:3-56; Wood, 1969:3-45).

8. During the early phase of the war, most Americans were probably ambivalent about separation from Great Britain. In fact, Washington himself toasted the Crown and flew a Union Jack flag from the time of his appointment as commanding general to the time of

the issuance of the Declaration of Independence. On the other hand, support for the policy of separation was considerable, and one reason for this support is that proponents of the "patriot cause" enjoyed almost absolute control over the press (Davidson, [1941] 1973:226). As it turns out, this monopoly was instrumental in containing the propagation of anti-Washington sentiments. The actual extent of these sentiments is difficult to ascertain, since positive as well as negative statements about Washington were made by the hard-line Tories (Borden and Borden, 1972:57-59, 61). As for the few Tory newspapers, they did what they could to undermine the deification of the American commander (to whom they often referred as "Mr." Washington), but eventually acknowledged his esteem by printing their propaganda messages over his name (see, for example, *Georgia Royal Gazette*, March 22, 1781).

9. Washington's extraordinary sensitivity to the uses of power in a republic (Morgan, 1980) was at least partly attributable to his understanding of and belief in the whiggish ideals of the revolution. In an analysis of book holdings of the founding fathers, Colbourn (1965:153) points out that among the 900 volumes in Washington's library were the writings of Burgh, Macaulay, and other English whig ideologies. Indeed, Washington corresponded with Catherine Macaulay (a lady "whose principles are so much and so justly admired by the friends of liberty and of mankind" [Washington, 1938:174]) from 1785 until her death in 1791. Washington was acquainted not only with the whig writers but also with the classical literature from which these writers drew part of their own inspiration. One of Washington's favorite plays (and a favorite of many other whigs) was Addison's *Cato*. Likewise, Wood (1969:50) and Montgomery (1936, 1960) attribute some of Washington's most conspicuous virtues — restraint, temperance, fortitude, dignity, and independence — to his devotion to the perceived ideals of the Roman republic.

10. Although his political views differed from those of the anti-Federalists and, later, the Republicans, vigorous public criticism of Washington (of which he was acutely sensitive) was actually infrequent. Antagonism toward Washington was probably greatest among the leaders of the Republican "faction" during his second term as President; however, their sentiments were not made public for fear of alienating most of the Republican constituency. As Thomas Jefferson complained, "Republicanism must lie on the oars, resign the vessel to its pilot, and themselves to the course he thinks best for them" (Flexner, 1969:276).

11. The tone is not uniquely Durkheimian. Indeed, the fact that it is heard at all in the United States, says Talcott Parsons (1968:67), is

partly due to the intellectual taste which Charles Horton Cooley helped to establish. Documentation of Parson's claim includes Cooley's ([1902] 1964:317-357) essay on leadership and personal ascendancy. Here Cooley prefigures Durkheim when he points out that the intangible values associated with a society become most vividly manifest in the people who embody them. Deep feelings about a nation, he says, "almost invariably connects itself with a personal image....The function of the great and famous man, [therefore], is to be a symbol." While the lines of analysis followed by Durkheim and Cooley are by no means identical, a common focus is given in their emphasis on the cultural and institutional setting in which the leader operates. In contrast to Weber, who sees great men and radical change as inseparable, the more general approach that has developed from Durkheim's and Cooley's work alerts us to the way social definitions of great men express the continuities, as well as the discontinuities, of history. Many students of heroic leadership have been influenced by this approach (Czarnowski, [1919] 1975; Case, 1933: Mecklin, 1941; Turner and Killian, 1957; Klapp, 1948, 1962, 1964; Cohen, 1979, Turner, 1974).

References

Adams, Samuel (1968). *The Writings of Samuel Adams*. Harry A. Cushing, ed. Vol. 3 and 4 (New York: Octagon Books).

Albanese, Catherine L. (1976). *Sons of the Fathers: The Civil Religion of the American Revolution* (Philadelphia: Temple University Press).

Ames, Fisher (1800). *An Oration on the Sublime Virtues of General George Washington* (New York: Smith and Stevens).

Apter, David E. (1963). *Ghana in Transition* (New York: Atheneum).

Bailyn, Bernard (1965). *Pamphlets of the American Revolution, 1750-1776* (Cambridge: Harvard University Press).

Baldwin, Thomas (1800). *A Sermon Delivered to the Second Baptist Society...Occasioned by the Death of General George Washington* (Boston: Manning and Loring).

Bancroft, Aaron (1800). *An Eulogy on the Character of the Late General George Washington* (Worcester, MA: Isaiah Thomas).

Bell, Daniel (1965). "Notes on Authoritarian and Democratic Leadership," in Alvin W. Gouldner, ed., *Studies in Leadership* (New York: Russell and Russell), pp. 395-408.

Benton, William A. (1969). *Whig-Loyalism* (Ruthersford, NJ: Fairleigh Dickinson University Press).

Boorstin, Daniel J. (1965). *The Americans* (New York: Random House).

Borden, Morton and Penn Borden (1972). *The American Tory* (Englewood Cliffs: Prentice-Hall).

Bryan, William A. (1952). *George Washington in American Literature, 1775-1865* (New York: Columbia University Press).

Buel, Richard, Jr. (1980). *Dear Liberty: Connecticut's Mobilization for the Revolutionary War* (Middleton, CT: Wesleyan University Press).

Burnett, Edmund C. (1934). *Letters of Members of the Continental Congress*. Vol. 7 (Washington, D.C.: Carnegie Institute).

Case, Clarence M. (1933). "Leadership and Conjuncture: A Sociological Hypothesis," *Sociology and Social Research* 17:510-513.

Charles, Joseph (1956). *The Origins of the American Party System* (Williamsburg, VA: Institute of Early American History and Culture).

Chinard, Gilbert (1940). *George Washington as the French Knew Him: A Collection of Texts* (Princeton: Princeton University Press).

Cohen, Abner (1979). "Political Symbolism," *Annual Review of Anthropology* 7:87-113.

Colbourn, H. Trevor (1965). *The Lamp of Experience* (Chapel Hill: University of North Carolina Press).

Cooley, Charles Horton [1902] (1964). *Human Nature and the Social Order* (New York: Schocken).

Cunliffe, Marcus (1958). *George Washington: Man and Monument* (Boston: Little, Brown).

Czarnowski, Stefan [1919] (1975). *Le Culte des Heros et Ses Conditions Sociales* (New York: Arno Press).

Daniel, John W. [1876] (1903). "Oration by Hon. John W. Daniel." *Dedication of the Washington Monument*. Senate Document, Vol. 21, No. 224 (Washington, D.C.: Government Printing Office), pp. 260-285.

Davidson, Philip [1941] (1973). *Propaganda and the American Revolution, 1763-1783* (New York: W.W. Norton).

Dow, Thomas E. (1968). "The Role of Charisma in Modern African Development," *Social Forces* 46:328-338.

Durkheim, Emile [1912] (1965). *The Elementary Forms of the Religious Life* (New York: Free Press).

Emmet, Dorothy (1958). *Function, Purpose and Power* (London: MacMillan).

Fagan, Richard R. (1965). "Charismatic Authority and the Leadership of Fidel Castro," *Western Political Quarterly* 18:275-284.

Fishwick, Marshall W. (1954). *American Heroes: Myth and Reality* (Washington, D.C.: Public Affairs Press).

Flexner, James T. (1965). *George Washington, 1732-1775.* Vol. 1; (1967). *George Washington, 1775-1783.* Vol. 2; (1969). *George Washington, 1793-1799.* Vol. 4 (Boston: Little, Brown).

Freeman, Douglas (1951). *George Washington.* Vol. 3 (New York: Scribners).

— (1968). *Washington.* Abridged by Richard Howell (New York: Scribners).

Friedland, William H. (1964). "For a Sociological Concept of Charisma," *Social Forces* 43:18-36.

Hay, Robert P. (1969a). "Providence and the American Past," *Indiana Magazine of History* 65:79-101.

— (1969b). "George Washington: American Moses," *American Quarterly* 21:780-791.

Holcombe, Henry (1800). *A Sermon Occasioned by the Death of Lieutenant General George Washington* (Savannah: Seymour and Wollhopter).

Hook, Sidney (1943). *The Hero in History* (New York: John Day).

Jefferson, Thomas [1814] (1926). "Letter to Dr. Walter Jones," in J.G. de Roulhac Hamilton, ed. *The Best Letters of Thomas Jefferson* (Boston: Houghton-Mifflin), pp. 187-192.

Kenyon, Cecelia M. (1955). "Men of Little Faith: the Anti-Federalists on the Nature of Representative Government," *William and Mary Quarterly*, 3rd series, 12:3-46.

Kerr, Harry P. (1962). "The Character of Political Sermons Preached at the Time of the American Revolution." Unpublished Ph.D. Dissertation. Cornell University.

Klapp, Orrin E. (1948). "The Creation of Popular Heroes," *American Journal of Sociology* 54:135-141.

— (1962). *Heroes, Villains and Fools* (Englewood Cliffs: Prentice-Hall).

— (1964). *Symbolic Leaders* (Chicago: Aldine).

Kuhn, Johannes (1932). "Address to George Washington Bicentennial Banquet, Dresden," in *History of the George Washington Bicentennial Celebration* (Washington, D.C.: George Washington Bicentennial Commission), pp. 142-143.

Lee, Henry (1800). *A Funeral Oration Prepared and Delivered at the Request of Congress* (Brooklyn: Thomas Kirk).

Main, Jackson Turner [1961] (1974). *The Anti-Federalists* (New York: W.W. Norton).

Mason, John M. (1800). *A Funeral Oration Delivered in the Brick Presbyterian Church in the City of New York* (New York: G.F. Hopkins).

McKeen, Joseph (1800). *Sermon Preached Before the Council, the Senate, and House of Representatives of the Commonwealth of Massachusetts* (Boston: Young and Minns).

Mecklin, John M. (1941). *The Passing of the Saint* (Chicago: University of Chicago Press).

Montgomery, Henry C. (1936). "Washington the Stoic," *Classical Journal* 31:371-373.

— (1960). "Addison's Cato and George Washington," *Classical Journal* 55:210-212.

Morgan, Edmund S. (1980). *The Genius of George Washington* (New York: W.W. Norton).

O'Neill, Edward H. (1935). *A History of American Biography: 1800-1935* (Philadelphia: University of Pennsylvania Press).

Padover, Saul K. (1955). "George Washington: Portrait of a True Conservative," *Social Research* 22:199-222.

Parsons, Talcott (1968). "Cooley and the Problem of Internalization," in Albert J. Riess, Jr., ed., *Cooley and Sociological Analysis* (Ann Arbor: University of Michigan Press), pp. 48-67.

Rheinhold, Meyer (1977). "The Classics and the Quest for Virtue in Eighteenth Century America," in *The Usefulness of Classical Learning in the Eighteenth Century* (University Park, PA: American Philosophical Association), pp. 6-26.

Robbins, Caroline (1959). *The Eighteenth-Century Commonwealthman* (Cambridge: Harvard University Press).

Rossiter, Clinton (1953). *Seedtime of the Republic* (New York: Harcourt, Brace and World).

— (1956). *The American Presidency* (New York: New American Library).

— (1959). "Our Two Greatest Presidents," *American Heritage* 10:13ff.

Royster, Charles (1979). *A Revolutionary People at War: The Continental Army and American Character, 1775-1783* (Chapel Hill: University of North Carolina Press).

Runciman, W.G. (1963). "Charismatic Legitimacy and One-Party Rule in Ghana," *Archives Europeenes de Sociologie* 4:148-165.

Scheer, George F. and Hugh F. Rankin (1957). *Rebels and Redcoats* (Cleveland: World Publishing).

Schlesinger, Arthur, Jr. (1963). "On Heroic Leadership and the Dilemma of Strong Men and Weak Peoples," in Arthur Schlesinger, Jr., *The Politics of Hope* (Boston: Houghton-Mifflin), pp. 1-22.

Schutz, John A. and Douglass Adair, eds. (1966). *The Spur of Fame: Dialogues of John Adams and Benjamin Rush, 1805-1813* (San Marino, CA: Huntington Library).

Schwartz, Barry (1982). "Basic Themes in the Veneration of George Washington." Unpublished manuscript.

Sewall, Jonathan M. (1799). *Eulogy on the Late General Washington at St. John's Church* (Portsmouth, NH: William Treadwell).

Spencer, Martin E. (1973). "What is Charisma?" *British Journal of Sociology* 24:341-354.

Trenchard, John and Thomas Gordon [1733] (1969). *Cato's Letters*. Vol. 2 (New York: Russell and Russell).

Tudor, William (1779). *An Oration Delivered...to Commemorate the Bloody Tragedy of the Fifth of March, 1770* (Boston: Edes and Gill).

Turner, Ralph and Lewis Killian (1957). *Collective Behavior* (Englewood Cliffs: Prentice-Hall).

Turner, Victor (1974). "Hidalgo: History as Social Drama," in *Dramas, Fields and Metaphors: Symbolic Action in Human Society* (Ithaca: Cornell University Press), pp. 98-155.

Washington, George (1931a). *The Writings of George Washington*. Vol. 3; (1931b) Vol. 4; (1938) Vol. 28. John C. Fitzpatrick, ed. (Washington, D.C.: Government Printing Office).

Weber, Max (1968a) *Economy and Society*. Vol. 1; (1968b) Vol. 2 (Berkeley: University of California Press).

Wector, Dixon (1941) *The Hero in America. A Chronicle of Hero-Worship* (Ann Arbor: University of Michigan Press).

Weems, Mason L. (1962). *The Life of Washington*. Marcus Cunliffe, ed. (Cambridge: Harvard University Press).

West, Samuel (1800). *Greatness the Result of Goodness: A Sermon Occasioned by the Death of George Washington* (Boston: Manning and Loring).

Willner, Ann Ruth (1968). *Charismatic Political Leadership*. Research Monograph No. 32 (Princeton: Center of International Studies).

91

Winthrop, Robert C. [1876] (1903). "Oration by Hon. Robert C. Winthrop." *Dedication of the Washington Monument.* Senate Document, Vol. 21, No. 224 (Washington, D.C.: Government Printing Office), pp. 234-260.

Wood, Gordon S. (1968). "Rhetoric and Reality in the American Revolution," in Frank O. Gatell and Allen Weinstein, eds., *American Themes: Essays in Historiography* (New York: Oxford University Press), pp. 55-80.

— (1969). *The Creation of the American Republic, 1776-1787* (Chapel Hill: University of North Carolina Press).

Wright, Esmond (1955). "Washington: the Man and the Myth," *History Today* 5:825-832.

PART TWO:

CONTRASTING MODELS

SAMUEL ADAMS AND SAINT-JUST: CONTRASTING EXAMPLES OF PROFESSIONAL REVOLUTIONARIES

Moshe Hazani

The American and French revolutions offer clear-cut examples of the two different, if not opposite, leadership styles. They are exemplified in the lives and work of two political leaders who were directly involved in the most dramatic events of their time: Samuel Adams, among the most outstanding radicals of the American Revolution, whom Jefferson called "Truly the man of the revolution"; and Saint-Just, one of the the most outstanding radicals of the French Revolution, who has become a legend, both as the "archangel of terror" and as the harbinger of the modern welfare state. Both leaders lived during approximately the same period; they participated in political activities which were influenced by one another; and they were both radical believers in republican democracy. It is against the background of these similarities that the differences in their styles of revolutionary leadership stand out.

Samuel Adams[1] was born in Boston in 1722 and graduated from Harvard College in 1740. He was active alongside his father, one of the leading patriots of his day, in the struggle against the British in the Land Bank affair. In the 1760s he was among the leaders in the struggle against the British over the Sugar Act and the Stamp Act. First elected to the General Court, the colonial legislature, in 1766, he was appointed Secretary, a position which gave him considerable influence behind the scenes. In 1768 the British army landed in Boston and the Boston Massacre occurred. Adams then succeeded in bringing about the removal of the army. Between 1769 and 1770, he struggled against the Townshend Duties, but did not succeed in convincing the colonists to break with England over them. Adams initiated and organized the Massachusetts Convention of Towns, an event considered by many as crucial to moving the colony in the direction of republicanism. In 1772 he founded the Boston Committee of Correspondence, a tool which unified the cities of New England for a joint struggle and reached the southern colonies as well. He was active in the struggle against the Tea Act of 1773 and was among the organizers of the Boston Tea Party.

Adams was a delegate to the first and second Continental Congresses and later a member of the Massachusetts convention which formulated the state's constitution. He was also a delegate to the Massachusetts convention which ratified the Federal Constitution and, through his struggle, the Bill of Rights was eventually added to the Constitution. He served as both lieutenant-governor (1789-93) and governor (1794-97) of Massachusetts. When national parties were established, he joined the cause of the Democratic-Republicans as a supporter of Jefferson. He died in 1803.

Louis-Antoine-Léon de Saint-Just[2] was born in Picardy in 1767 and grew up in the rural town of Blérancourt. After a stormy adolescence, including six months in a juvenile prison, he graduated in law at Reims in 1788 and moved to Paris. There he joined bohemian circles and published political-erotic satire, for which he was threatened with arrest. He was in Paris on Bastille Day, but did not participate in the events. He returned to Blérancourt, apparently without money, became active in local politics, and harbored an ambition to return to Paris. In 1791 he published a moderate political treatise, *l'Esprit de la Révolution et de la Constitution de France*, which earned him considerable popularity. That same year he was chosen as a district representative to the legislative assembly, but was disqualified for being under the minimum age of twenty-five. In 1792 he was elected to the Republican National Convention as its youngest member, two weeks after turning twenty-five. He immediately stood out with his radical speech calling for the trial and execution of Louis XVI. In May 1793 he was elected as a member of the well-known *Comité de salut public* and served on it until 9 Thermidor (July 27, 1794). The next day he was executed along with Robespierre.

As a political leader Saint-Just stands out for three major reasons: he initiated a centralist welfare state; he organized the defense of Alsace against the Austro-Prussian invasion, an operation he carried out with astonishing success; and he was the premier advocate of political terror, whose speeches sent Danton, Hébert, and their comrades to the guillotine. With this he became the personification of the reign of terror.

Saint-Just became a legend in France. Some saw him as a monster, while others viewed him as an enlightened social reformer who was ahead of his time. "He is found in that place at which legend and reality meet," wrote André Malraux.[3]

History has distorted the images of both Adams and Saint-Just. Adams was perceived until recently as a wild and unbalanced radical who stood at the head of a Boston mob and led his followers into unrestrained riots. Maier has now demonstrated that this description has no basis in fact.⁴ Adams was an astute and clever politician who was repelled by violence and who tried to stay within the rules of the game. Even his opponents, the Tories, did not see him as a mob leader.⁵ Modern research also shows that the people of Boston were far from a wild mob. For example, the notorious Boston Tea Party, organized by Adams and his colleagues, was a quiet action without damage to persons or property — with the exception, of course, of the tea. The British who were in Boston on the eve of the revolution commented in amazement that the people of Boston acted "from principle and under countenance."⁶

Saint-Just was seen as a member of a triumvirate headed by Robespierre and as essentially subordinate to Robespierre's political authority. This triumvirate was held responsible for the reign of terror, and their removal on 9 Thermidor brought an end to it. There had been a suspicion that Robespierre and his two junior comrades would establish a dictatorship in France.

Modern research refutes much of this view. Saint-Just was not subordinate to Robespierre, but rather was an independent leader who in every way acted on his own authority. By the summer of 1794, Robespierre wanted to stop the terror, and this could have been the reason for his removal. It has been found that Saint-Just also wanted to stop the terror and to push for the implementation of his ideas concerning a welfare state. Moreover, it seems that his execution was not demanded by the political situation, as he was not deeply involved in the factional struggles among the Jacobins.⁷

Boston

Samuel Adams was born in the South End of Boston, the son of Deacon Adams, who had established the neighborhood church. His father was also active in the South End Caucus, leading it for many years. The supporters of the Caucus were middle-class craftsmen, small businessmen, and storekeepers. The Caucus maintained ties with other local caucuses as well as with the Merchants Club of Boston. Together these bodies essentially controlled the town meeting. Adams, in his father's footsteps, became a leader of the South End Caucus.

Adams also frequented the popular taverns of the city, important centers of social activity. John Adams said that it is in the taverns that "bastards and legislators are frequently begotten." Samuel Adams realized that the common people were extraordinarily politically aware and held, when they so chose, the political power in the city. As the Tory leader, Oliver, said, "Such men chiefly composed the voters of a Boston Town Meeting."[8]

To better understand the nature of the Boston "mob," let us look at an accepted popular institution in New England: the Pope's Day. On the 5th of November of every year, the Pope's Day institutionalized riots were held in Boston in memory of the Catholic gunpowder plot of 1605 in England. The North End and South End gangs would fight one another according to an agreed format. Each gang would prepare an effigy of the pope and bring it on a carriage to the center of the city. There each gang would try to capture the rival gang's "pope." In the process they would exchange blows, and in 1752 one was actually killed. Still, the event was entirely institutionalized and never reached the level of an actual riot, with the possible exception of 1745. The city's leaders organized and tried to restrain the gangs' behavior on Pope's Day, but as it was a very popular custom, with many people enjoying the spectacle, their efforts met with little success.

After one of the gangs caught its rival's "pope," both of the effigies were taken to the gallows and burned. A crowd of thousands of people gathered to join in the festivities, which concluded with the return of the gangs to their respective neighborhoods. The crowd, led by the well-known Boston Mechanics, was quite disciplined, and Hoerder, who studied it thoroughly, saw the crowd itself as an institution.[9]

The tradition of the neighborhood gangs, now politically active, may also be seen in the struggle against the Stamp Act. At dawn on the 14th of August, 1765, two effigies were discovered hanging from the Liberty Tree. One was an image of Oliver, who was to serve as the Stamp Distributor in the colony. The second, a boot with a devil's image inside it, alluded to Lord Bute. When Hutchinson demanded that the effigies be removed, the "Sons of Liberty" would not allow it. The entire city enjoyed the spectacle. In the evening the effigies were taken down and carried in an orderly procession, joined by respected members of the community, while the crowd watched from the side. The effigies were burned on Fort Hill. Later, one of Oliver's nearby structures was destroyed, while his house was broken into and pillaged. At about midnight the crowd dispersed and the city enthusiastically received the event. When Oliver decided not to serve as stamp distributor, a crowd gathered at his house and cheered him for his patriotic decision.

On August 26th, local gangs attacked the houses of a number of people connected with the Customs House and the Admiralty. Afterwards they attacked and pillaged Hutchinson's house. In the action, according to Hutchinson's testimony, the "North End ragamuffins" were conspicuous. This outburst worried the patriot leaders. While the events of August 14th turned into a popular holiday, the events of the 26th were sharply criticized by Adams, among others. He said that they were "remote from any considerations of the Stamp Act." Adams suspected that such outbursts would distance the upper classes from the patriot cause and understood that the gangs had to be restrained. At the same time, he realized that the gangs were an important source of political power and that they also must not be estranged from patriotism.

Arrest warrants were issued for several leaders of the disturbances. Ebenezer Mackintosh, the leader of the South End gang, was imprisoned. Several of the city's leaders, Adams, among them, came to Sheriff Greenleaf and informed him that they were prepared to help him prevent further riots, on condition that Mackintosh was set free. He was freed and given a municipal job, thus making him subordinate to the city's patriotic leadership.[10]

Adams had also befriended Swift, the leader of the North End gang. Indeed, according to Miller, Adams was the initiator of the unification between the city's gangs.[11] On the 5th of November, 1765, instead of the traditional Pope's Day confrontation, the North and South End gangs met by the townhouse. At their head stood "General" Mackintosh and his second-in-command, Swift. They commanded a trained force of 150 men who marched in the streets of the city. A week later, a "union feast" was held in celebration of the new unification. Thus, three months after the August riots, Adams had succeeded in binding to him the active elements of the gangs, uniting them in the patriotic cause, and cultivating their pride, while at the same time preventing a rift between them and the upper classes.[12]

From August 1765 until June 1768, there were no riots in the city, despite the political tension of 1767.[13] Adams praised the citizens: "The people have listened with attention" to the *Gazette*, which "has been incessantly calling upon all to be quiet; and patiently wait for their political salvation — NO MOBS – NO CONFUSIONS – NO TUMULTS" (emphasis in original).[14] These episodes demonstrate Adams' ability to restrain the behavior of the gangs, an ability which derived from his involvement with the common people, from the respect which he felt for them, and from the direct contact which he always maintained with them.

While it is possible to claim that Adams' attitude towards the people derived only from his desire to exploit them for political purposes, this does not seem correct. Adams was a modest man, who saw himself as belonging to the lower-middle class. At the time that he was sent to the First Continental Congress, his friends needed to dress him specially for the journey, as his clothes were too modest. When, in his later years, he served as governor of Massachusetts and did not lack for funds, he continued to associate with the common people and with his old neighbors, without considering his exalted political status.[15] Indeed, in these years as well, the Boston Mechanics remained his loyal supporters, just as he remained loyal to them.

A few episodes and statistics will show this: In 1784, Boston's merchants sought to establish a local city government based on a mayor and municipal council, thus bypassing the traditional town meeting, which the Mechanics controlled. The merchants established a committee which recommended the change. Adams, a member of the committee, opposed it, but found himself in a minority. After he warned the Mechanics of the plan, they gathered as usual in Fanueil Hall to vote against it, but the idea remained alive. A year later the merchants tried again, but this time the Mechanics overcame them at the town meeting, brought about the dismantling of the previous committee, and established a committee chaired by Adams in which they had the majority. The plan was buried and the old system remained unchanged.

In 1788 Adams ran for the office of lieutenant-governor. He received only 17 percent of the vote statewide, while in Boston he received 56 percent, thanks to the support of the Mechanics. In the elections for Congress in 1788, Adams received only 14 percent of the votes in the commercial cities of Suffolk County, but in Boston he received 48.7 percent. His opponent, Fisher Ames, who defeated him, received 72 percent in the commercial cities, but only 49.4 percent in Boston.

In the election for the Massachusetts Convention that was

called to ratify the Federal Constitution, Adams was elected by the votes of the Mechanics, despite the campaign which the Federalists waged against him. This is testimony to the personal loyalty of the Mechanics to Adams, since ideologically they actually tended to favor the Federalists.

The Federalists attempted to attract Adams to their side and turned to the leaders of the popular caucus to request that they pressure Adams to accept the Constitution. The Mechanics gathered at the Green Dragon Tavern, their gathering place since the eve of the revolution, and decided to support the Constitution. According to a story told many years later, Adams was present at the meeting, and when he was asked not to "act contrary to the best interests, the strongest feelings...of the town of Boston," he announced, "Well, if they must have it, they must have it." While this story appears legendary, since Adams continued to oppose a constitution which was not accompanied by a bill of rights, it illustrates the strong ties between Adams and his supporters. This bond reflected a basic Bostonian solidarity rooted in the experience of generations. In the eighteenth century communal solidarity often preceded political outlook. Adams was a believer in the corporatist view which opposed splits in the social body on the basis of politics or class.[16] While this view declined toward the end of the eighteenth century as national political parties began to make their mark, it remained alive in Adams' consciousness and explains the unquestioned bond between him and the people of Boston.

Alsace

Saint-Just's stance towards the people was radically different from Adams'. "Le peuple est un éternel enfant," wrote Saint-Just in *l'Esprit*. Although he never denied democracy even during the Jacobin dictatorship, Saint-Just never relied on the political judgment of the people. He looked down upon them with a kind of aristocratic arrogance, which even his sympathetic biographer, Ollivier, notes.

Saint-Just considered the common people not only politically immature, but also morally evil. On the basis of the events of October 1789 he declared, "The people exercised a kind of despotism on their part....One sees that the people do not act for the elevation of anyone, but for the debasement of all."

To him the people were thus no better than the despots who ruled them. They worked for nothing less than the degradation of all, with a kind of all-encompassing popular tyranny. While Saint-Just could not deny that the conquest of the Bastille was carried out exclusively by the people, he wrote, "The people had no manners, but were full of life. The love of liberty erupted, and weakness gave birth to cruelty." His view was clearly from above, judging the people, while not identifying himself as a part of them. In his description of the cruelty of the people after the capture of the Bastille, he manifested the same anti-popular stance that was typical of the enemies of the people, both among monarchist circles and among the revolutionary bourgeoisie.

Saint-Just was suspicious of a popular uprising and opposed neighborhood organizations such as those which made the Bastille Day uprising possible. In his essay he called the organizations "promoteurs de la liberté," but in almost the same breath he praised the National Assembly for dismantling them. Thus he praised the popular local armed forces that spontaneously arose in the cities of France in 1789, but at the same time he feared them and worked to take away their power,[17] despite the fact that he, himself, was active in the organization of the National Guard in his home town of Blérancourt. Thus suspicion of the common people and lack of trust in their political judgment went hand in hand with opposition to any form of popular self-organization and led to leadership from above, not to leadership which proceeded together with its people out of respect for their social and organizational traditions.

In the autumn of 1793, the Republic was in danger of military collapse. Particularly desperate was the plight of Alsace, which the Austro-Prussian forces had invaded, pushing the barefoot revolutionary army all the way back to Strasbourg. In order to save the region, the Committee for Public Safety sent Saint-Just and his friend, Le Bas, in October 1793 as "representatives of the people," armed with "extraordinary powers" to organize Alsace for the repulsion of the invaders. The success in Alsace turned into one of the legends of the revolution. Palmer humorously recounts the story:

> Once upon a time...while a very young republic was struggling with an old, old Empire...all seemed lost, when suddenly two youths appeared...to save the day. The two youths went to work with a will. They punished the bad men, brought back the courage of the troops, gave them shoes, food and guns and soon the Emperor's army turned and fled. The two youths then

departed as quickly as they had come....This sounds like a story from the never-never land....And yet...a certain fairy-tale atmosphere still hangs over the mission of Saint-Just and his friend Le Bas to Alsace.[18]

In his mission in Alsace, Saint-Just revealed such great organizational and leadership abilities that Malraux equated him with Napoleon.[19] Through the use of Draconic orders, he achieved his goals, but at the same time he became the terror of all Alsace. Nodier, a youth in Alsace who closely saw Saint-Just in action, wrote of him:

> I am far from contesting the importance of the services which the rigid severity of Saint-Just might then render to the invaded provinces and routed armies; but nothing has ever seemed to me more frightful than the insulting conciseness of these proscriptions in a single line, which sometimes struck down a whole class of citizens at one blow, sudden, unexpected and mortal as a pistol shot....I cannot recall without trembling the persistent recurrence of that cruel word, Death, which armed them all at the end like the scorpion's dart.[20]

Saint-Just's commands were obeyed, for no one dared argue with the "terrible Saint-Just." For instance, he often placed tax violators on the guillotine that stood in the city square; the hint was well understood (all the more so when some of them were executed).

The most dramatic story — which turned into one of the myths of the revolution — was the affair of the soldiers' shoes. The republican army went barefoot. The municipality of Strasbourg was requested to supply 10,000 pairs of shoes for the soldiers, but it hedged. Saint-Just publicly ordered:

> Ten thousand men are barefoot in the army; you must unshoe all the aristocrats of Strasbourg within the day, and tomorrow by 10 a.m. ten thousand pairs of shoes must be on their way to headquarters.[21]

The order was obeyed, of course; in November Saint-Just and his comrade returned to Paris, and in December the enemy was entirely banished from France.

It is instructive to look at Saint-Just's attitude toward the people when there was no emergency, and this we can learn from his other actions in Alsace, those not directly related to the military situation. There were several types of local bodies in Alsace:

formal bodies of the local government, such as the municipalities or administrations of departments; informal political bodies, primarily voluntary Jacobin clubs; and popular bodies at the neighborhood level, like the popular sections of Strasbourg. At Saint-Just's initiative a new type of body appeared, committees appointed by Saint-Just, independent of the local population and subordinate to Saint-Just alone. Immediately upon arriving in the area, he established "une commission révolutionnaire," containing five members, for judging political and military criminals and with the authority to execute by gunshot. This committee stood above the local authorities, and even above the army. Its members were paid directly from the army treasury. When he arrived in Strasbourg, Saint-Just established the "Commission spéciale et révolutionnaire" which judged without being subordinate to any legal procedure, subordinate only to Saint-Just. Monet, the mayor of Strasbourg and a devoted Jacobin patriot, wrote to Saint-Just in protest. Saint-Just responded: "We are here, not to befriend the authorities, but to judge them."[22]

Armed with absolute authority, Saint-Just dismantled the administration of the departments of Bas-Rhin and Strasbourg. He also dismantled the municipality of Strasbourg and jailed its members, with the exception of Monet. He ordered the city's popular Jacobin club to assemble a committee which would take over the functions of the municipality. The club protested the dismantling of the municipality, but Saint-Just silenced this protest, and it soon carried out his orders. He subordinated the committee and its leader, Monet, to his own absolute authority. He also turned against the most popular bodies, imprisoning the presidents of the popular sections of the city. Yet on the previous day he ordered that 10,000 libres be transferred from the wealthy of the city to the poor of the sections, so he cannot be accused of antisocial policies.

It is interesting that Saint-Just injured even those bodies which he himself had formed, turning them into his puppets. He scolded the revolutionary committee which he had established immediately upon arriving in the area: "You were appointed to be prompt, just and severe, but remember that death is under the seat of the unjust judges as well as under that of the guilty."[23]

Saint-Just struck out at every local body; he did not leave any political authority in the hands of the people at any level. This stance cannot be explained in terms of security alone. The local Jacobin clubs, and especially their *comités de surveillance* (committees of inspection), were good patriots and could have willingly served Saint-Just as an important operational arm; he indeed sided with them, but only after he made them his puppets. Monet was a devoted Jacobin and could have helped Saint-Just in his struggle against the supporters of Germany in the area. However, Saint-Just's attitude towards the people brought on their alienation and even led to an exodus of the common people from the area. This can only be understood in light of his lack of trust in the people, his opposition to their spontaneous gatherings and bodies, and his blindness to their important role in the revolution. This was after the glorious days in Paris, in which it was the people who dethroned the king, brought down the Girondins, and brought the Jacobins to power.

Paris

Saint-Just held the same stance towards the people in Paris, although here he no longer acted on his own, but rather in the framework of the Committee for Public Safety. Still, it is possible to see that he was a partner in the hostility of the Committee to the Parisian people who had brought it to power.

Paris was a mosaic of neighborhoods of relatively well-defined populations. In the east of the city was Faubourg Saint-Antoine; its residents were the pioneering forces of the popular revolution alongside those of other neighborhoods such as Faubourg Saint-Marcel. Thompson viewed the neighborhoods as small republics and called the type of politics which spontaneously developed there "civic federalism." While the central authorities tried to repress the sovereignty of the sections, they struggled successfully to maintain their independent existence.[24]

Only with the fortification of the Jacobin government was the suppression of the sections successful. On October 10, 1793, immediately before he left for Alsace, Saint-Just delivered an historic speech in the Convention, in which he proposed turning the Convention into "a revolutionary government until the peace." The Convention did become the government. Formally the Committee was not a separate executive body. In practice, however, it directed all the operations. After this speech came the law of 14 Frimaire (December 4, 1793), which created the Jacobin dictatorship and liquidated the popular sections. Saint-Just's role in these events is clear; in his October 10th speech he made no mention of popular sovereignty because he did not support this idea. In the law of

Frimaire, popular power was put to an end. "Congrès ou réunions locales" were forbidden and collection of money by the sections was outlawed. Local committees were subordinated to the central government, militias were disbanded, and the Convention was turned into the "sole center of the impulse of the government."[25]

This law was not a temporary edict required by national emergency, nor was it a political maneuver directed against the opposition parties, as Ollivier suggested. It was in fact the logical conclusion of the anti-popular, though not necessarily anti-democratic, political philosophy which Saint-Just professed from the beginning of his career. Indeed it was he who wrote the introduction to the law.

Saint-Just took part in every Committee initiative to do away with popular bodies; on some of the orders given to undermine their strength, such as the edict of January 6, 1794, he signed along with his comrades. Repression of the sections continued systematically until the summer of 1794. At that time the Jacobin government fell due to its loss of popular support, according to Soboul.[26]

Saint-Just, who in 1791 had mixed feeling toward the local bodies, initiated and participated in their destruction as a political force in the years following 1793. When in Thermidor (July 1794) he tried to initiate a popular uprising, he was left on his own and eliminated by his political rivals.

The *Sans-Culottes* Ethic

The *sans-culottes*, the stormtroopers of the revolution, were the residents of the revolutionary sections of Paris such as Faubourg Saint-Antoine. They were puritans, not religiously, but in their social and moral ideals. They opposed wealth, conspicuous consumption, easy profits without work, idleness, and immoral sexual behavior. They were moral rigorists who professed simplicity, modesty, and manual labor. For the most part they were craftsmen, storekeepers, and small producers who believed in the sacredness of private property. At the same time they strove for equality; they rejected both exaggerated wealth and poverty. Therefore they favored inheritance taxes for the wealthy as well as progressive income taxes. The money thus raised was to support the needy. They professed moral education for their children, as well as for uneducated adults. On the whole these "menu people" abided by what Vedel has called the "handicraft spirit" of the industrious classes, and considered the upper classes, with their "mercantile spirit," to be wasteful and corrupt parasites.[27]

Saint-Just and the *sans-culottes* had the same world view. He hated bankers, speculators, war profiteers, and new bureaucrats who had arisen with the revolution and had gotten rich in their new-found positions. The word "corruption" appears often in his speeches. Not a few of these people were sent by him to the guillotine, even from among the radicals of the revolution, such as Hébert and his group. Saint-Just went so far as to attack the revolutionary bureaucracy that had become corrupted and had turned into a new parasitic class. Referring to it, he announced: "A people has but one dangerous enemy, its government." At the same time he stated, "The unfortunate are the power of the Earth." On the whole, his vision was of a society of small producers, farmers, craftsmen, and storekeepers, all living in modesty and diligence.[28] He attempted to create this society for all of France by means of the Laws of Ventôse, as we will see later.

As the absolute ruler in Alsace in the autumn of 1793, Saint-Just created a small welfare state. He took care of the poor of Strasbourg, residents of the popular sections, and transferred some of the property of the wealthy to them. From the wealthy he demanded an obligatory loan. The wealthiest man in the city opposed the loan, so Saint-Just stood him on the guillotine platform to convince the public to contribute. He placed controls on prices, punished profiteers, and confiscated the property of the executed, in accordance with the law of 5 Brumaire, for the benefit of the Republic. He took care of widows and orphans and set up hospitals and schools, and he also successfully curbed the inflation, which hurt mostly the lower classes. Monet, the local leader who was a radical Jacobin, announced proudly, "The mercantile spirit has disappeared from Strasbourg." Saint-Just rightfully claimed, "We have supported the weak against the strong," in the spirit of the *sans-culottes* ethic.[29]

After his experience in Alsace, Saint-Just thought about the national level. In the month of Ventôse (winter of 1794) he was at the height of his political power. His influence in the Committee was considerable, and he apparently planned his social revolution with the support of two additional members of the Committee. On 8 Ventôse (February 26, 1794), while serving as the President of the Assembly, he initiated the approval of a resolution declaring that the property of patriots was sacred, while the property of the enemies of the revolution was to be confiscated for the republican nation. On 13 Ventôse (March 3, 1794) he spoke out again to explain how the law should be carried out; he recommended that the appropriated property be transferred to the needy. According to the Laws of Ventôse, the radical committees all over France were ordered to send lists to the central government in Paris of all those designated for property appropriation.[30]

The ideas behind these laws were not new; various popular sections had proposed them before. Once they were accepted as the laws of the state, they were received by the *sans-culottes* with enthusiasm, and Saint-Just became their hero. In actuality, none of these laws were ever carried out. A majority of the members of the Committee including, apparently, Robespierre, had reservations about them. Yet since the "menu people" rejoiced, why did Saint-Just never become a popular leader?

The answer can be found in his behavior in Alsace, for he was extremely paternalistic, not respecting those who needed his social reforms, but despising them instead. He distributed money to popular sections, but imprisoned their leaders; he implemented the ideas accepted by Monet, but disbanded the municipality of Strasbourg, despite the latter's protests. He went so far as to dictate what was in people's hearts, ordering the women of Strasbourg to abandon German manners, "for their hearts are French." Freedom of conscience, therefore, was not acceptable to Saint-Just. In this he resembled an absolute ruler who wished to govern even the souls of his citizens, not a popular leader who respected his public. Michelet pointed this out, " The idea of a glorious tyrant...seemed to be fully realized in this astonishing young man."

The people were repelled by his paternalism, even though many agreed with his ideas. In fact, many who fled from Alsace included residents who were the backbone of *sans-culottisme*, small farmers and craftsmen who should have appreciated the new social order.[31] However, that social order was imposed from above, without the participation of the popular bodies in its establishment. The realization of the "handicraft spirit" failed, ultimately, not because of the opposition of the common people to its ideals, but rather due to their opposition to paternalistic government at bayonet point. Thus we see how a revolutionary leader who professes popular and rooted ideas can lose the support of the people due to his leadership style. We also see Saint-Just's blindness to the fact that without popular support for his ideas, he had no chance to implement them. Lost in his socialist utopia, Saint-Just ignored the public and failed to achieve his goals. In this he was completely different from Adams.

Massachusetts

> It is often stated that I am at the head of the Revolution, whereas a few of us merely lead the way as the people follow, and we can go no further than we are backed by them; if we attempt to advance any further, we make no progress, and may lose our labor in defeat.[32]

Adams' leadership style, summed up in this statement, is recognizable from several of the political struggles which he led. In each case, he acted not from above the people, but rather from within them, as an elder brother leading his younger brothers, through persuasion, in the direction which he advocated. Far from regarding the people as an "eternal infant," he believed in its "collected wisdom" and thought that "when they are satisfied they will proceed gently, but with constancy and finally attain the end."[33] If Saint-Just's style of activity was paternalistic, then Adams' style can be called fraternalistic.

For example, in 1767 the Townshend Duties were levied on the American colonies, and Commissioners of Customs and Admiralty Courts were appointed for their enforcement. The patriots of Boston responded with fierce protest. The Pope's Day was celebrated by political marchers chanting slogans such as "Liberty, Property and no Commissioners." However, the other colonies did not join in Boston's protest. In order to free Boston from its isolation, Adams succeeded in gaining the approval of the House of the Colony to send a circular letter to the other American colonies. This was achieved with great difficulty since the western agricultural cities of Massachusetts were rather indifferent to the fate of commercial Boston, the principal victim of the new customs levies. The letter disputed the right of the Parliament in London to levy duties solely for the purpose of income for the Crown; it also claimed that it was forbidden for the government to pay the wages of judges from this income.[34] At the same time, the letter was quite moderate; it recognized Parliament as the "supreme legislative power" of the Empire and did not dispute its right to levy duties for the purpose of regulating imperial trade (but not for the purpose of extracting a profit for the King).

John Adams did not understand why his second cousin

Samuel was satisfied with such a moderate letter, which did not attack the overall authority of Parliament in America. Yet Samuel Adams knew that it would be unwise for him to run too far ahead with his ideas when he was trying to attract an indifferent public to his side. The goal of the letter was the unification of the colonies, and it was essential that it not take too extreme a stand. American political thought at the time followed the moderate principles of John Dickinson, the "Pennsylvania Farmer"; even the Boston Town Meeting adopted his ideas, so Samuel Adams based his letter on Dickinson's opinion. John Adams is revealed in this instance as more radical than his cousin, being also blind to the danger that too much radicalism would distance the other colonies from the patriot cause.

The British insisted that the House withdraw the letter. When the House refused, it was disbanded by the British. They also insisted that the remaining colonies reject the letter, but this brought about the opposite result, winning greater support for Boston. When a favorable response arrived from Virginia, the second pillar of patriotism alongside Massachusetts, there was great rejoicing in Boston.[35]

Boston still remained isolated, however, from the western agricultural cities of Massachusetts. It was part of their tradition to antagonize her, the capital of commerce. "He is very bitter vs. the Town of Boston. I hate 'em from my Soul says he," wrote John Adams of the opinions of a man from Worcester.[36] These western towns were quite loyal to the Crown.

The first step in unifying the colony around Boston was the Massachusetts Convention of Towns which Adams initiated and organized. Whether its success was a result of circumstances, part of an inevitable process, or due to Adams' political savvy, the Convention illustrates Adams' fraternal style of leadership.

In 1768 there were only a few British troops in Boston to protect the customs agents. In the wake of the riots in the summer of 1768,[37] additional troops were due to arrive. When this became known in the city, it sparked considerable rage. A town meeting was called at the initiative of the Patriotic Caucus which Adams led. It requested an explanation from Governor Bernard as to the purpose of the arriving troops. The governor rejected the request, an act perceived by the public as an insult to the city, which had acted within the law up to this point. In response to the rejection, the Town Meeting requested that the governor summon the House of the Colony, which had been dispersed after the circular letter. The governor refused and once again was perceived as insulting the city, as well as the entire colony. (This was not the first appeal to summon the House, and every one had been rejected. However, this last rejection was considered the worst, since it related to the matter of the army, a particularly important and urgent issue.)

Boston had acted in a completely legal manner up to this point, but then it came time to turn to other methods. On September 12th, the Town Meeting approved a decision forbidding the stationing of troops in the colony without the agreement of the House. Since the governor refused to summon the House to discuss the issue, Adams proposed a convention of all the towns of the colony for this purpose. Boston accepted his proposal and invited representatives from throughout the colony.

The convention opened on September 22. Representatives of ninety-six towns and eight districts were present, an impressive number, especially when considering the short amount of time at the disposal of the organizers and the unconstitutional nature of the gathering. Many western towns sent representatives, and many new faces were present. Although some towns had opposed it, the convention was a tremendous success. Unrelated to the content of the discussions, which did not resolve many issues, its very existence contributed to "Boston's gradual dominance of New England."

The convention was especially significant in that it was an act against the authority of the Crown. Governor Bernard commented, "So daring an assumption of the Royal Authority was never practiced by any city or town in the British Dominion, even in the times of the great disorders, not even in the City of London when the great Rebellion was at the highest." Furthermore, the spontaneous gathering, without inviting the King's representatives, was a display of republicanism "with no ingredient of Royalty in it."

Hutchinson, then lieutenant-governor, said that Boston revealed in this convention "a greater tendency toward a revolution in government than any preceding measure in any of the Colonies." The gathering was more important than the city riots, in his opinion, for the latter did not constitute a "revolution in government," while the convention heralded a republican political system. It was, in fact, the first display of Republicanism in the American colonies.[38]

Throughout the confrontation, Adams took care to inform the public as to what was happening, and public opinion sided more and more with Boston. The city was perceived as moderate and law-abiding, taking a radical step only as a last resort. (This is permitted according to Locke's teachings, which were the political Bible of the colony). Most of the towns of the colony agreed to participate in the convention; most probably, if Adams had not followed the path which he did, he would not have succeeded in attracting the towns of the west to his side, for only two years before they had displayed conservative indifference to the plight of Boston.

On October 1st, with the landing of the troops, the convention dispersed, but its goal had been achieved. The patriots of Boston were now accepted throughout the colony, which had now experienced its first taste of republicanism.

The Colonies

The establishment of the Boston Committee of Correspondence followed a process very similar to that of organizing the Massachusetts Convention of Towns. Richard Brown has detailed the story of this Committee and Adams' role in building this tool which contributed so much to the revolution throughout the colonies.[39] As will be seen, the idea of a committee which would centralize the correspondence of the various towns of the colony was quite radical.

The "Boston Pamphlet," the first document which Boston sent to the towns of the colony, was sent to the recognized local leaders of these towns. The Boston patriots sought to take advantage of the recognized and accepted social structures of the public to which it turned; it did not try to circumvent them and certainly not repress them. In addition, Boston did not force any particular political point of view on the towns, but rather requested that they discuss the issue (in this case one of the traditional conflicts concerning the wages of the judges), such that "your wisdom and fortitude shall dictate." Boston did not even request that the cities set up committees of correspondence. On the whole, the Boston Committee kept a modest profile, and under no circumstances did it want to appear as a radical leader pushing others into action. Adams saw to it that the towns of Plymouth and Marblehead, among others, discussed the issue of the salaries of judges independently from Boston, so that Boston would not seem to be the only one involved in the struggle. His purpose was not only to calm fears in the peripheral towns of Boston's predominance, but also to calm some of the residents of Boston, who feared that they would remain alone in the field of action.

The towns, at their own initiative, set up committees of correspondence with Boston and with one another. Hutchinson, now governor of the colony, admitted on December 8, 1772, that the "doctrine Independence upon the Parliament...every day increases." In 1773, in view of the success in Massachusetts, the House of Burgesses of Virginia called for the establishment of intercolonial committees of correspondence, something which Adams had dreamed of since at least 1764, and the colonies began to unify into one body in the spirit of Adams' belief:

> When it once appears beyond contradiction, that we are united in sentiments there will be a confidence in each other, and a plan of opposition will be easily formed and executed with spirit.[40]

The historical importance of the Boston Committee of Correspondence has been recognized. In considering the extensive network of committees of correspondence, John Adams exclaimed, "What an engine!" and said that without a study of this correspondence network "the history of the United States never can be written."[41]

In the matter of leader-people relations, a leader can be seen as surrounded by an inner circle and an outer circle. In this case, the inner circle was the radical group which is partner to the leader's political world view; the outer circle was the broader group, consisting of an indifferent, and perhaps suspicious, public. Adams was integrated and interwoven into his inner circle, the Boston Mechanics, with ties of mutual loyalty lasting throughout the decades amidst mutual concessions. At the same time, he took care to bring the outer circle closer to him — the peripheral western towns of the colony, and even other colonies — acting pragmatically while taking advantage of opportunities as they arose and of the mistakes of the opposition. Throughout, he respected the traditional bodies of both circles and refrained from imposing his opinions upon others. As a true fraternalist, he always waited until the people came near to him before he took any additional step.

Saint-Just is Adams' near opposite; he exalted himself above his inner circle, the popular sections and the radical Jacobin clubs, and distanced this circle from him with his autocracy and with insults to its leaders. At the same time, he attempted to impose his ideas on the outer circle from above, whether through emergency orders as in Alsace, or with the aid of central national legislation as in Ventôse. His path was straight ahead, blind to the social and political realities surrounding him. As an extreme paternalist, he turned the local bodies into tools for his own policing and did not wait for a change in the consciousness of the people.

It is clear that the cases of Adams and Saint-Just do not exhaust all of the possible combinations. A combination of consideration of the inner circle and dependence upon it, for the purposes of forcefully imposing reforms on the outer circle, would be the tactic of elitist parties. An additional combination is possible — appealing to the outer circle, to overcome the inner circle's opposition; leaders have resorted to these tactics more than once. In any case, among the four theoretically possible combinations, Saint-Just and Adams represent two extreme combinations. The first entirely ignores the people, in both circles. The second considers, and even attracts, the people, and takes care to maintain ties with both circles.

A discussion of the various meanings of the concept "people" which were accepted by Saint-Just and Adams will shed additional light upon their leadership styles. The following discussion was influenced by Nisbet;[42] but while Nisbet was concerned with political theorists, we will show the practical implications of their teachings as these active leaders understood them.

A Metaphysical Whole

The "people," according to holistic philosophy, is a homogeneous and indivisible whole, existing beyond the concrete human individuals belonging to it. We cannot see it in reality; we see only individuals and human groupings, parts found within the whole, the sum of which do not constitute the whole itself. As Rousseau noted, "people" stands above them, as an abstract entity that stands above its concrete and chance manifestations and, being metaphysical, does not take on any earthly form.[43]

The more the concrete human collective is made homogeneous and uniform, lacking in internal divisions, the more it approaches the "whole," the "people," in the holistic sense of the concept. This was the ideal of the French Republic, which referred to itself in its official documents as *"une et indivisible,"* and this was Saint-Just's point of view. Sharing Rousseau's ideas, he declares *"La volonté générale est indivisible."* Yet in a later essay, *"De la Nature,"* in which he rejects Rousseau's teachings concerning the contract, he still states that *"La cité is indivisible,* for a society which is divided ceases to be a society."

Holism, therefore, is not necessarily tied to the contract teachings. On every occasion Saint-Just radically denounced any idea of division, "The territory is under the guarantee and the protection of the sovereign. It is, like it, indivisible." To the extent that division of the population is permissible, it is only for passing technical purposes such as elections. He clearly denounced federalism: "Federalism is not only a divided government; it is a divided people. You are ferocious beasts, you that divide the inhabitants of a republic."[44] He used the concept of federalism, as this study does,[45] in its broadest meaning: any method which builds one political entity from a number of political entities which do not lose their uniqueness and identity.

Holism is also related to certain conception of the legislative body, and of the relations between it and the people. According to Saint-Just, *"L'assemblée nationale est une et indivisible."*[46] The legislative body is a sort of microcosm which reflects the national macrocosm. Members in the legislative body do not represent the districts in which they were elected, but rather the entire people. Every representative, unrelated to the place from which he is elected, is swallowed up within the uniform legislature and breaks off his ties with his electoral region. This perspective is clearly revealed in the polemic surrounding the Condorcet constitution.

In the spring of 1793, a committee headed by Condorcet proposed a constitution for the fledgling French republic. The proposal was apparently influenced by the Massachusetts and New Hampshire constitutions. According to this proposal, *"assemblées primaires"* would have been established in the districts of France and would have continued to function for various purposes — discussion of new proposed laws, election of local authorities, judges and juries — even after the elections.[47] But this popular sovereignty violates, according to the holistic perspective, the higher national whole. In addition, their existence would make it likely that the legislative body would be comprised of representatives of defined districts that have not lost their independent existence — representatives who are likely to find themselves tied to their voters, thus undermining the wholeness and unity of the

115

central legislature. Saint-Just attacked the Condorcet proposal, "A general representation, formed of the particular representations of each of the departments, is not a representation any more but a congress."

"Congress" was a word of abuse, since it implied representatives who remain tied to the bodies that sent them. Saint-Just considered this dangerous, for it would bring about the disintegration of the republic. "All congresses rend the constitution federative; and whatever happens...the republic will dissolve one day, and its demise will come out of a representative congress."

The Americans, therefore, did not establish a true republic. "The United States of America...did not recognize...that the unity of the republic rests in the unity of the national representation....This confederated state is not, in effect, a republic."[48] He spoke these words in 1793, after the United States had accepted the federal Constitution and established a central government, with Washington serving as its president. As defined by Saint-Just, then, a republic must be a uniform whole with a unified legislature.

The Condorcet proposal was rejected, and Saint-Just was elected to the committee which formulated the Jacobin Constitution of 1793. The new constitution did away with the independence of the voting bodies; they were to gather only for the purpose of electing representatives, after which they would disperse. They were to have virtually no other functions.[49] In the Jacobin constitutional committee, Saint-Just was the most radical holist. He wanted one central list of delegates to serve in all of the electoral districts of France. The concept of constituency had no place in his philosophy, for it bordered on federalism, a sin against the republic: "It is necessary to extinguish federalism with harsh police."[50]

The holistic philosophy and the concepts deriving from it are important to our understanding of the relations between leaders and followers. The elected leader is not at all obligated to the voters; he owes everything to the national "whole." He does not take the particular interests of his region into consideration and maintains no ties with it. He thinks only of the "people," and only to it is he tied. Since the "people" reveal their will only at election time, the elected becomes an absolute ruler for the period between elections. Rousseau, although his perspective was holistic, took notice of the danger of a disconnection between the elected and the voters:

The English deceive themselves if they think that they are free. The only freedom they exercise is during the election of deputies to parliament. As soon as they have elected their representatives they lose this freedom entirely and become nothing more than slaves.[51]

Also among the revolutionaries, there were those who saw the danger of the formation of an "aristocracy of deputies" on the grave of the fallen aristocracy of the nobility, and they proposed constant assemblies which would keep a "watchful eye" on the representatives. The holistic approach claimed against them, "They do not realize how close they come to overthrowing the Republic when they convince the Sections that sovereignty resides in their midst."[52]

Holism won out, as is well known, and as noted earlier, Saint-Just does not even mention the term "popular sovereignty" in his October 10, 1794, speech.

The apparent paradox of a tyrannical democrat becomes clearer once we have understood the essence of holism. From the moment a person is elected to the Assembly, he becomes a part of the legislative body, which is independent of the concrete French people. From the moment the Assembly appointed Saint-Just as its special representative in Alsace, he was nothing less than the manifestation of the French "people," the metaphysical "whole," and in its name he could impose his will upon the residents of the area who were nothing but a small fraction of the "whole," lacking any independent status. The Draconian edicts that he proclaimed were the will of the "people." The desires of the Alsacians were nothing other than a particularistic revolt against the whole republic, for which they deserved punishment. The holistic democrat, therefore, could reach a radically paternalistic leadership style. Moreover, he could perceive this paternalism as concern for the concrete people, as the "aristocracy of the elected" knows better than the various citizen groups what is good for them. The elected representative is compared to a philosopher, who reads "objective truths" in the heavens and brings them down to his electorate. Thus a Platonic tone, reminiscent of Plato's parable of the cave, is evident in Saint-Just's statements on this matter: "The legislative body is like an immobile light which distinguishes the form of everything."

The people requested the legislature to "bring down" laws, as though the people had no part in the legislative process. Saint-Just exclaimed in his youthful treatise, *l'Esprit*: "O legislators! Give us laws that will force us to love them!"[53]

In sum, Saint-Just's holistic approach was characterized by three elements: the conception of the "people" as a metaphysical whole, the conception of the legislature as a "whole" with members not tied to particular popular groups, and the conception of the legislator as a "philosopher" who legislates according to his own wisdom, without involving the people in the process. Here lies the source of Saint-Just's paternalistic leadership style, which went together with the political philosophy or metaphysics that he and many of his colleagues shared.

A Community of Communities

The leadership style of Samuel Adams and the political tradition of New England reflected a very different world view. New England was built on a federation of concrete communities, the townships, made up of concrete individuals. They were related to each other and subordinate to a central legislature. They were not lost in an abstract "whole," and their representatives did not lose their local identity when they were elected to the legislative body — which was not uniform and indivisible. In Saint-Just's terms, the House of Massachusetts was a "Congress." Its members remained tied to the cities that sent them, and followed their instructions. This outlook was expressed rather naively by the residents of Lynn in a letter to Governor Hutchinson, who had attempted to violate the right of the towns to meet and discuss political issues, claiming that only the legislature had a right to do this. The town's residents wrote, "It appears to be a principle with his Excellency, that the Representatives in General Assembly have Authority to determine some points which their Constituents have no Authority to show their Sentiments upon." How, they asked, can a representative have any more authority than the public which sent him? Could it be that a servant had more authority than his master! The words of the governor were therefore absurd to them.[54]

This radically popular conception of representation — the elected as the servant of the city that sent him — is the polar opposite of the conception of the philosopher-legislator expounded by Saint-Just. It is also a fundamental concept of Adams. In a letter to Noah Webster, in 1784, he expressed his opinion of the institution of the Township: "While we retain these simple Democracies in all our Towns which are the basis of our State Constitution...it appears to me we cannot be enslaved and materially injured."[55]

The representatives of those same "simple Democracies" were obligated to follow the guidelines of those who sent them. Thus Adams began his political life in 1769 as a member of the committee of the city of Boston which formulated instructions for the representatives of the city in the House and brought them to the Town Meeting for authorization, making them binding on their representatives. In 1765, at the time of the struggle over the Sugar Act, he wrote in the name of the city to her representatives, "The Town of Boston cannot remain silent." In other words, the city is its own political entity, which instructs its representatives on how to act.

The towns guarded their uniqueness, and the "whole" created by the covenant between them did not swallow them up. "It is often necessary that the Circumstances of individual Towns should be brought into Comparison with those of the whole....The proportionate Part of each to the whole can be found only by an exact Knowledge of the internal Circumstance of each."

Adams understood the meaning of the word "people" as in, "A representative should be...well acquainted with the Internal Circumstances of the people whom he represents."[56] Here the word "people" related to the concrete urban population which sent its representative to the House and not to any abstract entity.

The Massachusetts Constitution speaks explicitly of a covenant binding the citizens into one people. The conception of a covenant between different parts which do not lose their identity and combine to form a united, but not uniform and homogeneous, whole guided Adams on the national level as well. This is perhaps less well-known because many historians mistakenly see him as an Anti-Federalist. Yet it was Adams who first called for unification of the colonies for the struggle against the British in 1764, and it was he who initiated the Stamp Act Congress in 1765 which was the first Congress on a continental level. Naturally enough, his initiative in 1764 was made in the form of an appeal to representatives of the city of Boston in the House of the Colony in a request that the House turn to the rest of the colonies to act together, for "by the united applications of all who are aggrieved, all may happily obtain redress."[57] Here we see the hierarchy of the components of the whole: city-colony-all of the colonies, while Adams' "whole" does not swallow up its parts. It constitutes, in St. Augustine's words, "a community of communities." For this idea, the toast "To the States United and to the States separate" is attributed to Adams.

In looking at the impact of the federalist perspective on relations between leaders and followers, we see that the elected leader owes much to those who elected him, for he remains tied to them and dependent on them even between elections. This does not imply that he cannot initiate radical courses of action, but if he does, he must lead the public, step by step, towards recognition of the necessity for such action, just as Adams, in fact, did. He is not the omnipotent father who rules his sons with a high hand, but rather the eldest brother, interwoven and integrated among his brothers, who is engaged in constant dialogue with them. Thus, if holism goes together with paternalism, then federalism goes hand in hand with fraternalism. Our two subjects are nearly ideal representations of these two combinations. Without entering into the question of causal relationships — does political philosophy lead to leadership style or vice versa — it is clear that their leadership styles consistently match their political thoughts, as well as the political traditions of the societies in which they acted.

The Team Player

Adams was a team player in the full sense of the term. He always acted among a group of partners to his struggle, and his power was in the caucus, in committees, and in the town meeting. An excellent example of this collective activity involves one of the struggles over the payment of judges.[58]

In 1774, the traditional conflict was renewed between the colony and the British government over the payment of judges' salaries. The government wished to pay them from its own treasury, but the House insisted on continuing a custom anchored in the Charter, according to which the colony controlled these payments. The judges of the colony sided with the House, but Oliver, Governor Hutchinson's brother-in-law, who served as chief justice and lieutenant governor, refused to accept the authority of the House. In contrast to what had occurred in August 1765, the protestors did not use violent means, seeking instead nonviolent methods to overcome Oliver.

John Adams related how once, when he sat together with some friends in an informal caucus, he got the idea of "a constitutional resource." He proposed that the lower House "impeach" Oliver, and that the Council (the upper House) and the Governor (Hutchinson) judge him. In the opinion of the colonists, Oliver's behavior was a violation of the constitutional authority of the colony's legislature, which had forbidden the judges to receive their wages from the Crown.

John told his idea to Samuel. Samuel then set up a committee of the House which, together with John, formulated the terms of impeachment. The document was brought to the House and authorized by an overwhelming majority of ninety-two to eight. Hutchinson refrained from attending the meeting of the Council to try Oliver. It was clear to him that, if he came, a discussion would develop over the powers and authorities of the House in the colony as opposed to those of Parliament in London, and he wished to avoid this. The president of the Council, Bowdoin, was a patriot who had been prepared in advance for the event. Samuel Adams opened the meeting before the Council, but was immediately interrupted by Bowdoin who noted the absence of the Governor. Adams replied, "The Governor is presumed to be present," and continued to read the impeachment before the members of the Council. Afterwards this was reported to the House, and it is written in the protocol of the House that Chief Justice Oliver was impeached before the Governor and the Council. The event received widespread publicity, and Hutchinson suspended the meetings of the House. Oliver's trial was never actually held, due to Hutchinson's absence.

Yet the patriots' victory was complete even without the trial. Hutchinson's absence was perceived by the public as an arbitrary violation of accepted constitutional procedures. In addition, the mere publication of the impeachment throughout the colony (all the representatives of the dispersed House returned to their towns with the story) was enough to awaken everyone to the question of principle. It was impossible to find anyone in the colony who would agree to serve on' a jury. John Adams recalled that in all of the towns of the colony they said "to a man" that they cannot sit as jurists as long as the charges against the Chief Justice remain pending. In September 1774, the High Court unwillingly closed its doors.

The success of the entire exercise depended upon the coordination and teamwork of all the participants. John Adams initiated the constitutional idea. Bowdoin made it possible to create a situation in which they could impeach Oliver, despite the absence of the governor (this was the deciding point in the exercise, which

Samuel Adams apparently had foreseen). Members of committees of the House cooperated in the struggle, and members of the House spread the story throughout the entire colony. Samuel Adams, of course, coordinated them all, totally dependent on his colleagues for his success.

There are many examples of Adams as a team player. Adams, Joseph Warren, and John Adams acted together to frustrate the efforts of the Tories in the matter of payment for the tea that was dumped into the water at the Boston Tea Party, when Samuel Adams acted from Salem. There were the historic decisions of Suffolk County that were passed under the leadership of Joseph Warren, raced to Philadelphia by Paul Revere, handed to the "brace of Adamses," and adopted by the Continental Congress. Even one of Adams' opponents, Galloway, complimented him on his ability for teamwork, when he said that Adams was the man "who managed at once the faction in Congress at Philadelphia and the factions in New England." The affair of the Suffolk County decisions, the outcome of this coordination, is a part of American history. According to Galloway, who opposed them, they were a "complete declaration of war against Great Britain."[59]

Adams was not merely a team player. He also had an explicit policy of building and training teams for the struggle over colonial rights. One of the "boys" whom he cultivated, John Adams, tells how his cousin invited "every rising genius in the New England seminaries" to the patriot club, so that they would be "embodied with the Whigs, and begin to taste of their spirit by being often in their company."

Among the young people drafted by Adams were (in addition to John), Josiah Quincy, Jr., Dr. Benjamin Church, Joseph Warren, and John Hancock. Apart from these Adams had other, more veteran partners. Among those, two particularly worth mentioning were Dr. Thomas Young and William Molineux, both of whom were avowed secularists. Although Adams himself was a strict Puritan, this did not prevent him from establishing contact with them. He cooperated even with the Freemasonry Lodge, despite his revulsion as a Puritan for their special rituals. Adams' tolerance for the opinions of his partners in his struggle, and the role this played in unifying the patriot camp, were well known to the Tories. They accused him of having "a religious mask ready for his occasions," but Adams maintained his loyalty to his friends. When the Tories tried to libel Boston in the eyes of the peripheral towns by describing her leaders as "virulent opposers of our Holy religion," Adams rushed to the aid of Dr. Young (at whom, among others, the accusation was directed) and said that he was an "unwearied assertor of the rights of his countrymen."[60]

It is difficult to know whether Adams' tolerance was only the result of tactical considerations, or whether he was tolerant in character. It is a fact that the Massachusetts Constitution of 1780 included Article III, which infringed somewhat on the rights of nonbelievers, and Adams was a member of the committee that formulated this constitution. However, at the time of the struggle Adams was able to rise above disagreements of conscience in order to achieve harmony within the patriot camp.

This tolerance was also revealed at the national level. Its most dramatic expression occurred at the opening of the First Continental Congress in Philadelphia. Adams knew that the southern and central colonies were suspicious of the Puritans, the "fire-eaters" of New England. He also knew that without the support of the southern Episcopalians, especially the Virginians, no unified front of colonies could arise. When a proposal arose that Dr. Duché, a respected clergyman of the Church of England, should deliver the opening prayer of the Congress, there were those who opposed it, claiming that the members of the Congress could not pray together due to the diversity of their religious beliefs. Adams then announced, "I am no bigot, and would hear a prayer from a gentleman of piety and virtue, who was at the same time a friend of his country." Dr. Duché delivered a moving prayer and the Congress opened. The suspicions of the other colonists against the northern Puritans were considerably reduced. Even the Tories, Adams' opponents, admitted that his act was "a masterly stroke of policy."[61]

Adams' tolerance for the purpose of protecting the ranks revealed itself in another affair at the Continental Congress. The radical minority requested that the colonies prepare for a confrontation with Britain, not wasting time on additional attempts at conciliation. The more conservative majority, headed by John Dickinson of Pennsylvania, preferred to send an additional petition to the King before taking another confrontational stand. John Adams sharply attacked Dickinson, widening the gap between the New England representatives and the more moderate members of the Congress to the point that Dickinson proposed that New England be allowed to go its own way, while Pennsylvania and the southern colonies attempted to reach a compromise with the King.[62]

Samuel Adams supported the presentation of an additional petition, since it was clear to him that, without this, Pennsylvania and the other colonies would not join the patriot camp. The failure of this attempt at conciliation would prove to the moderates, as well as to Dickinson, that there was no escaping the rift. This is indeed what happened, and the rest is history. It is nearly certain that, had Samuel acted according to John's advice, he would have alienated the influential Dickinson and weakened the power of the New England colonies in the Congress. Once again, he knew how to rise above political disagreements in order to maintain unity. John Dickinson and Samuel Adams in the same camp sounded a bit fantastic at the time, but it was precisely this reality which was created in the Congress, thanks to Adams' understanding of the importance of cooperative action. Adams' words of 1769, "One spirit animates all America...to quench that spirit, all the colonies must be absolutely destroyed,"[63] came to fruition in 1775.

This tolerance for the opinions of friends and opponents was joined in Samuel Adams by an additional characteristic — a rare personal modesty. In the early days of the struggle he served as second to James Otis, the brilliant but unstable leader of the patriots. Even when Otis suddenly revealed conservative leanings, Adams continued to work with him. When Adams set up the Boston Committee of Correspondence, he appointed Otis as its chairman. His relationship with Hancock was similar; Adams drafted Hancock to the patriot struggle and groomed him for leadership. In the end Hancock became the governor of the state and Adams his lieutenant, but Adams never showed any bitterness at his place in the leadership.

In summary, partnership, tolerance, and modesty are the personality characteristics which typified Adams as a leader. It is difficult to find him alone as a revolutionary star. He was always involved with his friends and colleagues, coordinating between them, working through them, conceding to them, and finally achieving his objectives. According to Miller, Adams' unsympathetic biographer, it was this characteristic which greatly advanced the implementation of independence, for Adams succeeded in assembling in Philadelphia a "caucus" that included such figures as John Adams, R.H. Lee, Thomas Jefferson, Patrick Henry, George Whyte and others, who drew the Congress after them in the direction of independence. At the time, Adams, the coordinator of the caucus, was considered by his enemies in London to be "the first politician in the world."[64]

The Uncompromising Individualist

Saint-Just was the polar opposite of Adams in this field, even more than in any other. He wrote, "You do not govern without friends," but in fact he avoided all teamwork, remaining an extreme individualist until his final day. He seemed to have had a partner in action in his loyal friend, Le Bas, who served with him in Alsace. However, Saint-Just revealed the true nature of their relations when, in the first report they sent from Alsace to the Committee, Saint-Just wrote "I have given you this detail," changed his mind, erased the word "I," and wrote in its place, "We."

In Alsace, Saint-Just demanded that the Committee remove all other representatives of the people who were in the region, all of whom with which he had quarrelled. For example, he requested the removal of his fellow Committee member, Hérault de Séchelles, judged his behavior as immoral, and ultimately sent him to the guillotine. He was unwilling to accept any opinion or behavior that differed from his own. As Palmer formulated it, he saw himself "supreme, believe[d] his policy [was] the only correct one, and distrust[ed] both the achievements and the intentions of those not of his opinion." (It is interesting to compare this with what Miller, Adams' unsympathetic biographer, wrote of him; he was willing "to agree with others' proposals as long as no vital principle was sacrificed...this 'pliableness and compaissance'...enabled him to succeed where a less adaptable man would have failed."[65]

Saint-Just wrote to Robespierre of his credo with regard to Republican purity and relations with colleagues. "Confidence no longer has value when shared with corrupt men; in that case [apparently meaning when confidence is not shared with the corrupt] a man does his duty for love of country alone, and this feeling is purer." Saint-Just was quick to attach the label "corrupt" to anyone who disagreed with him.

Saint-Just, however, was not only a political puritan who demanded ideological purity. He did not like to share his leadership with others, even when those others shared his views. An air of aristocratic haughtiness always accompanied him. Desmoulins mockingly called him "M. le Chevalier." Palmer described Saint-Just's arrogance: "Cold and superior in manner...he behaved like one who thought himself above humanity, and his admirers feel the presence of a demigod." Saint-Just himself, in writing of his struggle with Danton, saw himself as the chosen elect messenger of God, come to exorcise the corruption from the body of the Republic.

Saint-Just's leadership style, which distanced partners in the struggle, whether due to personal arrogance or doctrinal purity, cost the republican camp greatly, for its active faction steadily decreased in numbers, as did the number of sympathizers who would accept passively the republican principles. Instead of compromising and maintaining the unity of the camp, Saint-Just split it. "The French people is composed of patriots. The others are helots or nothing." He thus defined the "true" camp, carriers of the torch of the revolution, alongside a majority of ignorant slaves ("helots") who were "nothing." Such an elitist perspective was bound to fail, as soon as it became clear that the "helots" were too many and too strong. In any case, it invited a dictatorship of the "true" revolutionary minority, which tried to force its will upon the moderate majority. It is interesting to note Saint-Just's method of persuading the moderates, "A government has virtue for principle; if not, terror."[66]

This chain of logic led apparently to a legitimization of a regime of terror, as "The republic is not a senate, it is the virtue." Moreover, in his previously noted speech on 8 Ventôse, Saint-Just declared, "What constitutes a republic is the total destruction of those who oppose it."[67] Thus Saint-Just's purist-doctrinaire attitude leads to a dual world, of virtue on the one hand and corruption on the other; of the republic, on the one hand, and its enemies, on the other. The leader, in charge of Republican purity, must defend himself against his impure enemies, who are the majority of the people.

Owing to his doctrinaire extremism, Saint-Just became the symbol of the purge trials of the revolutionary leadership. He handled the execution of the Hébertists and, afterwards, of Danton and his supporters. These were the first political show trials in the new era, and they clearly damaged the Republican camp, which was already quite small. In the Danton trial, Saint-Just was aided by two additional radical members of the Committee, Billaud and Collot.

In the summer of 1794, the terror reached its peak.[68] There were those who wished to stop it, among them Robespierre, but this possibility frightened those whose hands were already full of blood (such as Collot), for they were convinced that Robespierre would want their heads. There were those who wanted it continued, but this aroused the opposition of the moderate majority of the Convention. Tension inside the Committee mounted to a near explosion, while other Convention members also feared for their own heads. The mutual distrust created pressures which were extremely difficult to withstand. Agreements were formed and broken; no one knew where he stood. "I can hardly trust anyone other than you; a man has so few friends....Were it not a crime, I would kill you and then kill myself; at least then we would die together" (Le Bas to his wife). "I have tired of people; if only I had a pistol in my hand, I would know nothing other than God and Nature" (Barère, among the more balanced and cool-headed of the Committee). "Tomorrow, Robespierre or I, one of the two of us will be dead" (Cambon, also among the more balanced in the Convention). Robespierre himself said, "Prepare for me a poison cup; I will wait for it on this holy platform." Saint-Just wrote, "The circumstances are difficult only for those who flinch from the grave." Billaud said that the leaders were treading upon the mouth of a volcano. And many years later Barère wrote, "At that time we were living on a battlefield."[69]

Despite all the talk of the "dictatorship" of the Committee, the Convention was stronger than a split Committee. Due to a lack of parliamentary tradition, Convention procedure became increasingly corrupt. A situation was thus created in which every leader feared lest an opponent obtain permission to speak before him, gain a majority in the Convention, and send him to the guillotine.[70] The order of the day for the Committee, then, was to hide its inner quarrels.

While Robespierre did not rule the Committee, despite the accepted legend, he did have magnetic influence on the Convention. The deputy Cambon said of him, "One man paralyzed the will of the National Convention."[71] When the conflict between Robespierre and Billaud and Collot broke, it was feared that he would take the Convention with him and "purge" the Committee. Still, no one dared attack him. On 5 Thermidor (July 23), all of the members of the Committee sat and tried to reach a compromise with Robespierre. It appeared that a compromise was achieved, and it was determined that Saint-Just, who was acceptable to all the Committee members, would deliver a speech in the Convention on

9 Thermidor, in which he would report on the unity that had returned to the ruling camp. There still remained considerable hostility toward the Committee in the Convention, both on the part of the moderate deputies, who were angry about the terror, and on the part of the ultra-radical deputies, who suddenly feared that the price the Committee paid to Robespierre for his conciliation on July 23 included their own heads. However, it was expected that Saint-Just's speech would overcome the Convention's resentment, by presenting a unified and powerful Committee, and reestablish its position of power.

Saint-Just chose to break the unified front. Contrary to custom, when he wrote his speech between 8 and 9 Thermidor, he did not show it to members of the Committee. When the meeting of the Convention opened on 9 Thermidor, the Committee members were amazed to hear Saint-Just reading a speech that had not passed their censor. His first words were, perhaps, the credo of the individualist who is not willing to belong to any group, "I am not of any faction; I shall combat them all."[72] Other members of the Committee came running to the plenary session; they were shocked by Saint-Just's words, for they knew full well what one well-aimed speech of his could do — he sent Danton to the guillotine with a similar speech. They silenced him, and an extended and disorganized argument began: the center was Robespierre. In the end, Robespierre, his brother Augustin, Saint-Just, Le Bas, and more were arrested and sent to jail.

Why did Saint-Just, who was not involved in the conflict for or against Robespierre and who was chosen by the Committee to present its unity, break the unity? We know that he bore some Committee members a grudge; we also know that he quarrelled with Billaud and Collot on the eve of his speech. Before he began it, he sent a note to the Committee: "The injustice broke my heart; I am going to open it in the National Convention."[73] But the real reason is a mystery, which Saint-Just took with himself to the scaffold.

Be that as it may, for Saint-Just, individualism was more than just a principle; it was a passion. In the opening sentences of his first known speech in the Convention, in the matter of the trial of Louis XVI, he pushed aside the two clashing proposals under discussion and arrogantly proclaimed, "And me, I say that the King must be judged."[74] With this speech he decided the fate of the King. In his last speech, he said, "I am not of any faction," and decided his own fate. On 10 Thermidor, after an unsuccessful attempted *coup d'état*, Saint-Just, alongside Robespierre, another passionate individualist, was led to the guillotine; and the Jacobin regime, already wracked with internal strife, collapsed.

Conclusion

Our descriptions of the activities of Adams and Saint-Just were idiographic; we tried to visualize the overall image of each leader to show each one more or less as a whole person. Nevertheless, our discussion was not a biography of these two men, since our primary interest was in the leadership style each one represented. This idiographic approach is a way of grasping the elusive concept of style; but it also can serve as a point of departure for the construction of a nomothetic frame of reference. Both Saint-Just and Adams had leadership characteristics so sharply defined that they are not too far from ideal types. At the one extreme, there is the fraternalistic leader, the team player, at one with his people, willing to compromise, seeking a democratic consensus. At the other extreme, there is the paternalistic leader, the individualist who stands above his public, who takes an "all or nothing" stance, and who relies upon a metaphysical democratic conception that borders on dictatorship. Any democratic revolutionary leader can be located on a continuum between these two ideal extremes, and evaluated in terms of his distance from them. This nomothetic tool, however, needs further elaboration, because the paternalistic/fraternalistic continuum is not the only relevant dimension characterizing revolutionary leaders. The limitations of the typological approach should also be remembered.

It is not our intention to claim that fraternalism is always good, while paternalism is always bad. It is highly doubtful whether the fraternalistic Adams would have succeeded in saving Alsace from the Austro-Prussian invasion. Saint-Just, on the other hand, succeeded, and there are many scholars who believe that his "guillotine democracy" was the only way to achieve success, given the circumstances. He apparently went a bit too far, but still it may well be that Saint-Just was the right man in the right place. This demonstrates that a researcher cannot evaluate the leadership style of a political actor on the basis of the typology alone, without also studying the place in which he acts. France and the American colonies at the end of the eighteenth century were two completely different worlds.

New England was the home of a rooted democratic tradition

built upon various kinds of local bodies, primarily the township. The large majority of New England residents were educated, including the "gang" leader Mackintosh, and were participants in the democratic process. In France, by contrast, there was a radically centralist tradition, at least since Louis XIV. Paris was the center of the world, and the *intendants* of the king ruled all the districts high-handedly. Alexis de Tocqueville described this in his book, *l'Ancien Régime et la Révolution*. Once the village community freed itself from feudalism, it was swallowed up into the district which was enslaved to administrative centralization. Tocqueville noted that in New England, however, the community turned into a township. Moreover, in his earlier book, *De la démocratie en Amérique,* he described the tendency, which the Americans had brought to "perfection," to create associations and to act together to achieve objectives, relying upon themselves rather than upon the central government, as in France.

In light of the above, it is doubtful whether Saint-Just could have achieved his objectives — such as passage of the Ventôse Laws, for instance — without centralistic enforcement from above. This is especially true if we remember that the majority of the French people at the time were illiterate and without experience in democracy. Saint-Just's style was, essentially, the centralistic style of the *ancien régime*, despite the revolutionary content of his ideas. His was a style which France had long been used to.

Adams' style was also not innovative. It was the same leadership style which New Englanders had long been used to, a style of action combined with public involvement and the formation of voluntary ties with assorted social and political groups. It is hard to imagine that a personality such as Saint-Just could have succeeded in leading the colonies in their struggle against the British. It would have been enough for him to make one false move — to alienate Virginia from Massachusetts on religious grounds, for instance, or to aggressively attack Dickinson — for the patriotic camp not to have crystalized. Adams was aware of these dangers and knew how to avoid them. He, too, was the right person in the right place.

In the introduction, we stressed the similarities between the American and the French Revolutions. It must be said, however, that despite the general similarities, there were also significant differences. The Jacobin revolution (we are referring only to this revolution, which was only one of a series of revolutions which took place in France in the course of the Great Revolution) sought a radical change of all the procedures of government and society, to such an extent that they strove to change man's very heart. The Jacobin revolutionaries strove to establish a holistic republic of *vertu*, which was a moral no less than a political being. In contrast, the revolution in New England included a notable element of conservatism. There were, indeed, social changes in the course of the revolution, but at its source, the struggle against the British was for the protection of the traditional rights of the residents of the colonies, in accordance with their traditional spirit. The conflicts that broke out were primarily in response to British innovations which conflicted with the colonies' political tradition.

A radical moral revolution requires a tougher leadership than a revolution which strives to protect traditionally accepted rights. This indicates that a leadership style must also be judged in light of the revolution's central goals. For example, Adams, as a leader, could rely upon the local groups of Massachusetts, for he was trying to protect them, and thus their good will towards him was all but guaranteed. Saint-Just, on the other hand, had no choice but to dismantle the local groups in France, for, from his ideological point of view, they were stumbling blocks to be overcome on the road to the fulfillment of the dream of the holistic republic. Since this was the case, he could not be a fraternalist, but had to combine paternalism with suppression. This is not meant to justify his actions. It merely demonstrates that there is a connection between the ideological content of a revolution and the leadership style appropriate to it.

One thing about Saint-Just that cannot be justified is his radical individualism. (This characteristic was typical of many Jacobin leaders.) As we have seen, internal tensions within an inner revolutionary circle may endanger the success of the revolution, particularly in the case of a moral-political revolution. Yet history teaches us that such revolutions are not necessarily doomed to failure and can succeed if they base themselves upon a unified revolutionary cadre which imposes a new order on the public. Perhaps the best example of this is the Bolshevik Revolution. Thus, in light of Saint-Just's radical individualism, it is hard to say that Saint-Just was the right man in the right place. It could well be that a certain degree of cooperation and teamwork are essential for any type of revolutionary leadership.

There are many possible varieties of revolutionary leadership, reflecting varied historical, social, ideological, and moral backgrounds. To properly evaluate a revolutionary leadership, one should go beyond typology and study the total context within which the leadership was active. We have learned this from the histories of Samuel Adams and Saint-Just, who not only approximate ideal types, but also reflect the New England revolution and the Jacobin revolution with their respective political traditions and values.

Notes

In order not to overload the reader with too frequent citations, we present them in groups at the end of the various sections of the text, except when a long quotation is made. The numbers of the pages of the grouped sources cited appear in the footnotes in the order in which they relate to the text of the article, which is not always their numerical order in the source itself.

1. For full biographies of Adams, see Chester Miller, *Sam Adams, Pioneer in Propaganda* (Stanford: Stanford University Press, 1966); William V. Wells, *The Life and Public Services of Samuel Adams* (Boston: Little, Brown, 1865); and Steward Beach, *Samuel Adams, The Fateful Years* (New York: Dodd, Mead, 1965).

2. For full biographies of Saint-Just, see Eugene N. Curtis, *Saint-Just, Colleague of Robespierre* (New York: Columbia University Press, 1935); J.B. Morton, *Saint-Just* (London: Longman, Green, 1939); and Albert Ollivier, *Saint-Just et la Force de Choses* (Paris: Gallimard, 1954).

3. Ollivier, p. 11.

4. Pauline Maier, *The Old Revolutionaries: Political Lives in the Age of Samuel Adams* (New York: Alfred A. Knopf, 1980). See also Beach; Robert E. Brown, *Middle-Class Democracy and the Revolution in Massachusetts, 1691-1780* (New York: Harper and Row, 1969; Richard D. Brown, *Revolutionary Politics in Massachusetts: The Boston Committee of Correspondence and the Towns, 1772-1774* (Cambridge: Harvard University Press, 1970; Stephen E. Patterson, *Political Parties in Revolutionary Massachusetts* (Madison, Wis.: University of Wisconsin Press, 1973); and Donald B. Chidsey, *The World of Samuel Adams* (Nashville, Tenn.: Thomas Nelson, Inc., 1974).

5. For a discussion of this topic, see Beach, pp. viii-ix, 23, 77, 171-72, 248.

6. Miller, p. 70. For discussions of the Boston mob, see Gordon S. Wood, "A Note on Mobs in the American Revolution," *William*

and Mary Quarterly, 3:23 (1966): 635-642; Dirk Hoerder, *Crowd Action in Revolutionary Massachusetts, 1765-1780* (New York: Academic Press, 1977); Beach, p. 136; Chidsey, pp. 141-142; R.D. Brown, pp. 145-146. See also Care Bridenbough, *Cities in Revolt* (New York: Knopf, 1955), p. 117.

7. Ollivier, 1954; Norman Hampson, *Maximilien Robespierre* (London: Duckworth, 1974); Moshe Hazani, "Forms of Consciousness and Political Behavior," Ph.D. dissertation, Hebrew University of Jerusalem, 1981 (in Hebrew). See also R.R. Palmer, *Twelve Who Ruled* (Princeton: Princeton University Press, 1973).

8. Miller, pp. 8, 38-39; Beach, p. 29; Bridenbaugh, pp. 221-22; R.E. Brown, p. 223; Van Beck Hall, *Politics Without Parties, Massachusetts, 1780-1791* (Pittsburgh: University of Pittsburgh Press, 1972), pp. 52-53.

9. Hoerder, pp. 72-73; Miller, p. 68. See also Chidsey's descriptions of Boston life.

10. Miller, pp. 61-68; Chidsey, pp. 48-52; Beach, pp. 81-84; Hoerder, pp. 97-110; R.E. Brown, pp. 215-220.

11. Miller, p. 69. Hoerder does not confirm Miller's position on this, but according to his research, Adams was active in the Mackintosh affair and influenced the "Loyall nine," the Sons of Liberty, who organized the 14 August events. See Hoerder, pp. 93-94, 96.

12. Miller, pp. 69-70; Hoerder, pp. 117-18.

13. Moreover, the 1768 riots, which led to the stationing of British troops in Boston and thus indirectly to the Boston Massacre, were an exception rather than the rule; they were triggered by British impressment of sailors which traditionally aroused bitter opposition in Boston, being the most serious infringement of a citizen's liberty. Historians often ignore the impressment and erroneously think that the riots reflected the city's true, "unruly" nature. As a matter of fact, riots caused by British impressment continued also in the 1790s, which shows that they were not directly related to the struggle for independence.

14. Hoerder, p. 156; Miller, p. 40.

15. Miller, pp. 313-314, 395.

16. Hall, pp. 171-173, 300, 312, 276; Miller, p. 379. For Adams' corporatistic views, see Patterson.

17. *Oeuvres Complètes de Saint-Just*, 2 vols. (Paris: Librairie Charpentier et Fasquelle, 1908), I: 258, 256, 330, 303.

18. Palmer, p. 177.

19. Ollivier, p. 15.

20. Curtis, p. 240.

21. *Oeuvres Complètes* II: 147.

22. *Oeuvres Complètes* II: 106-107. For a discussion of Saint-Just's measures, see Curtis, pp. 176-178; and Ollivier, pp. 278-279.

23. *Oeuvres Complètes* II: 126, 144-146, 134, 132; Curtis, p. 176.

24. James Thompson, *The French Revolution* (Oxford: Blackwell, 1947), pp. 111-112. For a description of the people of Paris, see Albert Soboul, *The Parisian Sans-Culottes and the French Revolution, 1793-94* (Oxford: Clarendon Press, 1964); Albert Soboul, *The Sans-Culottes* (Princeton: Princeton University Press, 1980); and George Rudé, *The Crowd in the French Revolution* (New York and London: Oxford University Press, 1959).

25. *Oeuvres Complètes* II: 74; Ollivier, p. 256; Soboul, 1980, p. 104; Soboul, 1964, pp. 205-206; Palmer, p. 127.

26. Ollivier, p. 256; *Oeuvres Complètes* II: 163; Soboul, 1964, p. 221.

27. For what we call "the *sans-cullotes* ethic," see Soboul, 1964, pp. 55-98; Soboul, 1980; Alfred Cobban, *The Social Interpretation of the French Revolution* (Cambridge: Cambridge University Press, 1964), pp. 120-131.

28. *Oeuvres Complètes* II: 238, 267; Maurice Dommanget, *Saint-Just* (Paris: Editions du Cercle, 1971), p. 71ff. See also Albert Soboul, ed., *Saint-Just, Discours et Rapports* (Paris: Editions Sociales, 1957), pp. 29-35.

29. Palmer, p. 186; Soboul, 1957, pp. 29-30; *Oeuvres Complètes* II: 145-146. For a description of Saint-Just's social policies in Alsace, see also Ollivier. Soboul, 1957, is particularly sympathetic to Saint-Just's policies.

30. *Oeuvres Complètes* II: 228-229, 247-248. For a detailed discussion of the laws, see Palmer, pp. 284-287, 312-314.

31. Soboul, 1957, pp. 24-25; Soboul, 1980, p. 207; *Oeuvres Complètes* II: 148; Michelet is cited in Soboul, 1957, pp. 29-30; Ernest Hamel, *Histoire de Saint-Just* (Paris: Poulet-Malassis et de Broise, 1859), p. 333.

32. Miller, p. 126.

33. R.D. Brown, "The Massachusetts Convention of Towns, 1768," *William and Mary Quarterly* 3:23 (1969): 79, 83.

34. According to the Colonial Charter of 1691, only the colony was entitled to pay the wages of the judges, not London. The people of Massachusetts stubbornly guarded this right so that the judges would not become dependent on the British rule. The Townshend Acts wished to infringe upon this right. Struggle on this issue

arose periodically during the eighteenth century and ended only with independence.

35. Miller, pp. 118-19, 125-31.

36. Quoted in Hoerder, p. 197.

37. See note 13 above.

37. For a thorough study of the Massachusetts Convention of Towns, see R.D. Brown, 1969. See also Miller, pp. 149-151, 164-165, 153. For the previous conservatism of the western towns, see Miller, pp. 111, 151. The quotations are drawn from these various sources.

39. R.D. Brown, 1970.

40. *Ibid.*, p. 85.

41. Miller, p. 75; R.D. Brown, 1970, pp. 80-81, vii.

42. Nisbet, 1974.

43. See, for example, in *Du Contrat Social*, Livre I, ch. 6-7; Livre II, ch. 2, 4. Rousseau refers to the "whole" as "une personne" and says that sometimes the name of this entity is "cité"; interestingly, Saint-Just uses the same name.

44. *Oeuvres Complètes* I: 434; Alain Liénard, *Saint-Just, Theorie Politique* (Paris: Editions du Seuil, 1976), p. 174; *Oeuvres Complètes* I: 434, 455; II: 373.

45. Federalism, as we use the term here, must not be confused with the "federalism" of the American political dictionary at the end of the eighteenth century.

46. Liénard, p. 202.

47. See Jacque Godechot, *Les Institutions de la France sous la Révolution et l'Empire* (Paris: Press Universitaire de France, 1951), pp. 242-244; and *Les Constitutions de la France dèpuis 1789* (Paris: Barnier-Flammarion, 1970), pp. 70-72.

48. *Oeuvres Complètes* I: 426, 432, 456.

49. Saint-Just's stance vis-a-vis the *communautés* is more complicated and lies beyond the scope of our discussion here.

50. *Oeuvres Complètes* I: 436-437; II: 371.

51. Quoted in Soboul, 1980, p. 109.

52. *Ibid.*, pp. 102, 116, 135.

53. *Oeuvres Complètes* I: 309, 292.

54. R.D. Brown, 1970, p. 116.

55. Harry A. Cushing, ed., *The Writings of Samuel Adams* 4 vols. (New York: Octagon Books, 1968), IV: 306.

56. *Ibid.*, I: 7-12, 67.

57. Miller, p. 75.

58. For a detailed description of the struggle, see Beach, p. 254ff.

59. Beach, p. 258; Miller, pp. 323-324.

60. Miller, pp. 98-99, 236.

61. *Ibid.*, p. 320ff.

62. *Ibid.*, pp. 338-341.

63. *Ibid.*, p. 201.

64. *Ibid.*, pp. 342-343.

65. Ollivier, p. 268; Palmer, p. 80; Ollivier, pp. 282-283; Palmer, p. 191; Miller, p. 61.

66. Palmer, p. 193, 74; Liénard, p. 304; Palmer, p. 194; Ollivier, p. 257.

67. Soboul, 1957, p. 141; *Oeuvres Complètes* II: 231.

68. The description of Thermidor, including Saint-Just's role in the events, is based mainly on Palmer, 1973; Hampson, 1974; Ollivier, 1954; Curtis, 1935; Albert Mathiez, *The Fall of Robespierre* (New York: Augustus M. Kelley, 1968); Richard Bienvenue, ed., *The Ninth of Thermidor: The Fall of Robespierre* (New York and London: Oxford University Press, 1968); George Rudé, *Robespierre* (New York: Viking Press, 1975); and Hazani, 1981.

69. Ollivier, pp. 542, 468, 514, 505; Liénard, p. 304; Hampson, p. 269-270.

70. F.V.A. Aulard, *The French Revolution, A Political History, 1789-1804*, 4 vols. (New York: Russel and Russel, 1965), II: 225-226.

71. Ollivier, p. 505.

72. *Oeuvres Complètes* II: 477.

73. Ollivier, p. 516.

74. *Oeuvres Complètes* I: 365.

Bibliography

Aulard, F.V.A. (1965). *The French Revolution, A Political History, 1789-1804* 4 vols. New York: Russel and Russel.

Bienvenue, Richard, ed. (1968). *The Ninth of Thermidor: The Fall of Robespierre*. Oxford University Press.

Beach, Steward (1965). *Samuel Adams, The Fateful Years*. New York: Dodd, Mead and Company.

Bridenbaugh, Care (1955). *Cities in Revolt*. New York: Knopf.

Brown, Richard D. (1969). "The Massachusetts Convention of Towns, 1768," *William and Mary Quarterly*, 3rd Series, XXVI, 94-104.

— (1970). *Revolutionary Politics in Massachusetts: The Boston Committee of Correspondence and the Towns, 1772-1774*. Cambridge: Harvard University Press.

Brown, Robert E. (1969). *Middle-Class Democracy and the Revolution in Massachusetts, 1691-1780*. New York: Harper and Row.

Chidsey, Donald B. (1974). *The World of Samuel Adams*. Nashville, Tenn.: Thomas Nelson, Inc.

Cobban, Alfred (1964). *The Social Interpretation of the French Revolution*. Cambridge University Press.

Curtis, Eugene N. (1935). *Saint-Just, Colleague of Robespierre*. New York: Columbia University Press.

Dommanget, Maurice (1971). *Saint-Just*. Editions du Cercle.

Godechot, Jacque (1951). *Les Institutions de la France sous la Revolution et l'Empire*. Paris: Press Universitaire de France.

— (1970). *Les Constitutions de la France depuis 1789*. Paris: Barnier-Flammarion.

Hall, Van Beck (1972). *Politics without Parties, Massachusetts 1780-1791*. University of Pittsburgh Press.

Hamel, Ernest (1859). *Histoire de Sain-Just*. Paris: Poulet — Malassis et de Broise.

Hampson, Norman (1974). *Maximilien Robespierre*. London: Duckworth.

Hazani, Moshe (1981). *Forms of Consciousness and Political Behavior*. Unpublished Ph.D. dissertation, Hebrew University of Jerusalem (in Hebrew).

Hoerder, Dirk (1977). *Crowd Action in Revolutionary Massachusetts, 1765-1780*. New York: Academic Press.

Lienard, Alain (1976). *Saint-Just, Theorie Politique*. Paris: Editions du Senil.

Maier, Pauline (1980). *The Old Revolutionaries. Political Lives in the Age of Samuel Adams.* New York: Knopf.

Mathiez, Albert (1968). *The Fall of Robespierre.* New York: Augustus M. Kelley.

Miller, John Chester (1966). *Sam Adams, Pioneer in Propaganda.* Stanford, CA: Stanford University Press.

Morton, J. B. (1939). *Saint-Just.* London: Longmans, Green and Co.

Nisbet, Robert A. (1974). "Citizenship: Two Traditions," *Social Research*, 41: 612-637.

Oeuvres Complètes de Saint-Just (1908). Paris: Librairie Charpentier et Fasquelle.

Ollivier, Albert (1954). *Saint-Just et la Force de Choses.* Gallimard.

Palmer, R.R. (1973). *Twelve Who Ruled.* Princeton: Princeton University Press.

Patterson, Stephen E. (1973). *Political Parties in Revolutionary Massachusetts.* University of Wisconsin Press.

Rude, George (1959). *The Crowd in the French Revolution.* Oxford University Press.

— (1975). *Robespierre.* New York: Viking Press.

Soboul, Albert, ed. (1957). *Saint-Just, Discours et Rapports.* Paris: Editions Sociales.

— (1964). *The Parisian Sans-culottes and the French Revolution, 1793-94.* Oxford: Clarendon Press.

— (1980). *The Sans-culottes.* Princeton: Princeton University Press.

Thompson, James M. (1947). *The French Revolution.* Oxford: Blackwell.

Wells, William V. (1865). *The Life and Public Services of Samuel Adams.* Boston: Little, Brown and Company.

Wood, Gordon S. (1966). "A Note on Mobs in the American Revolution," *William and Mary Quarterly*, 3rd series, XXIII, 635-42.

REVOLUTIONARY LEADERSHIP AND THE PROBLEM OF POWER

Morton J. Frisch

In 1783, George Washington, who had retired as commander-in-chief of the Continental Army, and Alexander Hamilton, who was a representative from New York in the Congress of the Confederation, were revolutionary leaders in the process of becoming founding statesmen. The problem which Washington and Hamilton faced at that time was what to do about the Articles of Confederation, a less than satisfactory political arrangement. By the time the Articles were finally ratified in March 1781, they were virtually inoperative. It almost seems as if that constitution, which had demonstrated its capacity to be by actually being, was never meant to be. One could never feel that it was rooted in reality. Washington wrote to James Warren in 1785 that "the confederation appears to me to be little more than a shadow without the substance." He further wrote to Thomas Jefferson in 1787 that "the situation of the general government, if it can be called a government, is shaken to its foundation...and unless a remedy is soon applied, anarchy and confusion will inevitably ensue."[1] Washington saw that America needed to restructure its entire system of government.

But Jefferson, a participant in the framing of the Articles, remarked as late as 1786 that "the Confederation is a wonderfully perfect instrument, considering the circumstances under which it was formed." He continued: "It has been said that our governments both federal and particular want energy; that it is difficult to restrain both individuals and states from committing wrongs. That is true, and it is an inconvenience. On the other hand that energy which absolute governments derive from an armed force, which is the effect of the bayonet constantly held at the breast of every citizen, and which resembles very much the stillness of the grave, must be admitted also to have its inconveniences. We weigh the two together, and like best to submit to the former."[2] Jefferson was willing, as he indicated, to sacrifice energy for liberty. Pursuing that line of thought, he wrote to James Madison the following year: "I own I am not a friend to a very energetic

139

government. It is always oppressive. The late rebellion in Massachusetts has given more alarm than I think it should have done."[3]

But despite his satisfaction with the Articles, Jefferson was not reluctant to recommend that, as a matter of course, constitutions be remade every generation. That recommendation assumes, needless to say, that the decisively architectonic function of statesmanship is a relatively simple task. Hamilton was less sanguine than Jefferson, for he well understood that serious errors have been committed in organizing (and reorganizing) political societies, and that "bad principles in a Govt. tho slow are sure in their operation, and will gradually destroy it."[4] He cautioned that "good constitutions are formed upon a comparison of the liberty of the individual with the strength of government: If the tone of either be too high, the other will be weakened too much. The problem therefore in forming systems of government is to find the best possible mode of conciliating those objects so that "the government will reach, in its regular operations, the perfect balance between liberty and power."[5] Jefferson ignores the fact that the act of founding a regime requires the greatest circumspection, for a change of regime is the greatest and most fundamental change which a political society can undergo. Hamilton would hold that only when a regime is in a state of complete disintegration, as was the Articles of Confederation, could its transformation into another regime become defensible.

It could be said that the dominant perspective of the American Revolution and indeed of the Articles of Confederation was that power tends to corrupt and that absolute power corrupts absolutely. Jefferson, under the influence of that view, wrote to Edward Carrington during the ratification debates in 1788 that "the natural progress of things is for liberty to yield and for government to gain ground."[6] But Hamilton was convinced that the abstraction of liberty from government is, practically speaking, impossible. He argued in the opening number of *The Federalist* that "the vigour of government is essential to the security of liberty; [and] in the contemplation of a sound and well informed judgment, their interest can never be separated." Hamilton was as fully dedicated to liberty as Jefferson, but he doubted the soundness of a perspective that placed a greater emphasis on liberty than on authority. He was not a simple believer in liberty.

Hamilton wrote in 1781, from the perspective of the problems of the Confederation, that "in a government framed for durable liberty, not less regard must be paid to giving the magistrate a proper degree of authority, to make and execute the laws with rigour, than to guarding against encroachments upon the rights of the community. As too much power leads to despotism, too little leads to anarchy, and both eventually to the ruin of the people. These are maxims well known, but never sufficiently attended to, in adjusting frames of government."[7] By this, he meant that the only way we might have liberty is by opening our minds to authority, whereas Jefferson's tendency, with his abstract enthusiasm for revolutions, was to depreciate political authority and thus weaken the force of government. Jefferson appears to have believed that government may be more and more replaced by society and indulged in sentimental visions of a society without government. He looked forward to the perfect freedom of self-government.

Hamilton says with perfect openness in *Federalist* No. 31 that "a government ought to contain in itself every power requisite to the full accomplishment of the objects committed to its care, and to the complete execution of the trusts for which it is responsible, free from every other control, *but* a regard to the public good and to the sense of the people."[8] It might appear from this statement, declaring the necessity of doing everything needful and possible for achieving the ends of government, that liberty be subordinated to authority in the interest of national self-preservation. But Hamilton believed that authority must condition itself or be conditioned by the ends or purposes of a free society and therefore be exercised under certain constraints or limitations. The necessary condition for liberty is government, but the absolute integrity of a government guaranteed by the rule of law and not the rule of force.

In his later defense of the government's suppression of the insurgents in the Whiskey Rebellion, Hamilton explained that power is the instrument by which a government must act, and it takes the form of either force or authority. If the authority of the law is undermined, then force must be substituted and there is an end to liberty. But according to Hamilton's account the real tension is between force and liberty and not authority and liberty, for he lays it down as a principle that a respect for the authority of law is "the sustaining energy of free government."[9] He understood that liberty must be limited in order to be possessed and reasoned that too much concern with liberty was a leading cause of the dissolution of political authority.

Hamilton had very specific ideas on how to reconstitute the regime under the Articles of Confederation. But while the Articles were widely perceived as a defective constitution, there was no general agreement as to whether they should be amended or discarded. It would be interesting to see how an amended Articles might have functioned, although it is hard to imagine how they could be substantially improved without being fundamentally changed. As Hamilton remarked in *Federalist* No. 15: "...the evils we experience do not proceed from minute or partial imperfections, but from fundamental errors in the structure of the building, which cannot be amended otherwise than by an alteration in the first principles of the fabric." The leading minds of the Convention — Hamilton, Madison, Gouverneur Morris, and James Wilson — were clearly intent on fashioning a more perfect political arrangement, and refashioning the Articles was furthest from their minds.

The collapse of the Articles of Confederation was the decisive moment in American history, for at that moment America had to restructure its institutions with a view to the realities of political power. What had brought down the Articles was the unreality of its regime, an awareness of which was induced by Shays' Rebellion. It could not be clearer that the Articles had provided for a government without power. Hamilton knew that all regimes and constitutions are not free from imperfections, but the tendency of the American Revolution to depreciate authority, where liberty in the radical sense was the dominant consideration, had to be corrected. His view, drawn from a recognition of the Confederation's imperfections, was that the best guarantee of liberty rests in a government with competent powers to act and a complex structure arranged to make it act wisely and responsibly. Otherwise stated, Hamilton thought that the best way to get a regime of liberty was through the right kind of formal constitutional arrangements — separation of powers and checks and balances, and a government equipped with the power to govern.

It is instructive to contemplate the impermanence of regimes and constitutions, as we are interested in the question of whether a political society free from impermanences and imperfections is indeed possible. America brought under revision its idea of a perfect commonwealth as a result of its experience with the Articles. The Founding Fathers were intensively concerned with the improvement of their establishment — a regime of liberty — and therefore were naturally drawn to the teachings of the political philosophers of the seventeenth and eighteenth centuries. Locke took the first step in the direction of the American Constitution by separating and equalizing legislative and executive power and by providing for the independence of executive power through prerogative. Montesquieu completed the transformation of thought which Locke had initiated through the introduction of a separate judicial power in order to make the regime of liberty more moderate. When Hamilton spoke of "the most approved and well founded maxims of free government, which requires that the legislative, executive and judicial authorities should be deposited in distinct and separate hands" in 1783, he was undoubtedly referring to the formulations of Locke and Montesquieu, formulations which were central to a revision of republicanism.[10]

Hamilton could substantially broaden the perspective of the Constitutional Convention because he believed that any fundamental restructuring of the regime would have to take its republican as well as its confederal defects into account. The confederal defects of the Articles of Confederation were generally recognized and understood in the mid-1780s, but its republican defects — the dominance of the republican assembly and the resultant lack of balance of power within the general government — were less visible. Hamilton saw the defective character of traditional republicanism in its inevitable tendency toward legislative usurpation. He had an opportunity to experience the deficient wisdom of representative assemblies and what he feared most was that there was no adequate counterpoise to legislative dominance in a government wholly popular and representative. He defined "limited government" as one which does not suppose the whole power of the nation to be lodged in the legislative body. Therefore the question of the limits of legislative power was for him the critical issue of republican government.

Hamilton was no advocate of legislative government and said in so many words that the legislative power is incapable of completely fulfilling governmental functions, the opposite of which was the confederate practice. He wrote to James Duane in September 1780 that "Congress is properly a deliberative corps and it forgets itself when it attempts to play the executive. It is impossible such a body, numerous as it is, constantly fluctuating, can ever act with sufficient decision, or with system."[11] The Confederation showed the ruinous character of a regime which had failed to differentiate between legislative and executive power by confounding legislative and executive power in a single body. It is fair to say that the government under the Confederation was virtually headless. What Hamilton seems to have believed was that republican government, supplemented and stimulated by energetic executive power, could provide more direction than legislatures are able to give, and at the same time furnish the necessary limitations on legislative power. He was not limited by the traditional republican perspective in the revolutionary phase of the American experience.

Hamilton's strategy for making republicanism more workable than it was under the confederal government required executive independence from the legislature through a real separation of powers. The principle of republicanism is necessarily limited or perfected by the separation of governmental power because the separation of power means the differentiation of power. The confederal government was characterized by undifferentiated power or the dominance of the republican assembly. Hamilton remarked to an unknown addressee sometime between December 1779 and March 1780 that "the Congress have too long neglected to organize a good scheme of administration and throw executive business into proper executive departments."[12] When members of Congress had at that time discussed delegating power to subordinate administrative agencies, they were primarily concerned with improving the efficiency of Congress and nothing more. But even after the creation of administrative agencies, the Continental Congress refused to remain within the bounds of what was properly its business and continued to concern itself with the details of administration. Congress was simply unwilling to divest itself of that power.[13] It was clear to Hamilton that the functions of government were not properly differentiated under our first republican government.

In unsubmitted resolutions calling for a convention to amend the Articles which Hamilton drafted in July 1783, he referred to the Confederation as defective in confounding legislative and executive powers in a single body and recommended the adoption of the principle of separation of powers, understood to mean the exercise of different functions of government by different departments.[14] Separation of powers is the doctrine designed to separate, to isolate the legislative and executive powers from one another in order to maintain a countervailing force to the popular assembly. The Lockean formulation of that doctrine never intended that the executive power would simply be limited to the function of executing the laws. The executive would have to exercise his prerogative in internal as well as foreign affairs. Locke established the executive as an independent and co-equal function of government within the complexity of a constitutional arrangement checking power with power. He must have had in mind that legislative and executive power would check each other by remaining in a state of tension. Hamilton followed Locke's construction, for he spoke in the New York Ratifying Convention of "the competition that ever subsists between the branches of government," the competition that keeps powers limited.[15]

It would be no exaggeration to say that the American Founding represents modern political philosophy in its best form, for it represents the transition from theory (Locke and Montesquieu) to practice through statesmanship rather than revolution. Hume had written that "liberty is the perfection of civil society; but still authority must be acknowledged essential to its very existence."[16] Hamilton's view of authority or power was that of separated and balanced power and accordingly does not imply an indifference to the end for which power is used or to be used, and this comes out clearly in his description of a good constitution as one which achieves a perfect balance between liberty and power.[17] He was for liberty and not against power. Hamilton was for the balance of a well-ordered republican government, for the rightly understood kind of power with no one power capable of gaining the decisive advantage. He guided his political actions consistently by the view that stable political rule cannot be based on liberty alone, and this was informed by his awareness of the corrupting influence of unlimited legislative power in a republican or popular regime. It became clear to Hamilton, from his experience with the Confederation, that republicanism could be made to work only insofar as it contained some ingredient of strong executive power to serve as a check on the legislature accomplished through separation of powers.

The critical period in American history offered Americans a singularly enlightening experience in politics and government, for the recovery or the rediscovery of the realities of power had to be made from under layers of republican prejudice. The Articles had failed, and this failure, considered in the abstract, was grounded in a distrust of political power inherited from revolutionary theory. It is abundantly clear that in 1787 the virtual obliteration of the American regime was at stake. Even the powers theoretically belonging to the general government, like those relating to the enforcement of treaties, were practically unenforceable, because the states seemed somehow not to realize that the Articles, inadequate as they were, had constituted a government. A more perfect political arrangement was needed to define and control the confederation of republics that constituted the American union.

Jefferson proceeded from the assumption that the Articles were a wonderfully perfect instrument considering the circumstances under which they were formed, and would have been well satisfied with something far less energetic than the American Constitution.[18] But it should not surprise us that Jefferson, although inclined toward radical change, was defensive of the Articles, for he was more thoroughly a rebel in thought than in action. The revolutionary boldness of his thought, as evidenced in the Declaration of Independence, was spectacular, but he remains a revolutionary theorist rather than a founder. Jefferson leans emphatically toward the view that revolutions are fundamentally liberating, whereas Hamilton unfolds the principles that guide the formation of constitutions. When speaking in the New York Ratifying Convention, Hamilton explained: "It is our duty to examine all those means [for the establishment of a republican government on a safe and solid basis] with peculiar attention, and to chuse the best and most effectual [in the formation of our government]. We should contemplate and compare the systems, which, in this examination, come under our view, distinguish, with a careful eye, the defects and excellencies of each, and discarding the former, incorporate the latter, as far as circumstances will admit, into our constitution."[19]

When there is a basic change of regimes, as there was in 1787-89, it takes theoretical thought to introduce the qualitative change, for theoretical thought (in this case the formulations of Locke and Montesquieu) guides and governs. What most distinguishes Hamilton from the other leading American founders was that he opened the whole issue of existing regimes and their respective merits in the constitutional proceedings which no narrow partisan of republicanism would ever do. When he thought about what kind of political constitution ought to replace the one in existence, he measured traditional republicanism by standards that transcended republicanism in an effort to bring about a perfected republican constitution.

Hamilton, unlike Jefferson, recognized that stable republican rule could not be based on the notion that only a small portion of power is requisite to government. In a way Jefferson knew this, but his doctrine made him forget it. From the perspective of

Hamilton, Jefferson ignored the fact that the real problem of politics is not the presence of power but its absence. Hamilton was very much more realistic than Jefferson because he understood that politics involves, in its most important respects, the responsible exercise of power, but he would deny that the ultimate reality is power and not principle. It was not Hamilton but Aaron Burr who may be described as a student of Machiavelli, for, although Hamilton would not divorce politics from power, he believed that the responsible exercise of power required the subordination of power to principle. Hamilton's realism was directed toward the highest excellence of which a statesman is capable, the establishment and improvement of regimes.

It must be mentioned that Hamilton viewed the American Constitution as a reasonable but imperfect document and said so in no uncertain terms when he signed it.[20] He was of the opinion that the executive was not sufficiently fortified by its constitutional powers, at least as those powers were generally construed at the time of the founding. He contemplated a stronger executive than that which the Constitution created, for he believed an energetic independent executive to be essential to balanced republican government. It was Hamilton's considered view that the Constitution lacked a truly secure balance of power, and that only in a political system where the power of the legislature is checked and balanced by an energetic executive (as well as an independent judiciary) could republicanism be established on a safe and solid basis. But although the Constitution's defects were real and he had serious doubts in his mind about the Constitution's future, this did not prevent him from working tirelessly for the Constitution's ratification and from making every effort after its ratification to further strengthen it in the direction of more balance.

Notes

1. George Washington, "Washington to James Warren, October 7, 1785," *The Writings of George Washington*, ed. by John C. Fitzpatrick, 39 vols. (Washington, D.C., 1938), XXVIII, 290; "Washington to Thomas Jefferson, May 30, 1787," *The Records of the Federal Convention*, ed. by Max Farrand, 4 vols. (New Haven, Conn.: Princeton University Press, 1966), III, 31. Hereafter cited as Farrand, *Records of Federal Convention*.

2. Thomas Jefferson, "Answers to Demeunier's First Queries, January 24, 1786," *The Papers of Thomas Jefferson*, ed. by Julian P.

Boyd, 21 vols. (Princeton, N.J., 1950-83), X, 14, 20. Hereafter cited as *Papers of T.J.*

3. Jefferson, "Jefferson to James Madison, December 20, 1787," *Papers of T.J.*, XII, 442.

4. Alexander Hamilton, "Speech on a Plan of Government, June 18, 1787," *The Papers of Alexander Hamilton*, ed. by Harold C. Syrett and Jacob E. Cooke (first 15 vols.), 26 vols. (New York, 1961-79), IV, 191. Hereafter cited as *Papers*.

5. Hamilton, "Speech in the New York Ratifying Convention, June 25, 1788," *Papers*, V, 81.

6. Jefferson, "Jefferson to Edward Carrington, May 27, 1788," *Papers of T.J.*, XIII, 208-209.

7. Hamilton, "Continentalist No. 2, July 12, 1781," *Papers*, II, 651.

8. The italics are mine.

9. Hamilton, "Tully No. III, August 28, 1794," *Papers*, XVII, 160.

10. Hamilton, "Unsubmitted Resolutions Calling for a Convention to Amend the Articles of Confederation, July 1783," *Papers*, III, 421.

11. Hamilton, "Hamilton to James Duane, September 3, 1780," *Papers*, II, 404.

12. Hamilton, "Hamilton to an Unknown Addressee, December 1779-March 1780," *Papers*, II, 246n.

13. See Charles C. Thach, Jr., *The Creation of the Presidency, 1775-1789* (Baltimore: Johns Hopkins University Press, 1969), Chap. 3.

14. Hamilton, "Unsubmitted Resolutions Calling for a Convention to Amend the Articles of Confederation, July 1783," *Papers*, III, 420-421.

15. Hamilton, "Speech in the New York Ratifying Convention, June 21, 1788," *Papers*, V, 38.

16. David Hume, "Of the First Principles of Government," *Essays, Moral, Political and Literary*, Part I, Essay iv.

17. Hamilton, "Speech in the New York Ratifying Convention, June 25, 1788," *Papers*, V, 81.

18. See Jefferson's letters to Madison dated December 20, 1787, *Papers of T.J.*, XII, 438-442; July 31, 1788, *Papers of T.J.*, XIII, 440-443; and March 15, 1789, *Papers of T.J.*, XIV, 659-662.

19. Hamilton, "Speech in the New York Ratifying Convention, June 24, 1787," *Papers*, V, 67.

20. Hamilton, "Remarks on the Signing of the Constitution, September 17, 1787," *Papers*, VI, 253.

JEFFERSON AND EXECUTIVE POWER: REVISIONISM AND THE "REVOLUTION OF 1800"

Gary J. Schmitt

In spite of the wide expanse of the Atlantic, the outbreak in 1793 of war in Europe between Great Britain and France seemed almost certain to entangle the young United States — an involvement it could ill afford. To avoid this, President Washington issued on 22 April what has come to be known as the Neutrality Proclamation; it declared that American policy would be impartial toward the warring European states. Opponents of the policy were quick to criticize the proclamation as an unconstitutional exercise of presidential power.

Alexander Hamilton, then Secretary of the Treasury, wasted no time in coming to Washington's defense. Writing under the pseudonym "Pacificus," Hamilton argued that the president was legally justified in issuing the proclamation based on powers inherent in the executive office. Hamilton's theorizing about the powers of the presidency led Jefferson to write James Madison in the hope that his good friend and political ally might pen a rebuttal to those "most striking heresies." Madison, writing as "Helvidius," did just that, rejecting Hamilton's arguments about the sweeping nature of the president's executive power.

From the tone and character of Jefferson's letter to Madison, it is not difficult to conclude that the Secretary of State saw himself as playing the part of Whig statesman to Hamilton's Tory villain.

> Nobody answers him and his doctrines will therefore be taken as confessed. For God's sake, my dear Sir, take up your pen, select the most striking heresies, and cut him to pieces in face of the public.[1]

Jefferson himself, of course, never disabused anyone who held

* This essay first appeared in *Publius: The Journal of Federalism* 17 (Spring 1987).

that view. Indeed, he fed such interpretations by writing letters like the following:

> Were parties here divided by a greediness for office, as in England, to take a part with either would be unworthy of a reasonable or moral man, but where the principle of difference is as substantial and as strongly pronounced as between the republicans and the Monocrats of our country, I hold it as honorable to take a firm & decided part, and as immoral to pursue a middle line, as between the parties of Honest men, & Rogues into which every country is divided.[2]

The stark division in political principles drawn by Jefferson in this letter was nothing new for most of his contemporaries. Most educated Americans had adopted one or another of the two opposed interpretations of British history — the Whig or the Tory. Both versions were defined largely in terms of the rise and fall of the crown. For the Whigs, history began with an idyllic Anglo-Saxon society where democracy ruled and liberty reigned. Its undoing dates from the time of the Norman Conquest and the imposition of a monarchy more befitting slaves than free men. For eighteenth century Whigs, the history of England was nearly synonymous with the history of the struggle to limit and control this alien imposition on the body politic. In sharp contrast, Tory historians maintained that the "golden age" of Anglo-Saxon history was in fact marked more by chaos and barbarism than real freedom. For them, the monarchy was critical in maintaining social stability and political order in England; the executive power of the crown was the shield behind which true liberty, civil liberty, could flourish. Jefferson, in couching his sentiments in language evoking the deepest sentiments of Whig history, appears to have appropriated its rhetoric to define the partisan struggles then taking place in the new regime.[3]

For Jefferson, a Whig reading of history provided insight not only into British affairs but the young nation's as well. America had been largely spared the disease of ministerial corruption associated with the English crown. When it had begun to take hold on these shores, the American Revolution had effectively uprooted it. Yet the Revolution, according to Jefferson and his followers, was in this matter in danger of being sabotaged by the machinations of Hamilton and his friends. To buttress his claims, Jefferson repeatedly referred to a conversation which he says took place between Vice President Adams, Hamilton, and himself during the first days of Washington's administration. By Jefferson's account, the question arose as to which form of government was best. To no one's surprise, Jefferson suggested the agrarian republic. Adams, to Jefferson's chagrin, claimed that monarchy was better and that the British system of government, if it could be purged of its corruption, would be the best that man could do. Hamilton, to the consternation of both, maintained that it was, in fact, only corruption that made the British government work and that, moreover, it was, as it stood, the most perfect system of government.

By Jefferson's account, such talk was not all that rare. Upon his return from Paris, where he had been the American minister to France and an active "witness" to the fall of the *ancien regime*, Jefferson settled into his new cabinet post and the political society that accompanied it. To his surprise, the table talk he found in the nation's capital was often the opposite of what he expected.

> I cannot describe the wonder and mortification with which the table conversations filled me....A preference of kingly over republican government was evidently the sentiment....I found myself for the most part the only advocate on the Republican side of the Question.[5]

For Jefferson, the Federalists were all too receptive to the idea of "kingly" government.

How genuinely surprised Jefferson was at this turn of events is difficult to determine. In a letter written to John Adams, long after the partisan rupture between the Federalists and Republicans, Jefferson ascribed that political division to the very nature of man:

> The same political parties which now agitate the U.S. have existed thro' all time...in fact the terms whig and tory belong to natural, as well as to civil history. They denote the temper and constitution of mind of different individuals.[6]

Jefferson apparently believed that the partisan struggle that had marked the country within its first decade was not traceable to anything so idiosyncratic as the personalities or individuals involved. Jefferson claimed that he had told Adams at the time that theirs was "no personal contest."

> Two systems of principles on the subject of government divide our fellow citizens into two parties. With one of these you concur, and I with the other....Were we both to die today,

151

tomorrow two other names would be in the place of ours, without any change in the motion of the machinery.[7]

In short, the contest between himself and Hamilton, the Republicans and the Federalists, was, in Jefferson's view, the inevitable collision of Tories and Whigs over political first principles.

Inevitable or not, for Jefferson's Republicans, "the victory of 1800 has rescued the nation from the threat of monarchic subversion."[8] The new president seemed determined to put an end to the pretensions of rank that had attached themselves to the Oval Office. For example, instead of riding around the capital in a coach and four with liveried outriders as Washington had done, Jefferson chose to ride his own horse accompanied by a single servant. As for his personal attire, it was republican to the core — simple and unpretentious. Indeed, so unpretentious was his dress as chief executive that some foreign dignitaries, accustomed as they were to the fashions and mores of the courts of Europe, believed that this former envoy to the court of France deliberately chose to affront them by wearing such attire when they met. This, combined with Jefferson's decision to host dinners at which it seemed that all distinctions and rank were ignored, gave social life in the capital a decidedly republican cast.

Jefferson carried out this role with the Congress as well. For example, prior to their first term in office, Presidents Washington and Adams delivered the constitutionally mandated annual address to the Congress in person. For Jefferson and the Republicans, this practice recalled rather too strongly the British monarch's address at the opening of Parliament. This president would submit his annual message in writing and, in doing so, evidence due deference.[9]

Such deference was a key element in the Republicans' plans to curtail the wide discretion and power previously exercised by presidents. In place of that discretion, the Republicans intended to substitute a party program which, while implemented by the president, would be controlled by the Congress and sanctioned by popular election.[10] Executive prerogatives and monarchic practices were to give way to the sentiments of the people and the will of their representatives. According to Edward Corwin, "Jefferson's conception of executive power came finally to be more Whig than that of the British Whigs themselves in subordinating it to 'the supreme legislative power.'"[11]

Jefferson's Conception of Executive Power

Corwin was not the first to hold this opinion. It was John Marshall's view, expressed while the election of 1800 was pending in the House, that were Jefferson chosen, he would "embody himself in the House of Representatives," thereby "weakening the office of the President."[12] This was evidently the common judgment among Jefferson's opponents — with one notable exception.

That exception was Alexander Hamilton. Hamilton, a cabinet colleague of Jefferson, was in a position to know. After all, he was privy to most of the counsel offered by the Secretary of State to Washington. To the general charge put forward by Marshall, Hamilton had the following to say:

> It is not true, as is alleged, that he is for confounding all the powers in the House of Representatives. It is a fact which I have frequently mentioned, that while we were in the administration together, he was generally for a large construction of the Executive authority and not backward to act upon it in cases which coincided with his views. Let it be added that in his theoretic ideas he has considered as improper the participation of the Senate in the Executive Authority.[13]

From Hamilton's point of view, whatever the Republican rhetoric, Jefferson was not to be counted among those who held simple-minded Whig convictions.

That Jefferson was a strong supporter of "Executive Authority" should not have been a surprise. Jefferson, as governor of Virginia during the War of Independence, was intimately familiar with the tribulations of running a government under a constitution marked by anti-executive features. As Robert Johnstone notes, Jefferson's being "responsible for defending his state against invasion caused him to have a dread of executive responsibility without power and of legislative omnipotence without responsibility."[14]

Jefferson's experiences while governor of Virginia were not unique. By the time of the Constitutional Convention, there seemed to be a general recognition that the fundamentally Whiggish state constitutions drafted in the wake of the Declaration of Independence were as incapable of governing well as the monarchy they replaced.[15] According to Jefferson, it was "no alleviation" that the powers of governing are "exercised by a plurality of hands, and not by a single one....173 despots" are "surely...as oppressive as one."[16]

If Jefferson had any doubt of the need for a vigorous, independent executive authority, such doubt was largely overwhelmed by his first-hand association with the incompetence displayed daily by the Congress of the Articles of Confederation. The Articles made no provision for an independent executive; the Congress was its own. But because of its plural composition, the Congress exhibited a threatening lack of energy and dispatch in prosecuting the war and an almost equally fatal want of secrecy and decisiveness in conducting the nation's foreign affairs. The more perceptive of the Founders recognized that these failings did not lie with particular members of Congress. To a large degree, the Congress was just being the Congress.[17] By the time of the Constitutional Convention, it was abundantly clear to a large segment of the framers that the national government, however it was finally configured, required an independent executive authority.[18]

Jefferson was not slow to come to this opinion. He joined the Congress in 1783 and within a relatively brief period concluded that it was both "rational and necessary" for the national government to have an independent executive arm. Jefferson reaffirmed this judgment the next year while serving as a member of a committee specifically charged with seeing how best to conduct the government's business over the summer months of 1784. Jefferson's proposal was to divide it into two, legislative and executive. If nothing else, such an alignment would, at least temporarily, quiet the "quarreling and bickering" by giving the government "a single Arbiter for ultimate decision."[19]

By the time of the Constitutional Convention, Jefferson had been sent by the government to be its minister to the court of France. As a result, he was not among that close circle of Virginians who were active in planning for Philadelphia. Nevertheless, Jefferson made known his desires. Specifically, he hoped that the delegates would reach beyond their more limited instructions on amending the Articles of Confederation and attempt a "broader reformation" of the government. According to Jefferson, a critical element in such reform was the adoption, in some form, of the doctrine of separation of powers. Creation of an independent executive authority would limit the Congress' "meddl[ing]" and confine it to "what should be legislative" and "enable the Federal head to exercise the powers given it, to best advantage."[20] "I think it very material to separate in the hands of

Congress the Executive and Legislative powers....The want of it has been the source of more evil than we have ever experienced from any other cause."[21]

By 1787, Jefferson clearly viewed the adoption of separation of powers, and with it an independent executive branch, as a rational division of the government's labor. What is not evident is Jefferson's understanding of exactly what powers should be exercised by the executive authority, especially in a republican form of government.

At first glance, Jefferson's definition of executive power is markedly Whiggish:

> By executive powers, we mean no reference to those powers exercised under our former government by the crown as of its prerogative, nor that these shall be the standard of what may or may not be deemed the rightful powers of the governor. We give them those powers only, which are necessary to execute the laws (and administer the government), and which are not in their nature either legislative or judiciary.[22]

Rhetorically, at least, the thrust of Jefferson's attempt at delineating the executive sphere is to limit it.

Yet the hole in this attempt to fence in the executive is Jefferson's use of the phrase — "and which are not in their nature either legislative or judiciary." The looseness of this construction leaves its meaning open to interpretation. Jefferson himself said that it was a matter whose "application" "must be left to reason."

Nevertheless, it was not a matter to which little thought had been given. Every educated eighteenth century American would have read Locke's and Montesquieu's discussion of the executive. In particular, Jefferson's claim that the executive's power includes those things neither legislative nor judicial would almost certainly have evoked in his reader's mind Locke's treatment of the wide range of powers associated with the conduct of foreign affairs, what he called the "federative" powers. These powers, according to Locke, were in theory separate from the executive, but his in practice.[23]

Jefferson appears to have had in mind something like Locke's discussion of the federative powers. In clarifying his definition, Jefferson explicitly excludes the "prerogative powers," such as erecting courts, fairs, markets, and the like. Left unsaid, but clearly implied, is the thought that these are powers exercised by monarchs, justified on conventional grounds, and not appropriate for executives in a republican form of government. These Jefferson would "expressly deny" the executive. What remains on his list, however, are precisely those powers that Locke would have described as being federative, powers integral to the conduct of foreign affairs: the power to declare war, conclude peace, contract alliances, and direct the military.[24]

Jefferson's broad conception of executive power before the Constitutional Convention is consistent with the views he expressed when holding the position of Secretary of State during Washington's administration. As a member of the cabinet, Jefferson was not, as Hamilton later pointed out, shy to argue for a "large construction of the Executive authority," nor "backward to act upon it."

Jefferson, of course, was not unmindful of Congress' prerogatives under the new constitution. On the other hand, he showed no Whiggish inclination to bring the president's powers under the simple control of a "supreme Legislature." Quite the opposite. In 1793, for example, Jefferson, as Secretary of State, met with Edmond Charles Genet, envoy to the United States from the first French Republic. Jefferson, the former American minister to Paris, was on the whole sympathetic to Genet's effort to move the United States toward a role more supportive of France in its war with Great Britain. The problem facing Genet was that President Washington had earlier issued a proclamation stating the nation's policy to be strict neutrality between the two belligerent powers, this in spite of a standing treaty of friendship with France. Yet even in this instance, Jefferson would hear nothing which suggested that the president's powers are anything less than complete in themselves:

> "[Genet] asked if they [Congress] were not sovereign." I told him no...."But," said he, "at least, Congress are bound to see that the treaties are observed." I told him no...the President is to see that treaties are observed. "If he decides against the treaty, to whom is a nation to appeal?" I told him the Constitution had made the President the last appeal.[25]

While it is to be expected that a Secretary of State would respond to a foreign envoy in such unequivocal terms, Jefferson in fact maintained this stance vis-a-vis the Congress as well. Washington and his cabinet officers were often asked by the Congress to supply papers and memoranda to support the administration's decisions and policies. The administration typically complied with such requests. However, Washington's cabinet was not slow to come to the opinion that, if the national interest so required, the president had the discretion to withhold material requested by the legislature.

The issue first arose after the stunning defeat of General St. Clair by the Wabash Indians in late 1791. The House committee created to investigate the defeat requested that Secretary of War Henry Knox turn over all papers connected to St. Clair's campaign. According to Jefferson, Washington called his cabinet together to discuss the request "because it was the first example, and he wishes so far as it should become a precedent, it should be rightly conducted."

Jefferson then noted that Washington believed that "there might be papers of so secret a nature, as that they ought not to be given up." In a subsequent cabinet meeting, called to resolve the administration's final position on the request, Jefferson reported that while the Congress might properly "institute inquiries" and "call for papers generally," the executive had every right "to refuse those, the disclosure of which would injure the public." Jefferson showed no signs that he disagreed with the administration's position; indeed, his notes outline a brief based on a famous debate in the British Parliament, in the case of Sir Robert Walpole, which supported the proposition that the executive authority had such discretion.[26]

Even in those areas in which the Constitution gives the Senate a share of the executive's responsibilities, Jefferson consistently argued for a reading to the president's advantage. For example, in the case of appointments, Jefferson would brook little interference from the upper house of the Congress. Writing to Washington early in his first administration, Jefferson advised him that "the Senate is not supposed by the Constitution to be acquainted with the concerns of the Executive Department. It was not intended that these should be communicated, nor can they therefore be qualified to judge of the necessity which calls for a mission to any particular place, or of the particular grade....All of this is left to the President. They are only to see that no unfit person be employed."[27]

Jefferson appears to have had a similarly limited view of the Senate's role in regard to treaty-making. The early days of Washington's presidency are punctuated with instances of his consulting the Senate prior to the start of negotiations. Historians have typically read Washington's behavior in these instances as adherence to the constitutional mandate of receiving not only the

Senate's consent but its advice. According to Jefferson, however, Washington's "habit of consulting the Senate previously" was a matter of common sense rather than constitutional prescription. Jefferson believed that it was "prudent to consult them" since "their subsequent ratification would be necessary."[28]

As Jefferson's words imply, it might be prudent at times *not* to consult. Jefferson seemed to believe that the president retained, as circumstances required, the discretion as to when and how to involve the upper house. Events did intervene to end Washington's practice of prior consultation. It became clear that the need for what *The Federalist* called "qualities...indispensable in the management of foreign negotiations [and which] point out the Executive as the most fit agent in these transactions" would lead Washington to abandon his habit of conferring with the Senate.[29] One of those "qualities" was a better capability of keeping things secret. In 1793, Washington had the Secretary of State begin and conclude negotiations with the western Indians without consulting the Senate over the terms of the treaty. According to Jefferson, "we all thought if the Senate should be consulted and consequently appraised of our line, it would become known to [British Minister George] Hammond, and we should lose all chance of saving anything more at the treaty than our ultimatum."[30] Jefferson never suggests that this precedent was in any way constitutionally objectionable — indeed, he participated in making it.

Time after time, Jefferson, as Washington's Secretary of State, participated in making decisions that upheld the independence and prerogatives of the nation's chief executive. There is no indication that he did so in an uninformed way or for reasons of simple political calculation. From the evidence at hand, Jefferson's rationale for supporting the newly formed office of the president was based on his principled understanding of the nature of the executive authority. As he wrote to Washington:

> The transaction of business with foreign nations is Executive altogether. It belongs then to the head of the department, *except* as to such portions of it as are specially submitted to the Senate. *Exceptions* are to be construed strictly.[31]

In Jefferson's view, whatever remnants of Whiggish sentiment found their way into the Constitution were strictly conventional, although perhaps prudent limitations on the natural and correct scope of the executive's power.[32]

Even on the issue which led to the great debate between

"Pacificus" and "Helvidius," the Proclamation of Neutrality, Jefferson agreed with his cabinet colleagues that the proclamation should be issued. He nowhere, even in his letters to Madison, suggests that Washington did not have the authority to make the declaration that he did. Moreover, to Washington's query of his cabinet whether the Congress should be called back in session early to consider the matter, Jefferson reported that the cabinet had "decided negatively." From this decision, Jefferson did not dissent. Whatever his ultimate concern regarding Hamilton and the "Monocrats," Jefferson never officially objected to Washington's assertion of authority, and he never publicly registered the smallest complaint.[33]

Jefferson's Exercise of Presidential Power

Jefferson, who had joined the administration in the spring of 1790, left at the end of 1793. By early 1798, he was describing a key difference between the two fledgling American political parties as being the Republicans' apparent affinity for the Congress and the Federalists' for the presidency.[34] Given those preferences, it was certainly to be expected that Jefferson and the Republicans' victory in 1800 would signal a major change in the pattern of executive-legislative relations that had been established by the Federalist administrations of Washington and Adams. What Jefferson himself described as the "Revolution of 1800" was looked to not only to alter the relationship between the federal and state governments, but also to shift power from the second branch of the federal government to the first.[35]

In fact, little seemed to change. This so frustrated John Randolph, leading Republican orator and majority leader in the House, that he bitterly declared that:

> [there are only] two parties in all States — the *ins and outs*; the *ins* desirous so to construe the charter of the Government as to give themselves the greatest possible degree of patronage and wealth; and the *outs* striving to construe it so as to circumscribe...their adversaries' power. But let the *outs* get in...and you will find their Constitutional scruples and arguments vanish like dew before the morning sun.[36]

Randolph's opinion that the difference between the Federalist administrations of Washington and Adams and the first

Republican administration was less than revolutionary is shared by others. According to Leonard D. White, student of both Federalist and Republican administrations, "Jefferson fully maintained in practice the Federalist conception of the executive power."[37] White is seconded by Abraham Sofaer, who finds that between the two "little changed." Indeed, if anything, Jefferson "probably increased the powers of the President at the expense of Congress."[38]

There is little reason to object to these assessments of Jefferson's presidency; for the most part, they accurately portray his practice. However, there are some things that cannot be so easily accounted for if one simply equates Jefferson's behavior while president with that of his Federalist predecessors.

The first of these was Jefferson's handling of the military expedition against Tripoli. The Pasha of Tripoli, dissatisfied with the amount of tribute he was exacting from the United States, had begun again to threaten American shipping in the Mediterranean late in Adams' term. Upon taking office, Jefferson ordered a Navy squadron under the commend of Commodore Richard Dale to the Mediterranean to protect the nation's property and ships. In early August, an American schooner, the *Enterprise*, encountered a Tripolitan cruiser which, after three hours of battle, was captured, stripped of its guns, and allowed to drift back to its home port.

Jefferson reported the *Enterprise*'s victory in his first annual message to the Congress. After describing why he had sent the squadron to the Mediterranean, he recounted the engagement and eventual release of the Tripolitan ship. He justified the cruiser's release thus:

> Unauthorized by the Constitution, without the sanction of Congress, to go beyond the line of defense, the vessel, being disabled from committing further hostilities, was liberated with its crew. The Legislature will doubtless consider whether, by authorizing measures of offence also, they will place our force on an equal footing with that of its adversaries. I communicate all material information on this subject, that, in the exercise of this important function confided by the Constitution to the Legislature exclusively, their judgment may form itself on a knowledge and consideration of every circumstance of weight.[39]

On reading Jefferson's justification, Hamilton went on the

attack. Writing in the *New York Evening Post* as "Lucius Crassus," Hamilton argued that attempts to draw such fine distinctions were chimerical. When one nation openly waged war against another, a declaration of war was hardly required. It was, according to Hamilton, "a very extraordinary position" that "between two nations there may exist a state of complete war on the one side and of peace on the other."[40]

Hamilton was not the only one who would have found Jefferson's reason for turning the Pasha's ship loose "extraordinary." So must have his Cabinet. In mid-May, prior to the expedition's departure, the Cabinet met to discuss the question of precisely what actions the Navy squadron could take against the Tripolitans if it were attacked. The near unanimous position of the Cabinet — the only dissent coming from Attorney General Levi Lincoln — was that once an act of war was perpetrated against the American ships, a state of war existed. From that point on, the squadron could, without question, search for and destroy the enemy's vessels wherever they could find them. And it was these orders that were cut for Commodore Dale.[41]

The historical truth is that the *Enterprise* cut the Tripolitan corsair free for operational reasons. Dale had ordered the captain of the American schooner to make his way to Malta for supplies for the squadron and not to waste valuable time by going out of his way to chase, capture, or sink the Tripolitan ships. There was nothing in the administration's orders to Dale, or in Dale's to his subordinate, that suggested that the *Enterprise* was legally bound to act as it did. Jefferson created the account he put forward in the annual message out of whole cloth, weaving novel threads into the constitutional fabric.[42]

Waging war with the Barbary pirates was not the only occasion in which Jefferson exhibited a talent for constitutional legerdemain. The second important instance is found in connection with his administration's purchase of the Louisiana Territory from France in 1803.

At the time, the purchase itself was hailed not only because of its size and the potential it held for the country, but chiefly because it, in the words of Jefferson, "remove[d] from us the greatest source of danger to our peace."[43] By gaining control of both the inland waterways and the port of New Orleans, Jefferson had with one stroke largely secured peace in the West. For his administration, the underlying issue was one of national security rather than of territory.

While Jefferson was adamant as to the necessity of the purchase, he nevertheless entertained questions concerning its legality. This is not all that surprising since strict constructionists within his own party were bound to point out that there was no specific grant of authority in the Constitution allowing the government to make territorial acquisitions of any dimension — never mind one doubling the size of the country. In January 1803, just prior to Monroe's going to France to complete negotiations with Napoleon, Jefferson asked his Cabinet about the constitutionality of the "proposed bargain" with France.[44]

Attorney General Levi Lincoln was the first to submit a reply. So convoluted was Lincoln's opinion that Jefferson turned to Secretary of the Treasury Albert Gallatin for his views. Gallatin "assumed a constitutional position which was virtually indistinguishable from the liberal construction of his predecessor Hamilton." It was Gallatin's position:

1st. That the United States as a nation have an inherent right to acquire territory.

2nd. That whenever that acquisition is by treaty, the same constituted authorities in whom the treaty-making power is vested have a constitutional right to sanction the acquisition.

3rd. That whenever the territory has been acquired, Congress have the power either of admitting into the Union as a new state, or of annexing to a State with the consent of that State, or of making regulations for the government of such territory.

Jefferson accepted Gallatin's analysis: "You are right in my opinion...there is no constitutional difficulty."[45]

Within Jefferson's official family, the constitutional question about the purchase was never really an issue. However, the president showed little inclination to state his case publicly along the lines Gallatin had argued and to which he had agreed. Again, Jefferson was apparently not above a little constitutional dissembling. To John Dickinson he wrote: "The general government has no powers but such as the constitution has given it; and it has not given it a power of holding foreign territory, and still less of incorporating it into the Union."[46] To political ally and Republican stalwart Senator John Breckinridge of Kentucky, Jefferson made the following argument:

The Executive in seizing the fugitive occurrence which so much advances the good of their country, have done an act beyond the Constitution. The Legislature in casting behind them metaphysical subtleties, and risking themselves like faithful servants, must ratify to pay for it, and throw themselves on their country for doing for them unauthorized what we know they would have done for themselves had they been in a situation to do it. It is the case of a guardian, investing the money of his ward in purchasing an important adjacent territory; and saying to him when of age, I did this for your good. I pretend to no right to bind you: you may disavow me, and I must get out of the scrape as I can: I thought it my duty to risk myself for you.[47]

These and similar letters were written in July and August of 1803. On 17 August, however, Jefferson received word from the American minister in Paris, Robert Livingston, that Napoleon was having second thoughts about the wisdom of selling Louisiana and was now looking for some pretense to void the agreement. Jefferson reacted to this news by concluding that nothing should be done which might give France an excuse to rescind the accord. Writing to his Secretary of State, James Madison, he stated: "I infer that the less we say about constitutional difficulties respecting Louisiana the better."[48] In the end, Jefferson made no further attempt to provoke a constitutional debate; nor, it should be added, did he attempt to publicize his private view that there was, in his words, "no constitutional difficulty."

A third episode worth reviewing was generated by the British warship *Leopard*'s attack on the American frigate *Chesapeake* in the summer of 1807. In late June, the British ship pulled alongside the *Chesapeake* as it left Hampton Roads, Virginia. The captain of the fifty-gun *Leopard* ordered the smaller American vessel to stop and submit to a search for British deserters. The *Chesapeake*'s captain at first refused. The *Leopard* then opened fire and disabled the *Chesapeake*, in the process killing and wounding some twenty seamen. The American frigate was then searched by the British, who impressed four of its crew.

News of the engagement caused an enormous uproar in the United States. Because war with Britain seemed imminent, Jefferson acted to prepare the country. In early July, he issued a proclamation excluding British warships from American waters. In late July, he ordered that all money which had been appropriated for the nation's fortifications and which remained available be used solely for fortifying New York, Charleston, and New Orleans. In addition, and most significantly, he ordered the purchase of 500 tons of saltpeter, 100 tons of sulphur, and sufficient timber for building 100 gunboats. Of these latter purchases, not a single dime had been authorized or appropriated by the Congress.[49]

The Congress went back into session in late October. In his annual message, Jefferson communicated to the Hill the steps he had taken. He made no attempt to hide what he had done, nor did he make any attempt to justify it constitutionally. Quite the opposite, Jefferson pleaded necessity in light of "the emergencies threatening" the nation:

> The moment our peace was threatened, I deemed it indispensable to secure a greater provision of those articles of military stores with which our magazines were not sufficiently furnished. To have awaited a previous and special sanction by law would have lost occasions which might not be retrieved....I trust that the legislature, feeling the same anxiety for the safety of our country, so materially advanced by this precaution, will approve, when done, what they would have seen so important to be done, if then assembled.[50]

Jefferson's actions did not go unchallenged. Randolph decried the president's deeds as being at odds with "the true old Whig doctrine." John Smilie, as did other House members, came to the president's defense: "Every gentleman knew that there were cases in which this form must be dispensed with, and in this instance he thought the circumstances of the case justified the measures adopted."[51]

Randolph believed Smilie's defense and Jefferson's action to be Republican "heresy." What it was, was a bold assertion of executive prerogative, the power to ignore the law if an emergency so dictates. Or, as Whig theorist John Locke described it:

> For the Legislators not being able to foresee, and provide, by Laws, for all, that may be useful to the Community, the Executor of the Laws, having the power in his hands, has by the common Law of Nature, a right to make use of it...where the municipal Law has given no direction, till the Legislature can conveniently be assembled to provide for it....This power to act according to discretion, for the publick good, without the prescription of law, and sometimes even against it, *is* that which is called *Prerogative*.[52]

Jefferson's decision to resort to prerogative is important to note; however, it is equally important that he made absolutely no attempt to give it the slightest constitutional justification.

Jefferson's actions in this instance can be usefully compared with Lincoln's in 1861. In the wake of his election in 1860, seven southern states seceded from the Union. After his inauguration the following March, Lincoln issued a call for the Congress to reconvene and undertook a series of actions, the propriety of which constitutional historians have long debated. While Lincoln believed that circumstances clearly justified the steps he took, he also went to great lengths to provide a constitutional argument for what he had done, invoking not only the Commander-in-Chief Clause and the Take Care Clause but also his presidential oath.[53]

Lincoln claimed that the Constitution authorizes the president to take extraordinary measures, otherwise not lawful, in such grave circumstances. His argument was not that "the Constitution is different" in such times but that "its application" may be.[54] Circumstances demand different things of a government. In making this case, Lincoln was not advancing a novel constitutional doctrine. It was *The Federalist* which had laid down as axiomatic that "a power equal to every possible contingency must exist somewhere in the government."[55]

Conclusion

Jefferson's presidency, according to biographer and historian Dumas Malone, "was much the most complicated part of Jefferson's career."[56] To one degree or another he confounded friends and foes alike, frustrating such principled opposites as Randolph and Hamilton.

While we know that Jefferson understood both the need for executive power and the strength of its embodiment in Article II of the Constitution, we also know that by the end of Washington's term, Jefferson had become concerned that through the office of the presidency the Federalists were "maneuvering" the citizenry into a "form of government, the principal branches of which may be beyond their control."[57] Even though Jefferson was never explicit on the point, it can be plausibly conjectured that to meet his concern he undertook to drain from the presidency as much of its formidable formal powers as was practical. This stratagem can be inferred not only from instances like those discussed above but from such other decisions as Jefferson's setting for himself a limit of two terms in office — undermining to some degree his formal powers with the creation of the "lame duck" term.

The substance of this endeavor was reflected in the style of his administration, by his "substituting what may be called 'republican simplicity' for Washington's 'republican dignity.'" Under Jefferson there would be "no great dinners, weekly receptions, personally delivered messages to Congress, none of the formalities that Jefferson associated with the monarchic executive."[58]

While in each of the three cases described above there are less esoteric reasons available to explain Jefferson's behavior, it is equally possible that he was moved to act as he did in these instances because he had concluded before taking office that the presidency, under the pressure of events and the influence of Hamilton, had become more powerful than he judged consistent with republican government. While Jefferson understood the constitutional potential for an expanded exercise of executive power, he was nevertheless surprised perhaps both by the degree and the swiftness with which it came to the fore, and the eagerness with which some saw it employed. Had what Jefferson expected to be exceptional become by the end of Washington's second term the norm?[59]

Jefferson would not have objected to Hamilton's axiom in *The Federalist* that "energy in the executive is a leading character in the definition of good government."[60] However, he must have questioned its constant and exclusive application. Since for Jefferson "a free government is of all others the most energetic," a single-minded and continual reliance on the formal instrumentalities of presidential authority by the Federalists betrayed their serious disregard for the republican basis of the polity.[61] Moreover, broad readings of the president's powers gave vent to that dangerous "preference of kingly over republican government" which Jefferson had found espoused at dinner tables throughout the nation's capital. To make reliance on the formal powers of the executive more difficult, he hoped in addition to some revisionism to employ a stratagem, where feasible, of strict constitutional construction:

> When an instrument admits two constructions, the one safe, the other dangerous, the one precise, the other indefinite, I prefer that which is safe and precise....Our peculiar security is in possession of a written Constitution. Let us not make it a blank paper by construction.[62]

The point is not that Jefferson did not appreciate that there would be times when a president would need to exercise extraordinary power. While he was apparently willing to see the formal scope of executive discretion trimmed back, Jefferson was also willing to advance in bold fashion the doctrine of extra-constitutional executive prerogative. It was this theory that he advanced, after having left office, to justify his purchase of Louisiana:

> A strict observance of the written law is doubtless *one* of the high duties of a good citizen, but it is not *the highest*. The laws of necessity, of self preservation, of saving our country when in danger, are of higher obligation. To lose our country by a scrupulous adherence to written law, would be to lose the law itself, with life, liberty, property and all those who are enjoying them with us; thus absurdly sacrificing the end to the means.[63]

In short, Jefferson understood as well as Hamilton the need for a potentially expansive executive authority; what they came to disagree about — if the conjecture above is correct — was what form such power might take and the ease and occasion on which it might be exercised. Jefferson presumably believed that if one could revise and scale down the formal, constitutional powers of the president while at the same time granting him, as circumstances warranted, the right to exercise extra-constitutional powers, one would make the use of such powers less likely.

Hamilton's rebuttal would certainly be that, while presidents might initially be reluctant to exercise such powers, their reticence was sure to dissipate over time. As *The Federalist* states, "every precedent...is a germ of unnecessary and multiplied repetitions."[64] What is initially extraordinary becomes ordinary through use. Moreover, Hamilton would argue that a resort to extra-constitutional powers was not conducive to the preservation of the public's deference to the idea of the rule of law. It is difficult to maintain respect for the rule of law in citizens and presidents alike when in the most critical instances they are publicly reminded of its radical insufficiency. As Hamilton had written in *The Federalist*:

> Wise politicians will be cautious about fettering the government with restrictions that cannot be observed, because they know that every breach of the fundamental laws, though dictated by necessity, impairs that sacred reverence which ought to be maintained in the breast of rulers towards the constitution

of a country, and forms a precedent for other breaches where the same plea of necessity does not exist at all, or is less urgent and palpable.[65]

In pointing toward a less imposing executive authority which nevertheless might break the bonds of the law as necessity dictated, Jefferson believed he was devising a presidency more in tune with the nation's republican character and less susceptible of abuse. Hamilton might have countered that necessity is often in the eye of the beholder and would have doubted whether such a presidential regime was in fact more likely to promote the rule of law and maintain republican mores.[66] Perhaps only someone as intimate with ambition as Hamilton could understand the dangers inherent in Jefferson's design.

Notes

1. Thomas Jefferson, *Writings*, 10 vols., ed. Paul L. Ford (New York: G.P. Putnam's, 1892-1899), vol. 6, p. 338.

2. *Ibid.*, vol. 7, p. 43.

3. See Forrest McDonald, *The Presidency of Thomas Jefferson* (Lawrence: University Press of Kansas, 1976), pp. 20, 33.

4. *Ibid.*, p. 20.

5. Jefferson, *Writings,* vol. 1, p. 160.

6. *The Adams-Jefferson Letters*, 2 vols., ed. L.J. Cappon (Chapel Hill: University of North Carolina Press, 1959), vol. 2, p. 332.

7. Jefferson, *Writings*, vol. 9, p. 296. Jefferson is recounting his conversation with Adams more than a decade later, in 1811.

8. James P. Ceaser, *Presidential Selection* (Princeton, N.J.: Princeton University Press, 1979), p. 89.

9. See Robert M. Johnstone, Jr., *Jefferson and the Presidency* (Ithaca, N.Y.: Cornell University Press, 1978), pp. 58-59.

10. See Ceaser, *Selection*, pp. 103, 121.

11. Edward S. Corwin, *The President: Office and Powers*, rev. ed. (New York: New York University Press, 1984), p. 18.

12. *Ibid.*

13. Alexander Hamilton, *Works*, 12 vols., ed. Henry C. Lodge (New York: G.P. Putnam's, 1904), vol. 10, p. 413.

14. Johnstone, *Jefferson*, p. 53. See, in general, Merril D. Peterson,

Thomas Jefferson and the New Nation (New York: Oxford University Press, 1970), pp. 166ff and John S. Pancake, *Thomas Jefferson and Alexander Hamilton* (Woodbury, N.Y.: Barron's, 1974), pp. 79ff.

15. See Charles C. Thach, Jr., *The Creation of the Presidency: 1775-1789* (Baltimore: Johns Hopkins University Press, 1929), pp. 49-52.

16. Jefferson, *Writings*, vol. 3, p. 223.

17. As John Jay wrote to Jefferson in 1787, "Those inconveniences arise, not from personal disqualifications, but from the nature and construction of government." *The Correspondence and Public Papers of John Jay*, 3 vols., ed. Henry P. Johnston (New York: G.P. Putnam's, 1890-1893), vol. 3, p. 223.

18. See Thach, *Creation*, pp. 55-75.

19. Louis Fisher, *President and Congress* (New York: Free Press, 1972), p. 263.

20. Thomas Jefferson, *Papers*, 20 vols., ed. Julian Boyd (Princeton, N.J.: Princeton University Press, 1954-in progress), vol. 10, p. 603.

21. *Ibid.*, vol. 11, p. 679.

22. *Ibid.*, vol. 6, pp. 298-299.

23. See Locke, *Second Treatise*, ch. 12, sec. 148 and Montesquieu, *Spirit of the Laws*, bk. 11, ch. 6.

24. Jefferson, *Papers*, vol. 6, p. 299. Jefferson's discussion is in the context of a proposal for a new state constitution. Jefferson's focus here is on the powers to be held by the governor under Virginia's new constitution. What he states is that these "other" powers are exercised "under the authority of the confederation" and, as such, fall outside the office of the state's chief executive. However, that he considers these "other" powers to be executive in nature is clear from the context of the discussion and his statement that "in all cases" where those powers are not exercised by the Confederation "they shall be exercised by the governor."

25. "Minutes of Conversation," 10 July 1793, *International Law Digest*, 8 vols., ed. John B. Moore (Washington, D.C.: U.S. Government Printing Office, 1906), vol. 4, pp. 680-681.

26. See Abraham Sofaer, *War, Foreign Affairs and Constitutional Power: The Origins* (Cambridge, Mass.: Ballinger, 1976), pp. 81-82.

27. Johnstone, *Jefferson*, p. 62.

28. Jefferson, *Writings*, vol. 1, p. 294.

29. Alexander Hamilton, James Madison, and John Jay, *The*

American Models of Revolutionary Leadership

Federalist Papers, ed. Clinton Rossiter (New York: New American Library, 1961), No. 75, p. 45. See also No. 64, p. 393.

30. Thomas Jefferson, *Anas*, ed. F.B. Sawvel (New York: Round Tables Press, 1903), pp. 108-111.

31. Jefferson, *Writings*, vol. 5, pp. 161-162.

32. See text to note 13 above.

33. See Sofaer, *War*, pp. 111-116.

34. Dumas Malone, *Jefferson the President: First Term* (Boston: Little, Brown, 1970), p. xviii.

35. Sofaer, *War*, pp. 168-169.

36. *Annals of Congress*, vol. 20, p. 70.

37. Leonard D. White, *The Jeffersonians: A Study in Administrative History* (New York: Macmillan, 1951), p. 30.

38. Sofaer, *War*, pp. 169, 224.

39. *Annals of Congress*, vol. 11, pp. 11-12.

40. Sofaer, *War*, p. 212.

41. *Ibid.*, pp. 209-210, 212-213.

42. Jefferson took a similar line with regard to military action against Morocco in 1802 — again, against the stated position of his Cabinet. Sofaer, *War*, pp. 221-224.

43. Malone, *First Term*, p. 284.

44. *Ibid.*, p. 311.

45. *Ibid.*, p. 312.

46. Jefferson, *Writings*, vol. 8, p. 262.

47. Jefferson, *Writings*, vol. 8, p. 244ff.

48. Malone, *First Term*, pp. 314-315.

49. Sofaer, *War*, p. 172.

50. *Annals of Congress*, vol. 17, pp. 14-17.

51. *Ibid.*, pp. 822, 826.

52. Locke, *Second Treatise*, ch. 14, sec. 159 and sec. 160.

53. "Message for Congress," 4 July 1861, *Collected Works*, 9 vols., ed. Roy P. Bassler (New Brunswick, N.J.: Rutgers University Press, 1953), vol. 4, pp. 429-430, 440; and "First Inaugural Address," 4 March 1861, *ibid.*, vol. 4, pp. 265, 270.

54. *Ibid.*, vol. 6, p. 302.

55. No. 26, p. 170.

56. Malone, *First Term*, p. xiii.

57. Jefferson, *Writings*, vol. 7, p. 280. See also, *ibid.*, vol. 7, p. 435

and the following reported statement by Madison: "I deserted Colonel Hamilton, or rather Colonel H. deserted me; in a word, the divergence between us took place — from his wishing to *administration*, or rather to administer the Government (these were Mr. M's very words), into what he thought it ought to be." Quoted in memoranda by Trist, 27 September 1834, reprinted in *Records of Federal Convention of 1787*, 4 vols., ed. Max Farrand (New Haven: Yale University Press, 1966), vol. 3, p. 534.

58. Robert Seigliano, "The Constitutional Governments of Hamilton and Jefferson" (Paper presented at the annual meeting of the American Political Science Association, New Orleans, 29 August-1 September 1985), p. 15.

59. To some extent, the enumerated powers found in Article II are deceiving in that they appear understated. By themselves, they do not explain the particular primacy the presidency has had in the governmental system since 1789. What helps to explain this fact is the presidency's radically different institutional characteristics, especially its unity of office. Because of its unique features, it enjoys — as the framers largely intended — the capacity of acting with the greatest expedition, secrecy and effective knowledge. As a result, when certain stresses, particularly in the area of foreign affairs, are place on the nation it will "naturally" rise to the forefront. Since those stresses existed at the beginning, it is not surprising that "the framework for executive-congressional relations developed during the first eight years differs more in degree than in kind from the present framework." Sofaer, *War*, p. 127. See also Alexis de Tocqueville, *Democracy in America*, vol. 1, pt. 1, ch. 8, "Accidental Causes that May Increase the Influence of the Executive Power."

60. No. 70, p. 423.

61. Jefferson, *Writings*, vol. 9, p. 201. "By weakening the presidential office in comparison with the original constitutional design and certainly in comparison with the status it held under Washington and Adams, the Republicans had brought about the situation in which energy, if it were to come from the executive, would have to rely on a non-institutional source." Ceaser, *Selection*, p. 102.

62. Jefferson, *Writings*, vol. 8, p. 247.

63. Jefferson, *Writings*, vol. 9, p. 279.

64. No. 41, p. 257.

65. No. 25, p. 167.

66. *New York Times*, 20 May 1977, page A-16. Interview with Richard Nixon by David Frost.

ALBERT GALLATIN: POLITICAL METHOD IN LEADERSHIP

Rozann Rothman

Albert Gallatin has been called America's forgotten states-man.[1] Little attention has been paid to his career either as a congressman or as Secretary of the Treasury under Jefferson and Madison. Even less attention has been paid to his writings, perhaps because he never shaped them into A *Disquisition on Government*. This gap in our knowledge is unfortunate. In spite of the scattered nature of his observations, contained primarily in speeches, letters, articles and a master plan for internal improvements, a coherent conception of the nature of a government is apparent in his works when they are examined as a whole. Moreover, a model of how to use the resources of the political system is implicit in the conception he outlines. The purpose of this article is a reconstruction of Gallatin's conception of the nature and the operation of government. His conception is valuable for its insight into the American system during its formative period and for the effect it had on the direction the system took.

Gallatin's contributions to the shaping of the American political system are impressive if only because he was instrumental in developing the means which permitted the reconciliation of an ideology with the demands of an emerging nation. An understanding of Gallatin begins with the recognition that conciliation of at times conflicting objectives was his primary goal. The element of conciliation is a major aspect of his work and gives a distinctive cast to his actions as well as to his explanations of the available options.

It must be stressed that the conception of the system and of the method needed to operate the system evolved gradually. The development was piecemeal, in response to immediate needs and only later, after use, do the principles become sufficiently explicit to be termed a conception of the system. In other words, Gallatin as a participant in government developed a style for resolving political conflict. This style was uniquely his but it was imitated by others, and thus had its effect on a developing system. Gallatin's contribution consisted of this conception of the system, the

173

means to operate it and a justification for the system which were interwoven to make a coherent whole. His contribution was to have a lasting impact.

In order to understand Gallatin's conception, it must be differentiated from the Hamilton model which preceded it and from the republican ideology to which it was related. The contrast may be drawn in the following terms: Gallatin is the first major American statesman to accept the realities of the political system created by the Constitution and to use these realities as a starting point for political action. In both Hamilton and Jefferson there is the noticeable tendency of trying to operate the political system as it might have been if either of them had been its sole architect. In other words, both Hamilton and Jefferson tended to use the political system as an ideological device to create the government and the support for the government that each deemed best. Gallatin is able to find a middle ground between Hamilton and Jefferson, which, as will be shown, is in certain respects a new ground. This discovery is possible precisely because he is not hindered by an ideological preconception of how the system ought to be or how it ought to work.[2] The difference between these three major participants in the formation of the American system are important in understanding Gallatin.

According to Henry Adams, only Hamilton and Gallatin should be studied by "persons who wish to understand what practical statesmanship has been under an American system. Public men in considerable numbers have run their courses in national politics, but only two have had at once the breadth of mind to grapple with the machinery of government as a whole and the authority necessary to make it work efficiently for a given object: the practical knowledge of affairs that enabled them to foresee every movement; the long apprenticeship which allowed them to educate and discipline their parties; and finally the good fortune to enjoy power when government was still plastic and capable of receiving a new impulse."[3]

Similarities between the careers of Hamilton and Gallatin are readily apparent. Nevertheless the differences between them are significant. The core of Gallatin's concerns are found in Jeffersonian doctrine and this differentiates him fundamentally from Hamilton. Yet Gallatin was more of a nationalist than Jefferson and the element of nationalism differentiates his style from the pattern of "old Republicanism," moving him closer to the Hamiltonian position. The necessities of a situation would be as apparent to Gallatin as to Hamilton, but in Gallatin's case, a Hamiltonian understanding of the necessities would be combined with a commitment to Republican ideology. It is this combination which is the foundation of Gallatin's position and the source of his method.

The primary component of Gallatin's position was commitment to the Union. He was a nationalist. The United States was made one nation by the Constitution and national development ought to be promoted. In this attitude towards the Union, he resembled Alexander Hamilton. This attitude also distinguished him from his fellow Republicans, Thomas Jefferson and James Madison. "The nullification of an Act of Congress has no fascination for him. Like other foreign born citizens, in this respect like Mr. Hamilton, himself, Gallatin felt the force of his larger allegiance to the Union more strongly than men like Jefferson and Madison, Fisher Ames or Roger Griswold, whose heartiest attachments were to their states and who were never quite at ease except on the soil and in the society of their birthplace....It is curious to observe that even in argument he rarely attempted to entrench himself behind states' rights without a perceptible betrayal of discomfort and a still more evident want of success. His triumphs must necessarily be those of a national leader upon national grounds...."[4]

A national leader upon national ground but only if those national grounds contained the Jeffersonian concern for liberty. Gallatin's double commitment would allow for the amalgamation of Federalist and Jeffersonian elements into a distinctive political position. Several examples early in his career illustrate the interweaving of the themes and their effect on his choice between alternate courses of action.

When a Federalist Congress placed an excise tax on the whiskey manufactured by the farmers of western Pennsylvania, Gallatin's constituents were touched in a most sensitive spot. To the farmers a tax on the one commodity they could convert easily into cash was an intolerable burden. The federal government was oppressive and the reaction was violent. When individuals were apprehended, they were prosecuted in accordance with regular procedures. However, their cases were heard in Philadelphia and objections were raised to the long, dangerous and expensive trip over the mountains. In July, 1794, while serving writs returnable to the federal court in Philadelphia, the United States marshal and the government inspector met opposition in Allegheny County. A

175

government man fired on a group of farmers, killing one and wounding six. This action produced open defiance by the opponents of the excise. They began a march on Pittsburgh.

Gallatin lived in Fayette County, next to Allegheny County. He offered himself as a delegate to a meeting called for August 14 at Parkinson's Ferry.[5] At this meeting he persuaded the farmers that the exertions of the government against them in support of the laws were coercive but not hostile. Almost alone, Gallatin convinced the western countries to submit to the authority of the government.[6] He drafted the Declaration of the Committees of Fayette County which urged their submission. In this Declaration his belief in the Union is clearly stated and so is the justification for this belief. The justification clarifies the differences between Hamilton and Gallatin.

Civil war will be the result, if the western countries resist the execution of the laws. "If any one part of the Union are suffered to oppose by force the determination of the whole, there is an end to government itself and of course to the Union. The excise law is obnoxious to us, another law may equally be so in another part, a third one in a different quarter and if every corner of the United States claims a right to oppose what they dislike, no one law will be obeyed. The existence of the government therefore depends upon the execution of the laws and they are in duty bound to enforce it."[7]

The situation of the citizens of Fayette County is fundamentally different from either the situation of the colonists or of the French before the Revolution. Resistance by force against oppression is lawful only when no legal and constitutional remedy is available, or when the evils arising from the oppression surpass the evils arising from resistance. The actual evil, the payment of the duty, must be balanced against the evils arising from resistance. The latter is nothing less than the "annihilation of the Union; for in order to conciliate so many and various interests as those of the several parts of the Union, mutual forbearance, manifestations of good will one to another, and reciprocal acts of friendship are as essentially necessary as a strict adherence to that Constitution which binds us together."[8] Gallatin's commitment is to the Union. His plea to the farmers of western Pennsylvania reflects this commitment.

The counties of western Pennsylvania are just one part of the Union. Laws passed by the whole must be accepted by the parts, even if the part feels the law is unjust. The people in this area have representatives in Congress and redress can be obtained through these representatives. If the people obey the law, then they may exercise their constitutional prerogatives. Perhaps Congress will listen and the law will be repealed.[9] Here is outlined the course of action Gallatin would follow during the crisis over the Alien and Sedition Acts. He did not appeal for the mobilization of powers inherent in a state. Instead the appeal was to Congress. Whatever powers inhere in the people of a state, they must be utilized within the structure of the Union.

The Union must be preserved. The federal republic is the finest monument men have yet erected to liberty. Peaceful measures must be adopted. They are indicated by "a serious consideration of the private interest of every individual amongst you, of the interest of the Western country, of the interest of the United States and of that solemn duty which you, as well as ourselves, owe to the government under which we live, to our fellow citizens here and throughout the Union, and to that being who has poured His choicest blessings upon us, by permitting us to live in this land of happiness and liberty."[10] Although Gallatin is as much of a nationalist as Hamilton, his nationalism is based on a different foundation. The Union must be preserved because it is a monument to liberty.

The main theme of the Declaration is devotion to the Union, a Union founded on liberty. Even, as a member of the opposition, Gallatin did not accept the states' rights doctrine. The Union could not be destroyed by its parts. But the Union was worth preserving only because it was a republican government. Thus Gallatin is able to reconcile federal and republican principles. And the instrument of reconciliation will be the Congress, that branch of government which republican theory saw as the mainspring of the system.

During the conflict over the Alien and Sedition Acts, Gallatin followed a course of action which differentiated his style from that of Jefferson and Madison. They retired from Washington in order to organize opposition in the states. Jefferson drafted the Kentucky Resolution while Madison drafted the Virginia Resolution. These resolutions contain the first statements of the doctrine of nullification. They represent a stress on liberty rather than union. States' rights were glorified in order to preserve liberty, an objective sufficiently important to warrant weakening the cement of union. The Constitution is a compact among the states. The Kentucky Resolution asserted that state legislatures have the right to nullify acts of Congress. The state is duty bound to interpose itself to arrest evil; therefore it could declare the Alien and Sedition Acts null and void. The theory is clear. The states are checks on the power of the national government, but it is equally obvious that if the states offered this kind of check, the union would not long endure.

Gallatin did not return to Pennsylvania. He remained in Congress and opposed the acts there. First, he rejected the acts on the grounds of expediency. The necessity of these acts was not proven. Their tendency to incite friction between the states and the general government was in itself ample cause for rejection.[11] Then he discussed the distribution of power established by the Constitution. The Constitution distributed power between the general government and the state governments. The purpose of the Tenth Amendment was to prevent the general government from assuming powers which were not intended for it. Since the Constitution neither gives power over alien friends to Congress, nor prohibits this power to the states, the Tenth Amendment will justify the assertion that power over alien friends remains with the states. Moreover, practice supports this interpretation. In 1788, slightly prior to the establishment of the Constitution, Congress resolved that the several states should take measures to prevent the introduction of certain types of persons into this country. It is inconceivable that Congress should ask the states to make such regulations if it possessed the power to do so itself. Practice confirms the theory. The Constitution limits power by distributing it; therefore the state and the general governments must operate within their respective spheres.

For our point, it is irrelevant that Gallatin's argument is weak. His reliance on the Tenth Amendment appears unrealistic from our present perspective just as his example of congressional action before the establishment of the Constitution appears devious. Our stress is on the fact that Gallatin's stand was taken in Congress. His stress is that the national legislature must itself respect the constitutional limitations on actions, not that the states can nullify national acts. Congressional precedents, not the moral duty of a state to interpose, are the supporting evidence for a denial of power to the present Congress. A check is proposed on national power within the framework of national institutions. If this check works, both liberty and union are preserved.

The fact that Gallatin acted in Congress rather than retiring to the state legislature is indicative of his attempts to reconcile liberty and union within the framework of the federal republic. It is also an example of his differences with prominent republicans. This distinction became clearer during the course of his congressional career. In a speech in the House of Representatives, he discussed the separation of powers and the system of checks and balances established by the Constitution. The conception of the system outlined in this speech illustrates fundamental variations from the conceptions of Hamilton and Jefferson.

His speech was designed to persuade the House of Representatives to oppose administration foreign policy. Although the effort was unsuccessful, a way to operate the American system as well as a sketch of the organization of the system was presented.

> Whenever the powers vested in any one department are sufficient to complete a certain act, the department is independent of all the others, and it would be an unconstitutional attempt in any of the others to try to control it. But whenever the powers have been so distributed between two departments in relation to another certain act, that neither of the two can complete the act by virtue of its own powers, then each department is controlled by the other, not in relation to the operation of its appropriate powers, but in relation to the act itself. Each department, in that case, may go as far as its own authority will permit but no farther. The refusal of the other department to exercise its powers in relation to that act, in the same direction and in concurrence with the first department is no abridgment of the legitimate powers of the first. It is the Constitution which in that case abridges the powers of both, and which has rendered the concurrence of both necessary for the completion of the act.[12]

There is nothing in this statement to indicate a lack of power in the national government or in any department of that government. The lack of emphasis on formal limitations on power can hardly be considered a Jeffersonian view. This is perhaps the crucial difference between Jefferson and Gallatin. In place of the Jeffersonian reliance on limited governmental powers, Gallatin has substituted a cooperative political process as a limitation on power. No department is limited with respect to the exercise of its appropriate powers. Each department is limited only in relation to what needs to be done, i.e., to the act itself. When an action (and there are few that do not fall within this category) needs the acquiescence of more than one department of government if it is to be undertaken, then the political process serves to limit power. Political process in the sense used here implies a bargaining procedure between equals or holders of nearly equal power. The substitution of political process for formal limitations on power is Gallatin's significant insight into the system and is the heart of his conception of the system. This insight is as applicable to the operation of federal-state relations as it is relevant for understanding the operation of a federal government.[13] The remainder of this article will be devoted to demonstrating the relevance of the insight. It provided the pattern for Gallatin's style of action and it became an integral part of a developing American system.

Gallatin has been classified by Leonard White as an "old Republican." He believed in rigid economy, in the rapid payment of the national debt, in the limitation of military and naval expenditures and in the reduction of administrative discretion. His belief in the importance of the legislature is more complex and will be dealt with in detail below. However, he leaves the company of the "old Republicans" on the question of the strict construction of the powers of the federal government. On this issue he anticipates the "new Republicans," Calhoun, Clay and John Quincy Adams, perhaps because he shares their nationalism. Gallatin stood for the broad construction of national power and for its active employment, for a Bank of the United States and for internal improvements.[14] His interpretation of the Constitution provided the grounds for a foreign policy which led to the further acquisition of territory.

Gallatin often differed with Jefferson on the question of the construction of the Constitution. At times Jefferson could be persuaded to adopt the broad position. The Louisiana Purchase is one such example. Gallatin's argument anticipates the "new Republicans." The United States as a nation has the inherent right to acquire territory. This power is sanctioned by the several constitutional provisions which authorize the general government to make war, to make treaties, and to govern the territory of the Union. If the acquisition of territory is by treaty, the President and the Congress have the constitutional right to sanction the acquisition. Congress has the power to admit into the Union new states from such territory or to govern the acquisition as a territory. The Tenth Amendment is not an obstacle to national power. The treatymaking power is not reserved to the states.[15] Although Jefferson felt it would be "safer not to permit the enlargement of the Union but by amendment of the Constitution,"[16] the necessities of the situation led to the completion of the purchase without an amendment.

Gallatin was only partially successful in allaying Jefferson's suspicions concerning the Bank of the United States. Gallatin supported the bank because his experience as Secretary of the Treasury strengthened his belief in its utility.[17] He was unable to save the bank in 1811. In 1831 when the bank was again at issue, Gallatin again defended the institution. At this time, he was on firm ground. The second bank had been established on a foundation of cooperation between the federal banking system and the state banks. The operation of the second bank conformed to the pattern that Gallatin had advocated. It was easy to defend the renewal of the charter in an article which considered the "concurrent and perhaps debatable jurisdiction of the general and the state governments."[18]

His interpretation is orthodox republican doctrine but only to a point. The Constitution consolidates the United States into one nation at least with respect to foreign affairs. The internal powers of the government are few but among these are the power to regulate interstate commerce and the power to control the monetary system of the country. In these areas the states were excluded "from any participation which might interfere with the controlling power of the general government."[19]

Article I, Section 8 of the Constitution gives Congress the power to lay and collect taxes, duties, imports and excises; to pay debts and provide for the common defense and general welfare; and stipulates that all such duties be uniform throughout the United States. "To provide for the general welfare," however, cannot be construed as a distinct, specific power of Congress. Congress does not have the power "to embrace within its jurisdiction any object whatever which it might deem conducive to the general welfare of the United States." Such an assertion would subvert the constitutional barriers which guard the rights of the states and the people. Acceptance is "tantamount to an assertion that there is not a Constitution and that Congress is omnipotent."[20] The correct interpretation is Jefferson's. The Constitution gives Congress the power to lay and collect taxes *in order* to pay the debts and provide for the general welfare.

Having paid his respects to republican orthodoxy, Gallatin shifts the ground of the argument by asserting that Hamilton in *The Report on Manufactures* accepted Jefferson's construction. Gallatin quotes Hamilton, "it is, therefore, of necessity left to the discretion of the national Legislature to pronounce upon the objects which concern the general welfare and for which under that description, an appropriation of money is requisite and proper. And there seems to be no room for a doubt that whatever concerns the general interests of learning, of agriculture, of manufactures, and of commerce are within the sphere of the national councils as far as regards an application of money. The only qualification to the generality of the phrase is that the object must be general and not local, its operation must extend in fact or by possibility throughout the Union."[21] According to Gallatin, there can be no objection to Hamilton's construction because this is not a sweeping grant of power. "A power to appropriate money with this latitude, which is granted, too, in express terms, would not carry a power to any other thing not authorized in the Constitution either expressly or by fair implication."[22]

Gallatin has synthesized the positions of Jefferson and Hamilton. He does not, as Jefferson did, explicitly deny that the objects which concern the general welfare, i.e., education, agriculture and manufacturing, are beyond the sphere of the national government. Rather he implies that they are within this sphere, but only so far as an appropriation of money. If the national government only has indirect power in these areas, the Constitution is not subverted, the Tenth Amendment is not contradicted and the powers of the national government are not as broad as Hamilton advocated. Although this interpretation of the general welfare clause is not needed to justify the bank, it does aid in explaining how the general government became involved in internal improvements. Gallatin's interpretation prepared the way for a constitutional understanding which would enable the federal government to appropriate money to the states for projects which the federal government could not undertake directly. In addition, this interpretation indicates that Gallatin's position differs from both Hamilton's and Jefferson's.[23] He wished to retain power for the general government and the discretion necessary to use the power, yet at the same time wished it limited by the exercise of a concurrent power in its application.

For the discussion of the bank, Gallatin can assume the validity of the contention that the general welfare clause refers only to powers expressly vested in Congress by the Constitution and is not itself a grant of power. The Constitution does contain the necessary and proper clause, and Gallatin relies on it. His interpretation echoes Hamilton's. The clause could not have been intended in that most limited sense, implying absolute impossibility of effecting the object without the law. It must mean such laws as are fairly intended and highly useful and important for the purpose.[24] Gallatin, however, remains a republican and qualifies his interpretation. "The means proposed for carrying into effect any special or expressed power vested in Congress should be highly useful and important, having clearly and bonafide that object in view which is the avowed purpose and not be intended under color of executing a certain special power, for effecting another object."[25]

A moderate position is defined; the two principles, nationalism and republicanism, coincide in Gallatin's interpretation of the necessary and proper clause. The government must have the power to achieve its objectives, but only those objectives fairly within its sphere. Tortured constructions that give Congress sweeping powers do not pass republican scrutiny. The second bank was chartered by Congress by reference to its power over the currency of the country, not by virtue of its power over interstate commerce. The bank is a highly useful means, fairly implied by the express power.

The alternative to a national bank is the utilization of state banks, but a national bank has more advantages than a state bank. "To insist that the operation of the Treasury may be carried on with equal facility and safety through the aid of the state banks without the interposition of a Bank of the United States would be contrary to fact and experience." The necessary concert does not exist between thirty different institutions. Moreover, to admit that "banks are indispensable for carrying into effect the legitimate operations of government, is to admit that Congress has the power to establish a bank. The general government is not made by the Constitution to depend, for carrying into effect powers vested in it, on the uncertain aid of institutions created by other authorities and which are not at all under its control. It is expressly authorized to carry those powers into effect by its own means, by passing the laws necessary and proper for that purpose and in this instance by establishing its own bank, instead of being obliged to resort to those which derive their existence from another source and are under the exclusive control of the different States by which they have been established."[26] This is Gallatin the nationalist. The general government was created to achieve certain objectives. It should not be dependent on institutions which derive their existence from and are dependent on the states.

Gallatin's position is as nationalistic as Madison's at the Constitutional Convention. At that time, Madison used similar arguments to secure the new government's right to supervise the elections of its representatives even though they were elected in the states.[27] This similarity illustrates a unique nationalism in the early days of the republic. Promotion of the Union had to recognize the political realities imposed by the previous existence of the states. They would retain their position in the system. Recognition of this position implies the need to secure the same kind of consent in intergovernmental relations that Gallatin had recognized as necessary for the operation of the national government. Independent sources of power, which must be conciliated if they are to cooperate, limit the exercise of power. When the conciliation and cooperation take place within the bounds erected by the Constitution, then the demands of both liberty and Union are secured. The necessities are most apparent in the case of internal improvements but they are also apparent when Gallatin defends the bank. In the latter case, recognition of the states functions to guarantee the republican character of the bank.

State banks do and should exist, but the problem is to fix their place in the system. The Bank of the United States is controlled by the general government. Its existence depends "on the correctness, prudence, and skill with which it shall be administered, [it is] perpetually watched and occasionally checked by both the Treasury Department and rival institutions [state banks]."[28] Because state banks check the Bank of the United States, the latter is a republican institution. There is no undue concentration of power with the possibility of excessive discretion. The second bank is justified both as a national institution and as a republican institution.[29] Gallatin can in this case promote a measure which strengthens the bonds of Union and, at the same time, oppose any usurpation of power by the general government. Since the state banks served to check the national bank, the latter can be considered a republican institution.

Ample justification could be provided for the bank. But in the case of internal improvements, the federal government's power was not as clearly specified. Gallatin advocated internal improvements for they promoted the bonds of Union. "Good roads and canals will...unite by a still more intimate community of interests, the most remote quarters of the United States. No other single operation within the power of government can more effectively tend to strengthen and perpetuate that Union which secures external independence, domestic peace, and internal liberty."[30] Again, the justification for the Union as its relationship to liberty.

But such justifications do not reduce the practical problem of the power to make internal improvements.

Gallatin was able with limited success to reconcile the need for internal improvements with orthodox republican doctrine. He devised the means by which the Cumberland Road was built.[31] Ohio was petitioning to enter the Union. If Ohio agreed to exempt the public lands from state taxation for ten years after payment of the purchase price, the United States would set aside one-tenth of the net proceeds of the land hereafter sold by Congress to be applied to laying out and making a turnpike or other roads; first from the navigable waters emptying into the Atlantic to Ohio, and then through the state. Such roads would be laid under the authority of Congress with the consent of the states through which the road must pass. The roads will cement those parts of the Union whose local interests have been considered most dissimilar.[32] The Cumberland Road is a national measure, yet it is also a republican measure. The general government must have the consent of Ohio and of the states through which the road passes before it can act.

The road was necessary but the general government could not undertake it alone. The consent of the states had to be obtained if only to satisfy republican consciences. Gallatin's political beliefs imply the necessity of securing the consent of the affected states to the Cumberland Road. Such concurrence reconciled national and republican beliefs. The limitation on power is the political limitation necessitated by the need for concurrence between different departments and, in this case, different governments. The general government cannot usurp power as long as the practice of obtaining consent provides checks on power.[33] Ohio as well as the states through which the road passed must consent to the Cumberland Road. When Pennsylvania objected to the route, Gallatin persuaded Jefferson to accede to the state's demands.[34] The bonds of Union could be enhanced even as checks on the power of the general government were preserved.

The Cumberland Road was a special case of internal improvements. The general government had the power to act in this case because Ohio was a new state, entering the Union. Article IV, Section 3 of the Constitution gives Congress the power to admit new states. The necessary and proper clause enabled Congress to fix the rules for admittance. The provision for the Cumberland Road was part of the compact by which Ohio was admitted and the procedure could not be extended from the special to the more general case. Gallatin's contemporaries — Jefferson, Madison and Monroe — thought internal improvements were necessary, but they thought a constitutional amendment equally necessary before the general government could undertake such projects.

Jefferson raised the question of internal improvements in the Annual Message of 1806. A budget surplus was accumulating and it should be applied to internal improvements and education. However, these subjects must be added to the constitutional enumeration of powers.[35] Gallatin commented on this message before it was delivered. Although it is unclear whether his acceptance of the Jeffersonian policy on this issue was due to necessity or whether it was voluntary, his remarks indicate that he accepted the need for an amendment.[36]

The Report on Roads and Canals which Gallatin submitted to Congress in 1808 assumed that an amendment would be adopted. Although the report is as comprehensive a plan for physical development as Hamilton's report on manufacturing was for economic development,[37] the constitutional question was not considered. Hamilton had considered the constitutional question in his report, but Gallatin contented himself with proving that only the general government could remove the obstacles to the construction of these improvements. The constitutional question was ignored because Gallatin assumed as Jefferson did that while the states deliberated "this extension of the federal trust, the laws shall be passed and other arrangements made for their execution."[38] *The Report on Roads and Canals* was part of these arrangements. In November, 1808, Gallatin again considered the question of a constitutional amendment. Nothing efficient could be done without an amendment. There is no power delegated by the Constitution to Congress which fairly implies the power to directly construct internal improvements.[39] The republican Gallatin must have been satisfied, but what of the nationalist?

The nationalist succeeded in modifying Jefferson's position in two respects. Jefferson in the draft of the message of 1806, wanted, once the constitutional amendment was adopted, to partition the surplus among the states in a federal and just ratio. Gallatin opposed this proposal and it was dropped.[40] Two years later the question was again raised. Commenting on the message of 1808, Gallatin reminded Jefferson that earlier he had been persuaded to omit the idea of an apportionment among the states. "For the same reason, I wish extremely that the words 'securing to each of them the employment of their proportionate share within their respective states' [should be omitted]. It may ultimately be necessary to insert such a provision in the Amendment in order to ensure its success but it is very desirable that it should be adopted without such restriction. A just apportionment will naturally result from the conflicting interests on the floor of Congress." Again, Gallatin has recognized the political realities of a situation. The power of the states in Congress was only too apparent. Congress, representing the nation, must retain the discretion necessary to insure the execution of a system of national communications.[41] Again, the political process and the bargaining necessary for such a process is substituted for a formal limitation on power. The need to obtain concurrence from equals on the floor of Congress is a sufficient limitation on power to satisfy Gallatin's republican conscience.

Conclusion

Gallatin's reconciliation of national and republican ideals is apparent. The general government was a limited government; its powers were restricted to those granted by the Constitution. But Gallatin was not a strict constructionist. The necessary and proper clause, properly interpreted, provided Congress with the power needed to carry into effect its delegated powers. A proper interpretation means that only those objects fairly implied by the express powers could be achieved by utilizing the necessary and proper clause. Because congressional action on internal improvements was not fairly implied, an amendment was necessary. If Congress was entrusted with additional powers, then the general government would be acting in its sphere. The states should not receive from the same amendment the power to insist on equal shares. The power of the general government should not be formally restricted because, in fact, the states possessed sufficient power to serve as a check. They had ample means to secure their share on the floor of Congress and did not need a formal guarantee.

If the government was to work, the consent of all parts of the Union had to be obtained on the floor of Congress. Much of Gallatin's practical political activity revolved around this institution. Although he cannot be considered a believer in legislative supremacy, much of his time and energy was spent in persuading

Congressmen. Early in his career he had organized the Ways and Means Committee. As long as the Federalists controlled the executive, this committee functioned as a counterweight to treasury influence. The situation was transformed when the Jeffersonians came to power. Congressional organization then became the means to organize and discipline a majority.[42]

The congressional structure was flexible in the sense that its function was determined by the needs of specific political situations but its position in the center of the system made it a significant factor in any political calculation. Even in a period of executive dominance, programs were tailored to win congressional support. The requirement for a just apportionment was omitted from the proposed constitutional amendment, but the *Report on Roads and Canals,* which needed congressional approval, contained a just apportionment. To forestall the objections of those parts of the Union less immediately affected by the plan, as well as gain their support, both justice and policy caused Gallatin to include in the plan construction of roads and canals of primarily local benefit.[43]

Gallatin had devised the means which enabled the government to build the Cumberland Road. The practices adopted during its construction, especially with respect to state consent, established a pattern of cooperation between the states and the federal government in an area where neither had exclusive power.[46] The states had neither the national view nor the resources, yet constitutionally the power to construct internal improvements belonged to them. The lack of a constitutional amendment forced the federal government to restrict its activities to the appropriation of money to the states for construction of these improvements. The power of both governments was limited in this area and the concurrence of both was necessary for the completion of an act.

Republican theory and nationalist practice could coincide. The necessity of obtaining consent functioned to quiet republican consciences. This same necessity also functioned to maintain the place of the states in the system. Their political power and their role was recognized. Unlimited power was the definition of tyranny. Such power was difficult, if not impossible, to obtain as long as the concurrence of affected groups had to be obtained in order to act. Concurrence could be obtained in Congress, which helps explain Gallatin's stress on that branch of government. It could also be obtained by negotiations between officials of the national government and state officials as Gallatin's correspondence indicates. If concurrence was obtained, then republican aspirations were satisfied. It should be stressed, however, that republican ideals were satisfied by the procedure adopted, and not by the content of the measures adopted. There is much in the Embargo Acts and their implementation that should make good republicans shudder. But the procedures which were utilized to pass and implement those acts were the "republican" techniques developed by Gallatin and Jefferson.[47]

Gallatin's position was consistent. Both in his writings and in his actions he attempted to harmonize the at times conflicting principles of republicanism and nationalism. When he could balance these principles, the result was an indestructible Union composed of indestructible states. The national government is supreme; a state may not nullify acts of Congress. But the states had power in Congress and for additional insurance, state consent to national actions within their boundaries had to be obtained. Thus the recognition and enhancement of the position of the states in the Union would secure liberty. The pattern of future development is implicit in this conception. As national supremacy was defined and solidified, state powers and responsibilities were not reduced.[48] Instead the states were preserved and developed.[49]

Gallatin was conscious of the importance of the states. Close connections with Jefferson and Madison created awareness of the potential of the states as a check on unlimited power, and the necessity of such a check was accepted. At the same time, Gallatin was more of a nationalist than either Jefferson or Madison, so the states had to function within the system. The political system provided countless opportunities for the states. There was no need for additional formal limitations on the power of the national government or for opposition to go beyond the bounds of the system.

For Gallatin, the Union was primary and must be promoted. It deserved allegiance because it embodied republican principles. These principles included checks on power, but Gallatin emphasized political checks rather than formal limitations. Political necessity demanded that consent be obtained from the diverse parts of the Union before action could be taken. The structure of the Union secured the position of the states, and the political process which derived from this structure provided the checks to limit power. The two principles, summed up in the denotation "federal republic," were thus balanced in Gallatin. His was the middle ground between Jefferson and Hamilton and his method of operating from the middle served as a model for his contemporaries as well as for later participants in government. Because the principles of Union and republicanism were not exclusive, "the two legitimate faces of American federalism" — the Union and the states[50] — could at the same time be preserved and promoted.

Notes

1. Frank Ewing, *America's Forgotten Statesman, Albert Gallatin* (New York: Vantage, 1959).
2. Daniel J. Elazar's suggestions were helpful in formulating this contrast.
3. Henry Adams, *The Life of Albert Gallatin* (Philadelphia: Lippincott, 1879), pp. 267-268.
4. *Ibid.*, p. 214.
5. Ewing, *op. cit.*, p. 63.
6. Adams, *op. cit.*, pp. 132-139.
7. Albert Gallatin, *The Writings of Albert Gallatin*, (ed.) Henry Adams (Philadelphia: Lippincott, 1879), Vol. 1, p. 5.
8. *Ibid.*, p. 7.
9. *Ibid.*, pp. 6, 8.
10. *Ibid.*, p. 8.
11. Adams, *op. cit.*, pp. 202-214.
12. *The Debates and Proceedings in the Congress of the United States*, Fifth Congress, May 15, 1797 to March 3, 1799, Vol. 1 (Washington, 1851), pp. 1129-1131.
13. See, for example, Morton Grodzins, "Centralization and Decentralization in the American System," Robert A. Goldwin (ed.), *A Nation of States* (Chicago: Rand McNally, 1963).
14. Leonard D. White, *The Jeffersonians, A Study in Administrative History, 1801-1829* (New York: Macmillan, 1951), pp. 13-15.
15. Gallatin, *op. cit.*, pp. 112-114.
16. *Ibid.*, p. 115.
17. *Ibid.*, p. 171. See also Gallatin, Vol. III, p. 328. On his stand on the second bank, see Daniel J. Elazar, "Banking and Federalism in the Early American Republic," *Huntington Library Quarterly*, Vol. XXVIII, No. 4 (August, 1965), pp. 301-320.
18. Albert Gallatin, *op. cit.*, Vol. III, p. 298.

19. *Ibid.*, pp. 319-320.

20. *Ibid.*, p. 321.

21. *Ibid.*, p. 323.

22. *Ibid.*, p. 323.

23. Gallatin persuaded Jefferson to omit from his message of 1806 a proposal urging an amendment to remove the general welfare clause from the Constitution. Gallatin, Vol. 1, p. 320.

24. Albert Gallatin, *op. cit.*, Vol. III, p. 326.

25. *Ibid.*, p. 327.

26. *Ibid.*, p. 329.

27. C.C. Tansill, *Documents Illustrative of the Formation of the Union* (Washington: U.S. Government, 1927), pp. 509-511.

28. Albert Gallatin, *op. cit.*, p. 333.

29. *Ibid.*, pp. 339-340. See also Henry Adams, *op. cit.*, pp. 156-157.

30. *American State Papers*, Class X, Miscellaneous, Vol. I (Washington, 1834), pp. 724-725.

31. Leonard D. White, *op. cit.*, p. 484.

32. Albert Gallatin, *op. cit.*, Vol. I, pp. 76-79.

33. Particularly instructive in this respect were the procedures used to implement the Embargo Acts. The content of the Acts was repressive but the procedures used to implement them satisfied republican theory. See Leonard D. White, *op. cit.*, pp. 423-473.

34. Albert Gallatin, *op. cit.*, Vol. I, p. 395.

35. Thomas Jefferson, *The Writings of Thomas Jefferson*, (ed.) H.A. Washington, Vol. VIII (Washington, 1854), p. 68.

36. Albert Gallatin, *op. cit.*, p. 476.

37. Leonard D. White, *op. cit.*, p. 476.

38. Thomas Jefferson, *op. cit.*, p. 68.

39. Albert Gallatin, *op. cit.*, Vol. I, p. 425.

40. *Ibid.*, p. 319.

41. *Ibid.*, pp. 424-425.

42. Ralph V. Harlow, *The History of Legislative Methods in the Period Before 1825* (New Haven: Yale University Press, 1917), pp. 180-184.

43. *American State Papers*, X, Vol. I, pp. 724-725.

44. Leonard D. White, *op. cit.*, pp. 423-473.

45. Daniel J. Elazar, *The American Partnership* (Chicago: University of Chicago, 1962), p. 134.

46. *Ibid.*, pp. 134-139.

47. Leonard D. White, *op. cit.*, pp. 423-473.
48. William Anderson, *The Nation and the States, Rival or Partners* (Minneapolis: University of Minnesota Press, 1955), p. 84.
49. Daniel J. Elazar, *op. cit.*, p. 328.
50. *Ibid.*, p. 328.

PART THREE:

LEADERSHIP IN
SUBSEQUENT GENERATIONS

LINCOLN'S POLITICAL HUMANITARIANISM: MORAL REFORM AND THE COVENANT TRADITION IN AMERICAN POLITICAL CULTURE

J. David Greenstone

"Had he lived to seventy," Richard Hofstadter has written, Abraham Lincoln "would have seen the generation brought up on self-help...build oppressive business corporations and begin to close off those treasured opportunities for the little man...[even as] his own party [became] the jackal of the vested interests." Lincoln himself, Hofstadter adds, "presided over the social revolution that destroyed the simple equalitarian order of the 1840s" (Hofstadter, 1948, p. 106). To Hofstadter, Lincoln is largely irrelevant to modern politics. His presidency may have resolved the issues of slavery and the supremacy of the national government, but he had little to say about the questions of class, ethnicity and even race so troubling to later generations.

Claims of this sort rest on two common themes in Lincoln's speeches and writings. One is the gospel of self-reliance. As Lincoln put it in 1859,

> If any continue through life in the condition of the hired laborer, it is not the fault of the system, but because of either a dependent nature which prefers it, or improvidence, folly or singular misfortune (Basler, 1953, Vol. III, p. 479).

The other theme celebrates individual rights. As he said in 1858, "true popular sovereignty" decrees that "each man shall do precisely as he pleases with himself and all those things which exclusively concern him..." (Basler, 1953, Vol. III, p. 405).

Hofstadter's interpretation is plausible but inadequate, primarily because it ignores the humanitarian character of Lincoln's political ethic. Hofstadter's reading cannot explain — save by invoking sheer filial piety — the reverence in which Lincoln was held by those later nineteenth-century social reformers who explicitly addressed the crises of an urban, industrial society. For example, Lincoln was revered by the settlement house movement, which in its own time emphasized the development of each individual's distinctively human faculties, and some of whose leaders subsequently influenced the New Deal (Addams, 1961, ch. 2).[1]

The argument developed here makes two basic claims about Lincoln's politics:

1. Like the ethic of the abolitionists, Lincoln's position on slavery was broadly humanitarian. For that reason he does not belong to the dominant wing of American liberalism that has concentrated on satisfying each person's individual determined preferences — be it directly through some form of utilitarianism, or indirectly through a commitment to individual rights. Instead he is part of a dissenting liberal tradition whose primary goal is the development of human skills and faculties.

2. Until Lincoln's time, the most prominent humanitarian reformers were more concerned with individuals and moral purity than with institutions and practicality. By contrast, Lincoln fashioned a persuasive humanitarian ethic that was political rather than personal; it required dedicating, or rededicating, the American regime — the nation's political institutions — to the moral, material and intellectual self-improvement of every citizen. Lincoln's commitment to American capitalism is obvious. But by politicizing the tradition of humanitarian reform he spoke powerfully to later generations.

In order to develop these two arguments it will be convenient to begin with an ethic that partially resembles Lincoln's: the humanitarianism of the ante bellum abolitionists.

The Abolitionists' Personal Humanitarianism

The abolitionists were America's quintessential humanitarians. For a time, they and they alone denounced chattel slavery as an intolerable sin that violated their most fundamental understanding of humanity and moral obligation. The peculiar institution, as William Lloyd Garrison maintained, bore "the awful guilt of debasing the physical and defiling the moral workmanship of the great God — creatures made little lower than the angels, and capable of the highest intellectual attainments" (Garrison, 1830, p. 7). Slavery blighted the moral development of the owners as surely as it stifled the intellectual development of the slaves. Elizur Wright, for example, believed that every person had the unavoidable "duty...to urge upon slaveholders *immediate*

196

emancipation so long as there is a slave — to agitate the consciences of tyrants, so long as there is a tyrant on the globe" (Wright, 1833, p. 12, his emphasis). Accordingly, the anti-slavery militants recognized a three-fold obligation: first, to exhibit one's own saintliness by attacking so evil an institution; second, to rescue the slaves so that they could develop their rational faculties; and third, to rescue the slave masters — regardless of their preferences — from the sin of owning other human beings.

This hatred of slavery epitomized a broader humanitarianism. As used here, "humanitarianism" means a belief in the imperative ethical obligation to help others develop their fundamental, distinctively human capacities — to make correct inferences and intelligent judgments; to act deliberately and take responsibility for one's actions; and finally, to master socially defined skills and practices as diverse as chess or English literature, painting or statecraft (Greenstone, 1982, pp. 13-18). Most abolitionists denounced every apparent obstacle to such development, including addiction to alcohol, discrimination against women, lack of education for the poor, and inhumane treatment of the indigent insane (Greenstone, 1979; Messerli, 1972; Walters, 1976, ch. 3-4). Thus, to use the philosophers' terminology, the abolitionists acknowledged a "perfect duty," that is, an obligation to help those particular individuals who lacked the opportunity for such self-development. Of this group, the slaves needed this help most, because their bondage so completely blocked their chances for self-improvement.

Equally important, the abolitionists hated slavery so fiercely because it was objectively wrong; it blighted both the intellectual development of its black victims and the moral development of its white beneficiaries. Its evil character did not depend on the slaves' preferences. Here was the source of the abolitionists' militance. From those reformers' perspective, there was no need to try to balance competing preferences or interests. It was simply immoral to block a person's efforts at self-development. For that reason, competing preferences or interests could not simply be weighted and balanced. In principle, there were no preferences, even those of southern whites and the slaves themselves that could decide the issue.

The anti-slavery militants framed their ethic in largely individualist terms. At first, they directed their moral suasion at individual slaveholders. When these overtures were angrily rebuffed, they began to stress their own suffering and persecution.

197

Later, in order to protect their personal moral standing, many of them withdrew from the political parties and the Protestant churches that they thought hopelessly compromised on the slavery issue. For Garrison and his followers, both the Union and the Constitution were themselves immoral (Walters, 1976, pp. 23, 129-131). Throughout, the plight of the individual slave dramatized the institution's sinfulness. Abolitionist propaganda made this plight a staple theme and embraced its quintessential expression in *Uncle Tom's Cabin*, even though it had been written by a relatively moderate New Englander (Garrison, 1852). And the movement's leaders denounced anti-slavery moderates like Lincoln for agreeing to laws that would help recapture fugitive slaves.

The abolitionists were also ethical perfectionists: some actions were imperative; other actions were simply unacceptable. The righteous must do the one and shun the other. Accordingly, they rejected consequentialist, cost-benefit arguments about the social and economic turmoil that would follow emancipation — or the political catastrophe that would follow secession. "Their attachment to the Union is so strong," Lydia Maria Child observed of her fellow abolitionists, "that they would make any sacrifice of self-interest to preserve it; but they never will consent to sacrifice honor and principle. 'Duties are ours; events are God's'" (Child, 1839, p. 69). "You must perform your duty faithfully, fearlessly, and promptly," Garrison told his followers, "and leave the consequences to God" (quoted by Chapman, 1921, p. 142; cf. Bartlett, 1965, p. 116; Child, 1839, p. 69; Garrison, 1837, p. 77).

A chasm separated these radical reformers from their contemporaries who simply disliked slavery, charitably wished the slaves well, and recognized in the abstract their right to freedom. Whether it grew out of benevolent feelings or a more activist belief in individual rights, this attitude did not demand immediate emancipation.

Ethical benevolence, as distinct from humanitarianism, prescribes personal charity to others primarily in order to alleviate their pain and suffering (cf. Davis, 1966, pp. 334-357, 376-382; Davis, 1975, pp. 179-182, 245-246). But because pain is intrinsic to the human condition, *everyone* is liable to suffering and is in need of succor and comfort. In the philosophers' terminology, benevolence prescribes an "imperfect" duty, because it does not indicate specific beneficiaries. That is, although benevolence requires me to help others, I am relatively free to select the particular persons I wish to assist. There is no particular group, even slaves, that I must help, come what may. In fact, slavery was so thoroughly enmeshed in the web of established social interests that a dislike or contempt for the institution did not entail a belief in immediate emancipation (cf. Davis, 1975, pp. 256-257). Many ante bellum Americans — including the partisans of Andrew Jackson — embraced democracy but rejected abolitionist principles. As Davis puts it, in his authoritative study, a belief in "the ideas of utility, social equilibrium, and the moral economy of nature" was more likely to encourage a complex weighing of opposed interests, fear of costly civil strife, and thus a quest for sectional compromise (Davis, 1975, p. 258; cf. Davis, 1966, ch. 13-14).

The abolitionists also rejected a rights-oriented liberal tradition which protected individual choices that did not interfere unfairly with other people. From this perspective, there were at least three main duties: 1) individuals should respect the rights of others when properly invoked; 2) the government should referee conflicts among individuals; and 3) each citizen should support a government that respects individual rights and impartially resolves disputes. These duties are indeed "perfect" in that they require one to respect the rights of particular persons. For example, contractarian theory requires us to help fellow citizens whose rights have been denied. Rights rather than duties were still prior. For one has the duty to help another only when that person invokes a right by identifying a goal and trying to pursue it (cf. Davis, 1975, p. 257).

In the case of slavery, therefore, the rights perspective was typically equivocal. In the abstract, there may have been a perfect duty to help free the slaves, but in practice, even running away was a crime, and it was virtually impossible for them to invoke their right to freedom. What is more, the rights tradition weighs competing claims. Although the slaves had a right to liberty, the slave owners had property rights, and all southern whites had a right to life which infuriated ex-slaves might threaten. Indeed, many liberals such as Thomas Jefferson and Henry Clay who espoused a doctrine of rights, only recognized the imperfect duty of treating the slaves considerately (Davis, 1975, ch. 4; Howe, 1979, pp. 133ff; Colton, 1857, Vol. V, pp. 151, 387ff; Koch and Peden, 1944, pp. 25-26, 698).

Because it placed duties ahead of a concern for benevolence, preferences and rights, abolitionist humanitarianism was often as paternalistic, as intermeddling and intrusive, as moralistically concerned with the affairs of others, as its critics maintained. But this relentless, often self-righteous agitation helped set off a fateful chain reaction. As southerners were provoked into defending slavery as a positive good and secession as a political right (Thomas, 1965b), their apologia became a sweeping indictment of the free states' culture, society and economy. In turn, this southern response increasingly antagonized moderate northerners. The result, in part, was the sectional conflict that finally destroyed the peculiar institution (cf. Friedman, 1982, p. 4).

Nevertheless, abolitionism was too perfectionist, too concerned with moral purity, to be directly political. It did not specify the practical way to implement its moral vision. Yet at another level, that same vision was clearly relevant to post-Civil War politics. For its humanitarian ethic represented a potential challenge to any social order, including industrial capitalism, that stifled individual self-development. On this point, Lincoln and the abolitionists converged.

Lincoln's Humanitarianism

"All nature — the whole world, material, moral, and intellectual — is a mine," Lincoln observed at the height of the slavery struggle in 1859. "Now it was the destined work of Adam's race to develop...the hidden treasures of this mine" (Basler, 1859, Vol. III, p. 358). During this development, the triumph of reason over passion was especially important (Basler, 1953, Vol. I, p. 114; cf. 1848, Vol. II, p. 4; 1858, Vol. II, p. 437; 1859, Vol. III, pp. 362, 480-481). "Every head," he added in the same year, "should be cultivated and improved by whatever will add to its capacity for performing its charge. In one word, Free Labor insists on universal education" (Basler, 1953, Vol. III, p. 480).

Lincoln followed these humanitarian precepts in his own life. As a boy, he read avidly; after serving in Congress, he taught himself geometry; as President he mastered military strategy. All through his life he appeared to fear the loss of reason more than death itself (Oates, 1977, pp. 77, 21; B. Thomas, 1952, pp. 130, 133, 292). As a state legislator, to be sure, he was sometimes reluctant to support appropriations for the public schools (Provenzo, 1982, esp. pp. 193, 196, but cf. Jones, 1927, p. 336ff). But he regularly favored government help to those who could not help themselves, and he began his political career by emphasizing the importance of education, and he made the government's responsibility for the common schools a tenet of his mature political thought (Basler, 1953, Vol. I, p. 8; 1854, Vol. II, pp. 221-222). As President, he broke with his Democratic predecessor by signing the Morrill Act that launched the American system of land grant colleges (Maccia, 1962-1963).

Like other humanitarians, Lincoln often placed the cultivation of faculties ahead of satisfying desires or preferences. Alcohol might be enjoyable to many, but he found that drinking left him "flabby and undone." If the style of his 1842 Temperance Address was charitable and ironic, it nevertheless attacked the passions and self-serving motives that enslaved the intellect. His goals were to free every dram seller from the lure of "pecuniary interest," and every drinker from "burning appetite" (B. Thomas, 1952, pp. 37, 111-112; Basler, 1953, Vol. I, pp. 274-275; cf. Walters, 1976, p. 56, on the abolitionists). Four years before, he had decried the "pleasure hunting masters of southern slaves" (Basler, 1838, Vol. I, p. 109). In 1854, he denounced indifference to slavery for assuming "that there is no right principle of action but *self-interest*" (Basler, 1854, Vol. II, p. 255, Lincoln's emphasis; cf. p. 267). During the war, he remarked that if anyone deserved to be enslaved it was those who "*desire* it for *others*" (Basler, 1865, Vol. VIII, p. 361, Lincoln's emphasis).

At least in principle, this humanitarianism extended to every human being. Like most abolitionists, he sympathized with several feminist goals, including the right to vote. He also privately rejected the nativism that attracted many of his fellow anti-slavery Whigs (Oates, 1977, pp. 33, 298; Basler, 1953, Vol. II, p. 323). Since most people would respond positively when given a genuine opportunity to improve themselves, the government ought to provide "for the helpless, young and afflicted," who might be unable to seek self-improvement (Basler, 1953, Vol. II, p. 221). Certainly, it was an error to assume "that the whole labor of a community exists within that relation [between labor and capital]....A large majority belongs in neither class" (B. Thomas, 1952, p. 197). In his youth, he recalled, "I was a hired laborer. The hired laborer of yesterday labors on his own account today, and will hire others to labor for him tomorrow. Advancement — improvement in condition — is the order of things in a society of equals" (B. Thomas, 1952, p. 197).

Slavery denied its victims just this opportunity. If passion and self-love undermined the slave owners' rationality and moral development, the institution was unforgivable — in part because it "clouded" the slaves "intellects" (Basler, 1953, Vol. V, p. 372). Bondage denied them the chance for "the weak to grow stronger, the ignorant wise, and all better and happier together" (Basler, 1953, Vol. II, p. 222). At the core of his politics was the "profound central truth that slavery is a wrong and ought to be dealt with as a wrong," that is, "with the fixed idea that it must and will come to an end" (Basler, 1953, Vol. III, pp. 368, 370). Despite his distaste for violence, he even found himself admiring the devotion to a cause that John Brown displayed at Harper's Ferry (Oates, 1977, p. 182). Lincoln himself never wavered on the issue of slavery's territorial expansion, even when anxious moderates warned him after his election about the dangers of secession (Oates, 1977, p. 205). Lincoln formulated his opposition in ultimately perfectionist terms. In the Garden of Eden, he reminded Douglas in 1854, there was a clear difference between right and wrong. God told Adam that "there was one tree, of the fruit of which he should not eat" (Basler, 1953, Vol. II, p. 278). Of course, no individual could attain perfection. But he interpreted the command of the New Testament, "be ye perfect," to mean that "he who did the most toward reaching that standard, attained the highest degree of moral perfection" (Basler, 1953, Vol. II, p. 501).

The Kansas-Nebraska Act was intolerable because it reversed this upward progress. Until Stephen A. Douglas steered the Act through Congress in 1854, the Missouri Compromise had barred slavery from the northern Louisiana Purchase. In defending his repeal of the Compromise, Douglas appealed to the doctrine of popular sovereignty, i.e., the right of a territory's white majority to decide the slavery question for itself. Because that majority in Kansas opposed slavery, Lincoln could clearly distinguish himself from Douglas only by invoking his humanitarian principles. His strategy, as Potter observes, was to "shift attention" to the "philosophic aspects" of the slavery question, "where he believed that their differences were specific and fundamental" (Potter, 1976, p. 338).

At one level, the overt issue was slavery itself. Where Lincoln insisted on treating and discussing slavery as a wrong, Douglas believed that, as a moral issue, it had no place in politics. At another level, the conflict was over humanitarianism. Douglas argued that the white people in a territory could best judge their own interests and circumstances. Letting each state or territory decide the slavery question for itself would therefore satisfy the preferences of as many persons as possible. But Lincoln insisted that the great issues could not be decided solely by self-regarding motives and preferences (Forgie, 1979, pp. 141-142, 144, 174; Basler, 1953, Vol. III, p. 310; Greenstone, 1984). On certain questions of principle, as he said in his last speech, he was "inflexible." Lincoln was certainly no abolitionist, but he thought his differences with these humanitarian reformers were primarily questions of means rather than ends. The abolitionists, to be sure, were not "properly" members of the Republican party. But Lincoln made it clear that the new party shared with the militants a belief that slavery was "a moral, social and political wrong." They differed, as he carefully put it, mainly on questions of "practical action" (Basler, 1953, Vol. III, p. 313).

This argument for Lincoln's humanitarianism can be readily challenged on three grounds: One objection stresses his enthusiastic belief in American capitalism. As a good Whig he consistently supported the party's program for economic development. In the 1850s, he embraced the Republican's free labor rhetoric that, as Hofstadter intimates, led to a later embrace of laissez faire. He was certainly not drawn to any moralistic meddling in the private affairs of others. As he said in his great speech at Peoria in 1854, "My faith in the proposition that each man should do precisely as he pleases with all which is exclusively his own, lies at the foundation of...[my] sense of justice" (Basler, 1953, Vol. II, p. 265).

But if the abolitionists are a relevant benchmark, this argument proves very little. In Lydia Maria Child's revealing words:

> The abolitionists...merely wish to have...the stimulus of *wages* applied instead of the stimulus of the *whip*. The relation of master and laborer [after emancipation] might still continue; but...even when human beings are brutalized to the last degree by the soul-destroying system of slavery, they still have sense enough to be more willing to work two hours for twelve cents than to work one hour for nothing (Child, 1839, pp. 63-64, emphasis in original).

Many humanitarian reformers despised slavery because it severely curbed the slaves' freedom and thus prevented them from developing their faculties. As they saw the American government continue to equivocate on slavery, some began to suspect any coercive exercise of political power (Walters, 1976, pp. 116ff). Lincoln himself never went this far. In his 1854 speech at Peoria, he rejected individual self-determination on slavery if it meant the government must allow one person to enslave another (Basler, 1953, Vol. II, p. 266). As we have seen, he also favored public as well as private action where necessary to improve American society. Moreover, both Lincoln and the abolitionists admired successful capitalists for essentially humanitarian reasons. The entrepreneurs' capacity for moral, intellectual and social self-development was simply a special case of the more general goal of self-improvement that Lincoln, like the moral reformers of his time, sought for every American. For both, "material prosperity...[was] the external sign of inner spiritual health" (Jaffa, 1959, p. 304; cf. Forgie, 1979, p. 72; Oates, 1977, p. 180; cf. Basler, 1953, Vol. V, pp. 51-52; on the abolitionists, see Walters, 1976, pp. 114ff).

A second objection stresses Lincoln's obvious ambition. Both Lincoln and his devoted law partner, William Herndon, acknowledged his passionate quest for political office (Oates, 1977, pp. 161 and 106; cf. 26 and Basler, 1953, Vol. III, p. 310). And Lincoln put as much distance as he could between himself and his family, particularly his illiterate father who symbolized the social obscurity, poverty and illiteracy that he fervently wanted to escape.

Once again, however, the distinction between Lincoln and the abolitionists is not very clear. For instance, anti-slavery militants exhibited the traditional piety of New England Protestantism (cf. Thomas, 1965b). And it has been a commonplace, at least since Weber's classic study of the Protestant ethic, that New England Calvinism strikingly combined morality and ambition. In demanding devotion to moral duty the Puritan's creed simultaneously commanded unremitting pursuit of success in one's vocation — be it the Protestant capitalist's worldly asceticism or a devotion to humanitarian reform. Certainly, the abolitionists exhibited this combination. Even though they shunned conventional politics, their notorious doctrinal and organizational rivalries suggest a drive for power and influence similar to Lincoln's (Walters, 1976, ch. 1; J. Thomas, 1965a, pp. 76-98; Wyatt-Brown, 1971, ch. 10). A number of scholars have also interpreted their militant zeal as an expression of anxiety over their social status. On this account, their movement was the response of an established intelligentsia newly challenged by a rising economic elite (Walters, 1976, p. 177, n. 17). In sum, the most fervent humanitarianism was no barrier to the pursuit of social and political success.

The abolitionists themselves had a third reason for

dismissing Lincoln's humanitarianism. Whatever his motives, they believed that his commitment to mainstream politics inevitably compromised any hostility he might have had to slavery. After all, he won his party's nomination for president because he was cautious enough to appeal to relatively conservative voters, particularly in the lower North for whom the abolitionists were much too extreme. As he made clear in the senatorial debate at Freeport, he would not demand repeal of the Fugitive Slave Law; he did not insist on abolishing slavery in the District of Columbia; and would not necessarily prohibit the slave trade between the slave states. He even agreed that a federal territory with a pro-slavery constitution would have to be admitted as a state, provided, of course, that slavery had been excluded up to the time the constitution was drafted (Johannsen, 1965, p. 76). As we have seen, the only issue on which he adamantly opposed the South was the one that united his party: exclusion of slavery from the federal territories themselves (Foner, 1979; Sewell, 1976, chs. 12-13; Potter, 1976; Fehrenbacher, 1962; Craven, 1971). Yet this stand on the territories was not obviously humanitarian. While it protected white settlers from having to compete with slave labor, it did nothing for the slaves, all of whom remained in the slave states.

More generally, Lincoln was clearly not a single-minded moral reformer. Unlike Horace Mann or Dorothea Dix, he did not throw all his energies into political action on behalf of unschooled children, the indigent insane, or other individuals denied a genuine opportunity for self-development. Nor was he an eastern intellectual (as were many leading abolitionists) whose jeremiads and solemn meditations denounced the slave owners' sins, the northern capitalists' greed, and the lower classes' inadequacies. The child of a mobile frontier society, he was unburdened, or unblessed, by the weight of a New England conscience. His ethical pronouncements were often relaxed, and sometimes even playful, and his instincts as a good politician led him to conciliate other members of his political community. Although he favored temperance, he had called in 1842 for *"persuasion"* or a "drop of honey" rather than "anathema and denunciation," and warned against trying to "dictate to the drunkard's judgment or to command his action" (Basler, 1953, Vol. I, p. 273, Lincoln's emphasis).

To the distress of many abolitionists such as Wendell Phillips, he was equally charitable to slave owners. "I surely will not blame" southern whites, he said at Peoria in 1854, "for not doing what I should not know how to do myself. If all earthly power were given me, I should not know what to do, as to the existing institution" (Basler, 1953, Vol. II, p. 255). At the same time, he always thought the abolitionists were misguided. While protesting against the anti-slavery resolutions of the 1837 Illinois legislature, he claimed the abolitionists' demands would only increase the evils of slavery. Later, he pointed out that by voting for the Liberty party's candidate in 1844, instead of Henry Clay, New York abolitionists had made possible the election of a pro-slavery Democrat, James K. Polk (B. Thomas, 1952, pp. 64, 112). Indeed, as a good Whig, he revered its author, Clay, as his "beau ideal" of a politician (Basler, 1953, Vol. III, p. 29). But this greatest of Whig politicians was himself a slave owner, and Lincoln's respect for him could hardly please the abolitionists. Not surprisingly, few supported Lincoln in 1860. Phillips called him a "huckster in politics," and Garrison denounced his party as "cowardly" (Oates, 1977, pp. 202-203).

Ultimately, however, the abolitionists' indictment is as inadequate as Hofstadter's. For one thing, it overlooks the humanitarian moral fervor that Lincoln's rhetoric both revealed and communicated. Lincoln won his party's nomination because that rhetoric appealed to its anti-slavery elements, especially in the upper North, as well as its conservatives. The real question, then, is not the breadth of his views but their coherence. Was Lincoln's feat just a matter of clever rhetoric, or did he really succeed in reconciling his politics and his ethics in a way that other northerners found persuasive and illuminating? And if so, how? To answer these questions, Lincoln's political ethic must be understood in terms of the political culture of the Whig party that he joined at the beginning of his political career.

Lincoln and the Political Culture of Northern Whiggery

Northern Whiggery reflected the political conscience, as well as the social aspirations and economic interests, of Protestant, and capitalist, New England (Howe, 1979). Now it is true that Lincoln's seventeenth-century Massachusetts ancestors were Quakers, not Puritans, and that his immediate forebears were Baptists from rural Kentucky and Virginia, not the cultured offspring of Yankee Calvinism (Oates, 1977, ch. 1; B. Thomas, 1952, ch. 1). Yet rather than identify with his illiterate frontier family, he fervently sought to rise above it. Starting out in the village of New Salem, he sought out the town's elite rather than the "meaner sort" who liked his humor (Oates, 1977, pp. 19-21). As a young man, he sought out better educated lawyers as teachers and colleagues, and the two women he courted came from upper class backgrounds (B. Thomas, 1952, pp. 80, 96). As a father, many years later, he was proud of his oldest son Robert's cultivation and easy familiarity with his Harvard classmates from established eastern families (B. Thomas, pp. 56, 80, 96; Oates, 1977, p. 34).

Most of these new upper class associates were Whigs. Lincoln joined the Whig party in his youth and stayed with it until its collapse in the mid-1850s. He served as its floor leader in the Illinois legislature, and later as a presidential elector, a Congressman and a member of its national committee (B. Thomas, 1952, p. 73, 78, 105; cf. Basler, 1953, Vol. II, p. 322; 1857, Vol. II, p. 400; Fehrenbacher, 1962, pp. 25ff). Although Lincoln gave his allegiance to a political party and not a church, Whiggery meant more to him than an economic program or a chance for political advancement or even a route to higher social status. As Daniel Walker Howe maintains, the party offered Lincoln an entire culture with which to shape his life. Whiggery, for example, had little room for the self-indulgent undisciplined individual. Instead, the Whigs were simultaneously concerned with the self-control and social progress, with the self-discipline and self-improvement that they thought essential for any well ordered society. Not surprisingly, Lincoln defended Whig values against the derision of Stephen A. Douglas and his Democratic followers, even in the late 1850s after the Whig party itself had died (Basler, 1953, Vol. III, pp. 356ff).

As we have seen, these traits also characterized the abolitionists, and like many humanitarian reformers, Lincoln's first party had strongly Protestant, indeed Yankee cultural roots (cf. Howe, 1979, passim). And within mainstream ante bellum politics, northern Whigs were much more sympathetic than Democrats toward both moral reform and anti-slavery. Where the two groups typically parted company was over the issue of the political community. It was in the name of community and the common good that the party's early leaders denounced the Democrats' self-serving, factional intrigues. From the 1830s on, the party justified its economic policies by arguing that a vigorous business community would benefit everyone. And it appealed to other social classes by celebrating community and polity as the source of essential moral standards (Howe, 1979, ch. 2; Greenstone, 1982; Benson, 1961, ch. 5). Accordingly, even strongly anti-slavery Whigs shied away from immediate abolition as a threat to the American political community which they revered. As the slavery crisis intensified, many conservative or Cotton Whigs, particularly in the eastern cities, tried to preserve national unity by supporting sectional accommodation and opposing moralistic attacks on the South. Yet the Whigs' split over moral reform could not be suppressed. In particular, Conscience Whigs of Massachusetts and their allies in the party's rural and western bastions detested slavery because it violated their belief in equality and universal self-improvement.

The Divided World of American Humanitarianism

Cotton Whigs, Conscience Whigs, and ante bellum moral reformers all shared the humanitarian goal of self-improvement. They differed among themselves in terms of two dimensions which must be separately identified before we can fully understand the character and importance of Lincoln's political humanitarianism. The first involves sainthood or moral purity vs. citizenship or loyalty to political institutions; the second pitted the value of instrumental rationality vs. the importance of piety, zeal or moral perfection. This pattern will be examined in terms of the nine-fold typology set out in Table A. (It must be emphasized that this analysis does not apply to utilitarian foes of slavery such as Richard Hildreth, or to those northern Democrats who opposed the slave owners as a competing economic and social interest — let alone Democrats like Douglas who urged sectional accommodation.)

The First Dimension: Unionism and Moral Purity

One of these dimensions exhibited conflicting conceptions of moral duty. How essential is it to maintain one's ethical purity as opposed to fulfilling one's obligations as a citizen? Much as the preceding generation of New Englanders had oscillated between the nationalism of the early Federalists and the secessionist

Table A

A TYPOLOGY OF 19TH CENTURY POLITICAL/ETHICAL POSITIONS THAT EVOLVED OUT OF COLONIAL CALVINISM

	Affirms the Place of Rationality in Morality	Affirms the Place of Both Piety and Rationality in Morality	Affirms the Place of Piety in Morality
Moral Obligations to the Polity	Daniel Webster and the Cotton Whigs	Henry Clay	Evangelical Supporters of Manifest Destiny
Affirms Both Obligations	William Seward and the Whig Modernizers (Lincoln before 1854)	Lincoln in 1854 and after	Joshua Giddings at the end of his career
Affirms Moral Obligations to Individuals	Secular (Anti-slavery) Utopian communities	Garrisonian Abolitionists	Quakers

tendencies of the Hartford Convention, the ante bellum generation witnessed a struggle between unionism (indicated by the top row of Table A) and political separatism (indicated by the bottom row). At one extreme, New England's Cotton Whigs, including Rufus Choate, Daniel Webster, and their capitalist allies, disliked slavery and objected for prudential reasons to its territorial expansion (Wilson, 1974, ch. 2). Like Lincoln, they tended to favor colonization rather than abolition. Webster, for example, believed that the union's providential place in history as an arena for economic and cultural improvement meant that conflicts over slavery must give way to sectional accommodation. But unlike Lincoln, these conservatives resisted any attempt to make slavery into a moral issue, lest it tear the Union apart and undermine the social basis on which freedom and improvement rested (Webster, 1860, Vol. 5, p. 332). They feared that without the union, liberty and improvement would not be secure for the people of any race. Accordingly, although Webster and Clay died in the early 1850s, many of their followers refused to vote for the Republicans in either 1856 or 1860 (Potter, 1976, pp. 263, 416).

At the other extreme, as we have seen, anti-slavery militants insisted on a moral purity that could not be found in most social, religious, and political institutions. Leading a genuinely holy life meant separation, that is, establishing real communion only with the truly righteous. In the eighteenth century, the Pennsylvania Quakers, the first major group to denounce slavery in the New World, were offended by their colonial government's use of force against the Indians. Later, they could not accept the constitutional compromise (which Lincoln explicitly embraced) that tolerated slavery in the South. From the mid-1700s on, therefore, orthodox Friends followed a separatist course in politics; in the next century, they took little part in the political side of the anti-slavery struggle (Baltzell, 1979, pp. 154ff). Instead, as Baltzell points out, the Friends sought ethical purity and attacked slavery not through political action but by reforming their own private and religious conduct. In the same decades in which they abandoned political activism, they purged their own religious community of slaveholders. Before the Civil War, they issued moral appeals and made a personal statement by helping individual fugitive slaves to escape to Canada.

Some abolitionists, including the strongly anti-slavery Transcendentalists, were directly influenced by the Friends. Garrison himself was converted to abolition by a Quaker (cf. Watters, 1976, p. 51). Indeed, Harriet Martineau thought he acted like a Friend, and one of Garrison's own converts compared him to the Quakers' founder, George Fox (Martineau, 1835, p. 116; Walters, 1976, p. 52; cf. Child, 1839, p. 68). On the issue of unionism vs. moral purity the two groups had similar beliefs. Although most anti-slavery militants recognized the value of private organizations maintained on righteous principles (Walters, 1976, pp. 8-9), they also believed that American society's established institutions were ethically compromised. The polity was particularly suspect. Garrison, who declared his country to be mankind, held that "the governments of this world...are all Anti-Christ"

(Garrison, 1837, p. 78; cf. Walters, 1976, p. 12; Massachusetts Anti-Slavery Society, 1844). Even worse, the abolitionists own government tolerated slavery within its borders. Not surprisingly, perhaps, a separatist creed was adopted by a congeries of radical anti-slavery anarchists and perfectionists who withdrew into utopian communities (Perry, 1973, chs. 3, 5).

Other anti-slavery groups took positions between the abolitionists and the Unionist Whigs. Some non-Garrisonians affirmed the Constitution by reading it as an anti-slavery document; others, notably members of the Liberty party, were willing to take the campaign against slavery into electoral politics (National Liberty Party Convention, 1843, pp. 96-97). Still, the Liberty party and Lincoln's Republicans differed over both the intrinsic moral worth of the Union and the policies it had adopted. For the Republicans, and before them for the nationalist but anti-slavery Whigs, the Union continued to be the great republican experiment of providential importance, which rightly deserved their allegiance, even if it temporarily tolerated slavery. Most Liberty members disagreed. Although some of their leaders eventually became radical Republicans, many rejected the maneuvering and compromises essential to institutional life, just as they withdrew from the major churches, just as they "came out" from the major parties — a step the politically ambitious Lincoln evidently never considered (J.L. Thomas, 1965b, p. 247; Walters, 1976, pp. 15-16; Ball, 1982, pp. 34, 32). In their view, the Missouri Compromise revealed the Union's hypocritical default on its republican commitment to freedom, for it allowed slavery in the southern part of the Louisiana Purchase (Ball, 1982, p. 20). By contrast, the great Whig leader Henry Clay had fought for the Compromise, and, as we have seen, Lincoln himself bitterly lamented its repeal. For him, the Compromise stigmatized slavery by barring it from the northern areas of the Purchase.

The Second Dimension: Instrumental vs. Consummatory Action

The second dimension involved conceptions of social action and ethical and political reasoning. In brief, should one reason in consummatory terms in order to obey the commands of the moral law, i.e., do only that which is intrinsically right without requiring an elaborate analysis of the likely consequences of these actions? Or ought one to view one's actions instrumentally as means for achieving desirable ends, and therefore reason instrumentally about the most likely way to achieve these goals?

On one side were most of those whom Howe calls conservative or modernizing Whigs (located in the left hand column of Table A) who evaluated legal arrangements and political actions instrumentally, i.e., in terms of their likely further consequences. Such reasoning, of course, depended on a stable, predictable context, and they saw a stable polity and legal system as essential for personal improvements, social progress and economic development. It followed that politics was less an exercise in morality than an applied science that focused on securing these outcomes. One's political duty was to shun a fanatical pursuit of ethical perfection in favor of dispassionate reasoning about the results of one's conduct, and to invoke patriotic sentiments where they would have beneficent outcomes. To convert politics into a morality play — as Webster thought the abolitionists wanted to do — was reckless and self-defeating. It was reckless because it risked destroying the Union. It was self-defeating, in that era, because destroying the world's one large, viable republic would make it much more difficult to achieve a humane, genuinely free society.

Not every instrumentally oriented politician was so totally opposed to making moral appeals. William H. Seward, for example, was a nationalist deeply committed to economic development. Yet his belief in individual improvement for all led him to reject nativism and denounce slavery. In the early and middle 1850s, he argued against the slave power, in the name of a law "higher" than the Constitution. Still, Seward had a rather serene trust in the ability of instrumental reason to control social and economic modernization, and, by the later 1850s, he worried about the negative consequences of moralism. During the secession crisis, he proved less militant than Lincoln.

The opposed conception (whose proponents are in the right hand column of Table A) insists that one's actions are intrinsically right just when they profess or affirm truly moral commitments. What is required, therefore, is consummatory reasoning in which one does one's duty and takes a certain action because it is consistent with such a moral code. To the ante bellum humanitarians who espoused this view, a preoccupation with effectiveness could become the idolatrous worship of efficiency. Many Quakers, for example, believed that instrumental political calculations inexorably led to moral compromise, especially to the use of force as the most effective means. As already noted, they avoided this trap by bearing personal rather than political witness against slavery, i.e., by acting as private citizens to help runaways escape (Potter, 1976, p. 135). This consummatory view was shared by others who had more positive, even Unionist, feelings toward their regime. Although Joshua Giddings, a leading anti-slavery Whig and then Republican Congressman, valued the Union, he drifted out of conventional politics as he underwent religious conversion. As he increasingly focused on achieving spiritual purity, he came to justify political actions almost entirely in terms of their ethical content (Stewart, 1970, pp. 280ff, and ch. 12).

Once again, there was a spectrum of positions between the instrumental and consummatory poles. Among Republicans, radicals like Charles Sumner tended to merge moral and political concerns, though he tolerated politically expedient positions more willingly than Giddings. On the other side, many Garrisonians did not fully share the Quakers' negative view of political action, as long as that activity did not involve a commitment to the Union and its institutions. As they saw it, their commitment to developing and exercising human faculties required them to use their own reason instrumentally in attacking slavery, mainly by arousing public opinion. Wendell Phillips argued at length that only agitation and propaganda could reach and convert an indifferent if not hostile society (Filler, 1965, pp. 34ff). Yet even within this group there were detectable shades of difference. By embracing non-resistance, Garrison rejected violence and by extension the political realm which so often used it. But Phillips' call for disunion suggests a concern with the regime's specific aims rather than its necessary and intrinsic defects. A government that had redeemed itself by separating from the South might perhaps merit his support.[2]

Lincoln's Synthesis

To understand Lincoln's politics it is necessary to understand the extent to which his ethic embraced both sides of each of the tensions that divided Yankee culture. Throughout his life, Lincoln carefully calculated the consequences of his political acts. In his famous Lyceum speech of 1838 he sounded the typically Whiggish call for the rule of law and reason, and thus, a due concern for the results of one's deeds (Basler, 1953, Vol. I, p. 115). His early

Temperance Address explicitly shunned moral denunciation as ineffective, in favor of a more effective appeal to the drunkards' and dramsellers' good sense. Throughout his adult life, he revelled in the effort to find the most effective legal tactics and political strategies, even on the slavery issue, in a way that most abolitionists could not stomach. But the great black abolitionist Frederick Douglass had also objected to the abolitionists' disunionism in instrumentalist terms. Allowing the South to secede, he observed, simply dissolves "the Union and leaves...the slave to free himself" (Douglass, 1855, p. 127). By the same token, when the Free Soilers of 1848 insisted that "they would do their duty and leave the consequences to God," Lincoln countered that duty required that we rely "on our most intelligent judgment of the consequences" (Basler, 1953, Vol. II, p. 3). Accordingly, he rebuked the minor anti-slavery parties because they helped elect proslavery Democrats.

Until 1854, this instrumentalist orientation seems to have largely dominated Lincoln's political outlook. To use Howe's term, he was for the most part a 'Whig modernizer' who had a calculating attitude toward his career and the rather complacent loyalty toward his society that one might expect of a provincial lawyer of apparently limited moral passion (Howe, 1979, ch. 8; cf. B. Thomas, 1952, p. 143). Even slavery's continued existence could be comfortably rationalized because it was limited to the South where it would eventually die. Lincoln never abandoned this commitment to instrumental reasoning. As he saw it, the only effective way to oppose slavery was to build political coalitions within a Union that stigmatized slavery as evil. Before he entered the White House, he tried to appeal to all Republicans regardless of their positions on issues other than slavery. Later, he pursued political success by joining together with northern Democrats and border state Unionists. During his presidency, he called on all his abilities as a political tactician and strategist to surmount an endless series of crises.

Yet Lincoln was too much of a humanitarian to reject all consummatory reasoning. The same speech that used instrumental arguments against the Liberty party campaign of 1844 conceded the sovereignty of "divine or human law" on those issues where it spoke clearly (Basler, 1953, Vol. II, p. 4). By 1854, chattel slavery had become just such an issue, and Lincoln repeatedly invoked the moral law in his struggle against the Kansas-Nebraska Act. Come what may, he insisted that the Union must adopt "practices and policies" that would both stigmatize slavery as immoral and eventually end it (Basler, 1953, Vol. II, p. 276; cf. p. 54). On this point, he and his party could accept neither compromise nor elaborate calculations about consequences. As he said in his last senatorial debate with Douglas,

> The real issue in this controversy...is the sentiment on the part of one class that looks upon the institution of slavery as a wrong, and of another class that *does not* look upon it *as a wrong*....[That anti-slavery position] is the sentiment of the Republican party. It is the sentiment around which all their actions — all their arguments — circle, from which all their propositions radiate.

What he detested about the Democrats was their doctrine that

> You must not say any thing about...[slavery] in the free States *because it is not here*. You must not say any thing about it in the slave States *because it is there*. You must not say any thing about it in the pulpit, because that is religion and has nothing to do with it. You must not say any thing about it in politics *because that will disturb the security of "my place"* (Johannsen, 1965, pp. 316, 318, Lincoln's emphasis).

At the same time, Lincoln exhibited a Unionist's devotion to social and political institutions — in a way that neither the abolitionists nor conservative Whigs could accept. On one side, he affirmed good citizenship by rejecting separatism in all its forms. Any valid ethic must seek to redeem the American republic as well as particular individuals within it. As a nationalist and a Whig politician, he fervently believed in the importance of social and political institutions. As a boy, he had responded enthusiastically to Parson Weems' portrait of Washington as a national hero. As a young politician, he praised education because it fostered an appreciation of the nation's free institutions (B. Thomas, 1952, p. 15). On economic issues, he believed in using the government to help expand opportunities for individual capitalist enterprise (Howe, 1979, chs. 8, 11).

Sentiment reinforced social vision. At the age of 29, he devoted his remarkable Lyceum address to "the perpetuation of our political institutions." He hoped that "reverence for the laws...becomes the *political religion* of the nation" in order to sustain "the temple of liberty" (Basler, 1953, Vol. I, pp. 108, 112, 115, Lincoln's emphasis). Lincoln shared that feeling with fellow Republicans and anti-slavery Whigs such as John Quincy Adams, William H. Seward and Joshua Giddings (all of whom occupy the middle row of Table A). As Potter points out, Lincoln took from Clay and Webster a romantic, even sentimental, reverence for the Union and its government (Potter, 1976, p. 343). "Our republican robe is soiled and trailed in the dust," he lamented in 1854, after passage of the Kansas-Nebraska Act. "Let us repurify it. Let us turn and wash it white, in the spirit, if not the blood, of the revolution, so...that succeeding millions...shall rise up and call us blessed to the latest generation" (Basler, 1953, Vol. II, p. 276). The Civil War, he so memorably asserted at Gettysburg in 1863, would test "whether any nation" that was "conceived in liberty and dedicated" to democratic principles "could long endure" (cf. B. Thomas, 1952, pp. 268-269; Basler, 1953, Vol. V, p. 424; 1864, Vol. VII, p. 528).

Yet Lincoln's enthusiasm for institutions did not obliterate the belief in individual development that we have already observed. Indeed, competition was an integral feature of his social vision (Basler, 1953, Vol. III, pp. 471ff). Like other Whigs, he believed that the progress and improvement of society and the individual were almost inseparably joined. As he saw it, the collective activities of past and present generations were morally worthy because they were indispensable for the cultivation of individual human reason. In his most interesting discussion of this question in 1859, at the height of the slavery crisis, Lincoln examined the connection between the "habit" of individual ratiocination, that is, "*reflection* and *experiment*," and the most important discoveries and inventions. In this view, the process of rational inquiry is essentially communal. Not only is "the inclination to exchange thoughts with one another...probably an original impulse of our nature," but, especially when language becomes written, it is this exchange — sometimes across generations — that enables "different individuals to...combine their powers of observation and reflection, greatly [facilitating] useful discoveries and inventions....What one observes...he tells to another...[and a] result is thus reached which neither *alone*...would have arrived at" (Basler, 1953, Vol. III, pp. 358-360, Lincoln's emphasis).

This argument casts in a progressive, egalitarian and somewhat pluralistic form the familiar Whig belief in the importance of social and historical development. Anticipating the arguments of late nineteenth-century Pragmatists, Lincoln emphasized the importance of a community of inquiry and practice that depended on both socially established habits and socially shared language. As a number of authors have suggested, Emerson can be seen as a link between the Puritans and the Edwardean focus on nature as God's handiwork and the Pragmatists' philosophic naturalism (Conkin, 1976). So, too, Lincoln represents a link between that same tradition's focus on society and the Pragmatists' pervasive emphasis on community and scientific collaboration.[3]

Here, perhaps, is the most fundamental justification for Lincoln's Unionism. The full exercise and development of human reason requires not the intimacy of a small, morally homogeneous community, but the diversity and freedom of a geographically and temporally extended republican society. The object here was self-improvement for *"every"* individual, but this goal required a republican society large and complex enough to sustain human inquiry and progress.[4] For Lincoln, in sum, there was a symbiotic relationship between individual improvement and the institutional life of the community. Lincoln argued explicitly against secession because the Union had a world historic mission as an exemplary republic, and because an independent South would make slavery permanent. This discussion suggests another compelling reason: secession would cut American society in two and very possibly arrest that society's growth and heterogeneity that was essential for the fullest level of inquiry and self development.

Lincoln's Political Ethic

During the 1850s, many moderate Republicans shared Lincoln's complex position on the questions of individual purity vs. devotion to the Union and consummatory vs. instrumental reasoning. In policy terms, his position was a moderate variant of the "freedom national" doctrine advanced by his fellow Republicans Salmon Chase and Charles Sumner (Sewell, 1976, p. 310; cf. Donald, 1974, p. 227ff. and Foner, 1970, chs. 3 and 4). Slavery, they insisted, should only be sustained by the authority of the states, and never legitimated by the federal government. Lincoln's version — his political humanitarianism — is distinctive primarily because he so carefully articulated both its political and ethical elements, and then fused them into a consistent and viable whole. This feat propelled him to the White House from the relative obscurity of provincial Illinois politics. But the achievement was intellectual as well as political. Or, more precisely, he succeeded politically in part because he succeeded intellectually. In a sentence, he was able both to institutionalize and historicize his ethic, while still retaining its strongly moral content.

At a number of points in his career, Lincoln took actions that sacrificed the welfare of many individuals because they seemed politically necessary. Before the war, as has often been observed, he tolerated (however unhappily) the recapture of individual fugitive slaves. As president he sentenced war deserters to death (although he issued many pardons), imprisoned those who attacked the northern war effort, and exempted from the Emancipation Proclamation the slaves of masters loyal to the Union. Above all, he led the nation into a war in which millions of people suffered (Rogin, 1982). Although Lincoln was troubled and even tormented by these decisions, they were consistent with his basic outlook. According to Lincoln's moral code, he was not required to provide direct or immediate assistance for every individual who merited it on humanitarian grounds. Because his humanitarianism was political rather than personal, his responsibility was to provide that help through political action. His obligation was to further policies directed toward perfecting those social and political *institutions* that would — in turn — help such persons develop their faculties. In 1854, at the beginning of his crusade against the Kansas-Nebraska Act, he denounced the "monstrous injustice of slavery" in part because "it...enables the enemies of free institutions, with plausibility, to taunt us as hypocrites" (Basler, 1953, Vol. II, p. 255). Thus his first goal was not to abolish slavery but to have the regime treat it as a wrong in a way that mattered. The Union must adopt "practices and policies" — notably preventing slavery's further expansion — that would guarantee slavery's ultimate extinction (Basler, 1953, Vol. II, p. 276, cf. p. 54). But this condition required instrumental reasoning. One could be serious about political institutions taking a moral stand against slavery only if one tried to take actions that were politically effective.

This concern with effectiveness was closely related to a second feature of Lincoln's humanitarianism. If one must first secure the moral commitment of the regime and then try to commit its institutions to working for individual improvement, success will be achieved through a temporal process. As we have seen, what mattered most about political institutions was not some immediate result, but their moral stance, i.e., their treatment of slavery as an evil. So, too, what mattered about this process was not its immediate outcome, but the morally relevant *direction* in which it moved. Although delay was acceptable, retrogression was not. Once the political community had morally stigmatized slavery, for example, by barring it from certain territories, any reversal such as the Kansas-Nebraska Act was intolerable. In the same spirit, he insisted in 1863 and 1864 that those slaves freed by the Emancipation Proclamation must never be re-enslaved. A similar "directed" gradualism seems to have shaped his policies on reconstruction.[5]

This complex position had wide appeal among Lincoln's fellow Republicans. On one side, Lincoln appealed to the party's militants by demanding that the federal government stigmatize slavery as a wrong. On the other hand, he appealed politically to northern moderates by embracing the nation's political institutions and calling for gradual progress. But Lincoln's ethic has had lasting importance because it was more than a skillful exercise in political coalition-building. By so firmly embracing humanitarian values he escaped the ethical relativism of Douglas's popular sovereignty, which left slavery's moral status to the decision of the white majority in each state or territory. By insisting on the central place of political institutions that had to operate through a morally directed process over time, he recognized the danger of the moral absolutism, i.e., the arrogance of the self-righteous, against which Lincoln had preached as early as his Temperance Address of 1842. Only by respecting the tolerant and deliberative character of popular and republican institutions could the anti-slavery movement contain its own impulses to unwarranted power that made slavery itself so repulsive. It was this double meshing of moral reform with political understanding that, pace Hofstadter, enabled Lincoln to appeal so powerfully to later reformers like Jane Addams. To be sure, his specific vision of a society of small entrepreneurs failed to anticipate either the structure or the human costs of late nineteenth-century industrial capitalism. But he contributed to humanitarian reform at a much more general level. By making that tradition politically relevant, he provided Addams and her colleagues with an ethic that embraced the institutional and temporal complexities of politics while still maintaining the integrity of its moral commitment.

These considerations do not support a cultural determinism in which Lincoln's thought and practice somehow caused later social reform movements. Such a claim is clearly either false or meaningless. The argument instead is that Lincoln inspired the actions of Addams and her colleagues, in part by offering them a perspective that helped them address the problems of their time. His example provided them with a model to emulate, a cultural resource to use as they pursued their own goals. Much as he insisted that the government must ultimately destroy the institution that had blighted the slaves' opportunities for self-development, so, too, Addams and her colleagues could call on the government to commit itself to individual self-development for even the least privileged members of their urban industrial society. Just as Lincoln joined perfectionist goals to gradualist political tactics, these later reformers could work not for the immediate transformation of society but for steady progress in building a social order that would encourage self-development for all its members. Here, indeed, was a political legacy for the generations that would follow.

Notes

1. Daniel J. Elazar reports that Paul Douglas, perhaps the most prominent liberal reformer in twentieth-century Illinois politics, hung Lincoln's portrait in his office next to those of Jane Addams and John Peter Atgeld, two of his state's most famous progressive social reformers (personal communication).

2. I should like to thank Diana Schaub for making this point to me.

3. I wish to thank David Tracy for making this point clear to me.

4. I am grateful to Gayle McKeen for making this point to me.

5. Lincoln contemplated extending to the ex-slaves some civil rights but not full political or social equality. And he evidently believed that any progress beyond this point required the revival of the South's political institutions (Basler, 1953, Vol. VIII, pp. 402-404). In some ways, it should be added, this position was at least as advanced as that of Garrison himself who (unlike Wendell Phillips) favored dissolving the American Anti-Slavery Society once all the slaves were legally freed. Indeed, Lincoln cannot be included among those laissez faire Republicans who assumed after the war that the problem of the ex-slaves would take care of itself without extensive governmental intervention.

Bibliography

Addams, Jane. (1961). *Twenty Years at Hull House*. New York: New American Library.

Ball, Robin. (1982). "Making Politics Religious and Religion Political: The American Anti-Slavery Society and the Liberty Party." Unpublished Bachelor's Paper, University of Chicago.

Baltzell, E. Digby. (1979). *Puritan Boston and Quaker Philadelphia*. New York: Free Press.

Bartlett, Irving H. (1965). "The Persistence of Wendell Phillips" in Martin Duberman, ed., (1965).

Basler, Roy P., ed. (1953-1955). *The Collected Works of Abraham Lincoln*, 8 vols. New Brunswick, NJ: Rutgers University Press.

Benson, Lee. (1961). *The Concept of Jacksonian Democracy: New York as a Test Case*. Princeton, NJ: Princeton University Press.

Bercovitch, Sacvan. (1975). *Puritan Origins of the American Self*. New Haven, CT: Yale University Press.

—. (1978). *American Jeremiad*. Madison: University of Wisconsin Press.

Birney, James G. (1840). Letter to Myron Holly, Joshua Levitt and Elizur Wright, cited in J.L. Thomas, ed., (1965a), pp. 80-84.

Chapman, John Jay. (1921). *William Lloyd Garrison*. New York: Moffat Yard and Co.

Charnwood, Lord Godfrey. (1916). *Abraham Lincoln*. London: Constable and Co.

Child, Lydia Maria. (1839). *Anti-slavery Catechism*. Newburyport, MA: C. Whipple. Reprinted in J.L. Thomas, ed., (1965a), pp. 63-69.

Colton, Avery, ed. (1857). *The Works of Henry Clay*. New York: A.S. Barnes and Burr.

Conkin, Paul K. (1968). *Puritans and Pragmatists: Eight Eminent American Thinkers*. Bloomington, IN: Indiana University Press.

Converse, Philip E. (1964). "The Nature of Belief Systems in Mass Publics" in David E. Apter, ed., *Ideology and Discontent*. New York: The Free Press of Glencoe.

Craven, Avery. (1971). *The Coming of the Civil War*, 2nd ed. Chicago: University of Chicago Press.

Davis, David Brion. (1975). *The Problem of Slavery in the Age of Revolution: 1770-1823*. Ithaca, NY: Cornell University Press.

—. (1966). *The Problem of Slavery in Western Culture.* Ithaca, NY: Cornell University Press.

Donald, David. (1974). *Charles Sumner and the Coming of the Civil War.* New York: Knopf.

Douglass, Frederick. (1855). "The Anti-slavery Movement" in B. Thomas, (1965a), pp. 126-131.

Duberman, Martin, ed. (1965). *The Anti-slavery Vanguard: New Essays on the Abolitionists.* Princeton, NJ: Princeton University Press.

Elazar, Daniel J. (1970). *Cities of the Prairie.* New York: Basic Books.

Fehrenbacher, Don E. (1962). *Prelude to Greatness: Lincoln in the 1850s.* Stanford, CA: Stanford University Press.

Filler, Louis, ed. (1965). *Wendell Phillips on Civil Rights and Freedom.* New York: Hill and Wang.

Foner, Philip S. (1950). *The Life and Writings of Frederick Douglass,* 4 vols. New York: International Publishers.

—. (1970). *Free Soil, Free Labor, Free Men: The Ideology of the Republican Party before the Civil War.* London: Oxford University Press.

Forgie, George B. (1979). *Patricide in the House Divided: A Psychological Interpretation of Lincoln and His Age.* New York: W.W. Norton.

Frederickson, George M., ed. (1968). *William Lloyd Garrison: Great Lives Observed.* Englewood Cliffs, NJ: Prentice-Hall.

Friedman, Lawrence J. (1982). *Gregarious Saints: Self and Community in American Abolitionism 1830-1870.* Cambridge: Cambridge University Press.

Garrison, William Lloyd. (2/12/1830). "Henry Clay's Colonization Address" in *Genius of Universal Emancipation.* Reprinted in J.L. Thomas, ed., (1965a), pp. 6-7.

—. (1/1/1831). "Opening Statement of the First Issue," *Liberator.* Reprinted in Frederickson, ed., (1968), pp. 22-23.

—. (12/15/1837). "No Union with Slave-Holders," *Liberator.* Reprinted in J.L. Thomas, ed., (1965a), pp. 76-79.

—. (3/26/1852). "Review of Uncle Tom's Cabin," *Liberator.* Reprinted in Frederickson, ed., (1968), pp. 56-58.

Genovese, Eugene D. (1965). *The Political Economy of Slavery: Studies in the Economy and Society of the Slave South.* New York: Pantheon.

Geertz, Clifford. (1973). "Ideology of Cultural Systems" in *The Inter-pretation of Cultures*. New York: Basic Books.

Gramsci, Antonia. (1971). *Selections from the Prison Notebooks*. New York: International Publishers.

Greenstone, J. David. (1979). "Dorothea Dix and Jane Addams: From Transcendentalism to Pragmatism in American Social Reform," *Social Service Review*, Vol. 53, pp. 527-559.

—. (1982). "The Transient and the Permanent in American Politics: Standards, Interests, and the Concept of 'Public'" in J. David Greenstone, ed., *Public Values and Private Power in American Politics*. Chicago: University of Chicago Press.

—. (1982 draft). "Was Lincoln Really the Great Emancipator?" University of Chicago.

Hartz, Louis. (1955). *The Liberal Tradition in America*. New York: Harcourt, Brace and Co.

Heimert, Alan. (1966). *Religion and the American Mind: From the Great Awakening to the Revolution*. Cambridge, MA: Harvard University Press.

Hofstadter, Richard. (1948). *The American Political Tradition*. New York: Vintage Books.

Holt, Michael F. (1978). *The Political Crisis of the 1850s*. New York: John Wiley and Sons.

Howe, Daniel Walker. (1979). *The Political Culture of the American Whigs*. Chicago: University of Chicago Press.

Jaffa, Harry V. (1959). *Crisis of the House Divided: An Interpretation of the Lincoln-Douglas Debates*. Seattle: University of Washington Press.

—. (1965). *Equality and Liberty: Theory and Practice in American Politics*. New York: Oxford University Press.

Jefferson, Thomas. (1820). "Letter to John Holmes." Reprinted in Koch and Peden, eds., (1944).

Johannsen, Robert W. (1965). *The Lincoln-Douglas Debates*. New York: Oxford University Press.

Jones, Henry C. (1927). "Abraham Lincoln's Attitude Toward Education" in *Iowa Law Review*, Vol. 12, No. 4 (June).

Kammen, Michael. (1972). *People of Paradox*. New York: Alfred A. Knopf.

Koch, Adrienne and Peden, William, eds. (1944). *The Life and Selected Writings of Thomas Jefferson*. New York: Random House.

Maccia, George S. (1962-1963). "Lincoln and the Morrill Act," *The Educational Forum*, Vol. XXVII, (November), pp. 35-46.

Martineau, Harriet. (1835). "An English Radical Describes a Meeting with Garrison" in Frederickson, ed., (1968), pp. 116-118.

Massachusetts Anti-Slavery Society. (1844). "Twelfth Annual Report" in J.L. Thomas, ed., (1965a), pp. 87-93.

Messerli, Jonathan. (1972). *Horace Mann: A Biography*. New York: Alfred A. Knopf.

Miller, Perry. ((1956a). "Errand into the Wilderness" in *Errand into the Wilderness*. New York: Harper and Row.

—. (1956b). "The Marrow of Puritan Divinity" in *Errand into the Wilderness*. New York: Harper and Row.

—. (1961a). *The New England Mind: The Seventeenth Century*. Boston: Beacon Press.

—. (1961b). *The New England Mind: From Colony to Province*. Boston: Beacon Press.

—. (1970). *Roger Williams: His Contribution to the American Tradition*. New York: Atheneum.

Moore, Barrington. (1966). *Social Origins of Dictatorship and Democracy: Landlord and Peasant in the Making of the Modern World*. Boston: Beacon Press.

Morgan, Edmund S. (1965). *Visible Saints: The History of the Puritan Idea*. Ithaca and London: Cornell University Press.

National Liberty Party Convention. (1843). "Emancipation Extra, Tract Number 1" in J.L. Thomas, ed., (1965a), pp. 94-98.

Oates, Stephen B. (1977). *With Malice Toward None: The Life of Abraham Lincoln*. New York: New American Library.

Perry, Lewis. (1973). *Radical Abolitionism: Anarchy and the Government of God in Anti-slavery Thought*. Ithaca, NY: Cornell University Press.

Pocock, J.G.A. (1975). *The Machiavellian Moment*. Princeton: Princeton University Press.

Potter, David M. (1976). *The Impending Crisis 1848-1861*. New York: Harper and Row.

Provenzo, Eugene F. (1982). "Lincoln and Education," *Educational Studies*, Vol. 13, No. 1, Summer, pp. 190-202.

Rogin, Michael. (1982). "The King's Two Bodies: Lincoln, Wilson, Nixon, and Presidential Self-Sacrifice" in Greenstone, ed., (1982), pp. 71-108.

Sewell, Richard H. (1976). *Ballots for Freedom: Anti-slavery Politics in the United States, 1837-1860.* New York: Oxford University Press.

Stampp, Kenneth M. (1959). *The Causes of the Civil War.* Englewood Cliffs, NJ: Prentice-Hall.

Stewart, James B. (1970). *Joshua Giddings and the Tactics of Radical Politics.* Cleveland: Case Western Reserve University Press.

Thomas, Benjamin P. (1952). *Abraham Lincoln.* New York: Alfred A. Knopf.

Thomas, John L. (1963). "The Liberator: William Lloyd Garrison" in Frederickson, ed. (1968), pp. 164-170.

—. ed. (1965a). *Slavery Attacked: The Abolitionist Crusade.* Englewood Cliffs, NJ: Prentice-Hall.

—. (1965b). "Anti-Slavery and Utopia" in Duberman, ed. (1965), pp. 240-269.

Walters, Ronald G. (1976). *The Anti-Slavery Appeal: American Abolitionism after 1830.* Baltimore: Johns Hopkins University Press.

Walzer, Michael. (1965). *The Revolution of the Saints: A Study in the Origins of Radical Politics.* Cambridge, MA: Harvard University Press.

Warner, W. Lloyd. (1961). "The Cult of the Dead" in *The Family of God.* New Haven, CT: Yale University Press, pp. 216-259.

Weber, Max. (1958). *From Max Weber: Essays in Sociology.* H.H. Gerth and C. Wright Mills, eds. New York: Oxford University Press.

Webster, Daniel. (1860). "The Constitution and the Union" ("Seventh of March" speech) in *Works.* Boston: Little Brown, Vol. V, p. 332.

Wilson, Major L. (1974). *Space, Time and Freedom: The Quest for Nationality and the Irrepressible Conflict, 1815-1861.* Westport, CT: Greenwood Press.

Wright, Elizur, Jr. (1833). *The Sin of Slavery,* Ch. 5. Reprinted in J.L. Thomas, ed., (1965a), pp. 11-17.

Wyatt-Brown, Bertram. (1971). *Lewis Tappan and the Evangelical War Against Slavery.* New York: Atheneum.

WHERE HAVE ALL THE LEADERS GONE? RULING ELITES AND REVOLUTION SINCE WORLD WAR II

Steven L. Spiegel

At the death of Franklin Delano Roosevelt, Walter Lippmann wrote:

> The final test of a leader is that he leaves behind him in other men the conviction and the will to carry on....The genius of a good leader is to leave behind him a situation which common sense, without the grace of genius, can deal with successfully.[1]

The American Revolution as a Contemporary Model

George Washington was not only such a leader, but he possessed the ability both to inspire his forces in revolution and to guide his people with a sense of principle and purpose once that revolution had been won. Thus, on July 2, 1776, he told his troops:

> Let us therefore animate and encourage each other, and show the whole world that a Freeman, contending for liberty on his own ground, is superior to any slavish mercenary on earth.[2]

Having succeeded in the War of Independence, he was telling his fellow Americans in his First Inaugural Address on April 30, 1789:

> The preservation of the sacred fire of liberty, and the destiny of the republican model of government, are justly considered as deeply, perhaps as finally staked, on the experiment entrusted to the hands of the American people.[3]

The same Washington who could speak in terms of an American mission was also the President who in his farewell address cautioned his countrymen against the dangers of emotional attachment to any foreign power lest it impede the pursuit of the

227

national interest — an unabashed reliance on *realpolitik* rarely present in the annals of the conduct of U.S. foreign policy. "It is our true policy to steer clear of permanent alliance with any portion of the foreign world."[4]

Washington was a revolutionary leader in the sense that he successfully guided his society from colonial dependence to sovereign rule, but he was a successful leader because he, like the other Founding Fathers, was able to make the transition from revolt to constructive formation of a new polity.

As has often been pointed out, the American Revolution was not a social revolution in the pattern of the French, Russian or Chinese Revolutions, but primarily a conflict over who would have the right to rule the thirteen colonies. It is this distinction by which the American model should be judged when applying it to the modern era. Any revolution must be evaluated by its objectives, its scope, its means, and its principles. A revolution may be aimed at freeing a society from the yoke of foreign rule, as the American Revolution was and several revolutions in the Third World since World War II have been. To the extent that it is limited to ousting a foreign ruler, the level of violence in a revolution may well be relatively restrained, as we see in such cases as the British in India or the French in Morocco, especially when the foreign ruler is willing to accept constraints. But revolutions today are more often directed not at foreign intruders but at indigenous rulers who are seen as illegitimate or oppressive. Unless they are immediately successful, these revolutions often result in chaos or serious violence, frequently leading to civil war as in Spain, China, Russia, France, and ultimately in India and Ireland. As hostilities become more sweeping, the ideas for which each side stands assume a dynamic which exacerbates divisions.

In the current era these conflicts over ideas, often rooted in class distinctions, are frequently overladen with ethnic, racial and religious tensions — witness such disparate countries as Indonesia, Cambodia, Malaysia, Zimbabwe, and Iran — adding to the ferocity and lasting bitterness and resulting in massive deaths or exile or both.

The leadership of any struggle is responsible for the conduct of the revolution and ultimately for its success or failure. Here the Washington model is indeed applicable, for the combination of principle, purpose, and pragmatism is a unique set of qualities that has only rarely been repeated. It is often forgotten by critics who disparage the revolutionary content of the American uprising that it was the wisdom and unusually high quality of its leadership which enabled American society to navigate successfully the transition from colony to nation. If the transition appears facile in retrospect, it is in large measure because instead of a Robespierre there was a Jefferson; instead of a Trotsky, a Madison. The Founding Fathers were able to combine philosophy and practice in a way that made the evolution of the new United States of America appear natural because of the skill they demonstrated in molding the new society.

In his First Inaugural Address, Jefferson demonstrated the ease with which the early leaders had meshed practice and philosophy. In a political version of "honesty is the best policy," Jefferson suggested that liberty is the most secure approach to government. After discussing the freedoms guaranteed by the new society, he added, "should we wander from them in moments of error or alarm, let us hasten to retrace our steps and to regain the road which alone leads to peace, liberty, and safety."[5]

No leader can be completely successful without a touch of revolution, without offering his countrymen a new order and a new philosophy, while also demonstrating his capacity to address pragmatically the policy issues of the day he confronts. The dearth of successful leadership in the current era is testimony to the difficulty of the task. It is striking that the failures have occurred equally among the industrialized and the newly independent states — although the tasks faced by each are certainly divergent. We propose to review recent leadership trends in the West and revolutions in the South, before moving to examine the new world leadership and revolution in the East.

The West: Craving for Revolutionary Leadership

In the industrialized countries few contemporary leaders have demonstrated an ability to inspire a populus to action on behalf of particular principles while also conducting day-to-day governmental affairs. Churchill, Roosevelt, and de Gaulle — all of whom rose to power in crisis — stand as rare giants. Churchill not only stood for opposition to tyranny and totalitarianism, even if that meant resorting to military force, but when the ultimate test came, he proved able to lead his nation in war. Roosevelt gained office in a period of economic depression and then presided over the development of a new philosophy of American government.

The process later repeated itself in foreign policy as the President skillfully but painfully guided the American people out of isolation and through the greatest war in U.S. history. Charles de Gaulle stood for a new unity of purpose for a French nation torn by division abroad and ineffectual government at home, but the principle was converted into practice when he effectively maneuvered the French departure from Algeria, established a stable government in the Fifth Republic which continues secure more than twenty years after he left office, and provided a previously declining European state with a dynamic new role in world affairs. Like the achievements of the Founding Fathers, leadership effectively exercised appears inconsequential if not inevitable in retrospect. But to gauge the scope of the achievement in each case, we can only compare these men to the failing record of their predecessors — Chamberlain, Hoover, and the "revolving door" prime ministers of the Fourth Republic.

By contrast, the current period is marked by leaders who are unable to convert principle into practice either because they lack the expertise to deal with successive social, economic and foreign crises, or because they are unable to inspire their electorate with a vision of where they are heading, or because they are unable to do either.

The last twenty years have been particularly instructive. In the early and mid-1970s, with the energy crisis and worldwide economic recession, Western electorates turned to pragmatic leaders, men and women who offered mastery of techniques and detail, "can-do" politicians who claimed they could master the fine points of difficult problems confronting their countries. Thus, Callahan in Britain, Giscard d'Estaing in France, Helmut Schmidt in West Germany, Yitzhak Rabin in Israel, Jimmy Carter in the United States all offered expertise and efficiency to electorates starved for answers to complex technical problems.

However, none of these leaders inspired a vision of where their country was heading or how they would deal with the economic and political dilemmas of current politics. All they offered was problem-solving techniques, and when unemployment, inflation and international crises grew worse, their *raison d'etre* in the eyes of their voters disappeared. Since the technocrats' appeal depended upon a continued reputation for competence and highly proficient performance, when major problems developed, they were particularly vulnerable because they had no alternative argument with which to claim a right to continue in power. Typical of the problem was Jimmy Carter's litany of the difficulties in resolving any single issue.

Since the election of Menachem Begin as Israel's Prime Minister in 1977, we have frequently witnessed the emergence of a new breed of leaders who speak to the deeply held values and faith of individual societies. In an era when the novel fails to tell a story, music has no melody, and art does not convey a picture, the electorate seeks purpose from the politician. In a period when traditional roots have been broken and television focuses on personality and only the broadest of themes, the man of belief and ideas — no matter what his ideology — seems to triumph over the man of practice. Thatcher in Britain; Reagan in America; Mitterand in France; Gonzalez in Spain; Papandreou in Greece; Hawke in Australia all share with Begin an approach rooted in a sweeping program which claims to be applicable to many levels of foreign and domestic policy. Each has understood that to be elected and to govern in the 1980s demanded the continuing assertion of a global vision. Simply put, in the 1980s the ideologue frequently triumphed over the technocrat in Western countries.

The advantage of the visionary leader is that he does not base his own legitimacy on competence or immediate results. Thereby, his own expectations and those of his followers are not as high as the standard of the technocrat, and the failure of at least some of his programs does not necessarily lead to his defeat. He can actually substitute inspiration for achievement, even if his "position in the polls" drops temporarily. When people pessimistically conclude that no one can resolve the terrible contradictions societies confront, they will opt for leaders who offer a different approach entirely: faith and aspiration instead of detailed accomplishment.

Yet there is also considerable danger in this type of leadership. Because of the importance of inspiration in the standing of these leaders and because small defeats are likely to be excused, the leeway they are given can have disastrous consequences. The Iran-Contra affair under Reagan, the Lebanon War under Begin, the widespread scandals under Papandreou, the severe economic crisis of confidence in France in the mid-1980s are all part of the same parcel: a grand vision will not be discredited until it fails spectacularly. Even then, as in the cases of Reagan and Mitterand, the leader may be able to recoup. Begin clearly could have if he had had the willingness to do so. Papandreou almost did.

Begin was the epitome of the new style — the first to be elected

231

and re-elected and the first to leave office. The peace treaty with Egypt, the defense of the Christian Lebanese, the vigorous assertion of Jewish rights in the wake of the Holocaust, and the decades-old conflict with the Arabs all appealed to a sense of renewed Jewish destiny. By contrast, Begin's opponent, Shimon Peres, seemed to represent an outdated style of leadership in his pragmatism and his timid conduct of the 1977 and 1981 election campaigns. It was a style that could not overcome Begin's dynamism.

Begin was also typical of the new leaders because he was far less popular abroad than at home. This characteristic of the new order is not surprising because the new style demands an attempt to speak to the fundamental values and mores which govern a particular civil society. By appealing to the deep yearning of his own people, the new leader will frequently disappoint and confuse other statesmen and foreign elites. Simply put, technocrats tend to be more universalistic; visionaries more particularistic.

In the case of Begin, the phenomenon was most acute, making the contrast between his position at home and abroad stark for several reasons. Begin ruled the smallest country of those conforming to the pattern, but one that is constantly under the microscope of the world's press and media. He was also the most intense of these leaders — in personality and ideology. Leaders like Thatcher, Reagan and Mitterand also speak in terms of national revival, but because of Israel's size and insecurity, Begin's assertions appeared more shrill and defiant than the others who lead larger, more secure, and diverse nations. Furthermore, foreign policy was more central to Begin's ideology, whereas the others concentrated relatively more attention on their own societies, thereby deflecting the effect of their positions on other countries.

If the latter years of Begin's political career became an ironic model for other political developments in the West, they may also constitute a prophecy of the future. The visionary leader presents himself as the head of a movement. Even after he has bequeathed office to a less charismatic successor, his party may be deceptively difficult to unseat, no matter how unsuccessful its program may appear, especially abroad. People are likely to be reluctant to turn to the opposition if it seems to represent a technocratic politics as usual. Thus, Ronald Reagan's popularity helped George Bush to gain the presidency in 1988 over the technician Michael Dukakis. Thus, by 1984, Begin's policies had left Israel with the most acute economic crisis in its short history and with a severe political-military dilemma created by the disastrous invasion of Lebanon.

Yet, Peres could still not muster a clear mandate, finally settling for a tenuous government of "national unity." In 1988, the second "national unity" government was formed without a rotating Prime Minister. Shamir was its chief, with Peres relegated to Finance Minister and Deputy Prime Minister.

Of course, if the opposition gains a new visionary leadership of its own or if the leadership in power leaves widespread disillusionment throughout society, then the prognosis for the continued success of the government in power will be negative. The failure of Papandreou is a dramatic case in point, although given the widespread corruption in his government and the severe economic distress of the country, it might have been surprising how close he came to retaining power. We learn from the "Begin revolution" in Israel and the "Reagan revolution" in the United States that once a new vision takes hold, it will be slow to dissipate, at least without a crisis.

If the Israeli election of 1977 was instructive of a new trend, the 1983 German election and the subsequent survival of Helmut Kohl would appear to move in a different direction. Actually, however, the German results are instructive of how a technocratic leader can succeed. Helmut Schmidt was the archetype and the most successful of the 1970s-style technocratic leaders. He was finally brought down after eight years in power by the combination of a declining economy and a growing ideological ferment within his own party with which he was not in sinc. Kohl won because his opponents had moved further to the left than the national consensus while offering unexciting leadership. Based on the lessons of the 1970s, the continued ideological ferment of the Social Democrats and the entry of the Greens into Parliament at first offered danger signals for Germany's new leadership. Since Kohl is largely a political manipulator (a particular form of the technocratic leader), he was held to high standards of performance in such areas as the economy and relations with the U.S. If he had come to be widely viewed as unsuccessful and if the Social Democrats produced a dynamic leader, the conservative government could have been in real danger of defeat and still could be in the 1990s. The key test will be Kohl's ability to adapt to the new opportunities and challenges offered by the changes in East Europe and the prospects of German unification. Kohl's manipulative adaptability may serve him well in this delicate period.

Western industrial societies today are likely to waver between technocratic and visionary leadership as events, particular problems, and personalities vary. Just as there was a trend in the 1970s toward the first, the 1980s were more distinctive of the second. Whatever the pattern, recent events in the politics of industrialized societies confirm again what every revolution teaches us: the overarching importance of leadership in the conduct of political affairs. No matter how intricate party or parliamentary structures may be in particular countries, the President or the Prime Minister or the Premier or the Chancellor sets the tone of the national debate and selects the key figures in the cabinet or the White House who assist in running the government. No matter how entrenched and powerful the permanent bureaucracy, this leadership makes critical decisions of policy and accounts for changes when new directions occur. No matter how compelling external challenges or internal crises, it is the particular set of leaders in power who must deal with the issues at hand. We can never be sure that another group of leaders would have reacted similarly; indeed, the weight of logic suggests otherwise.

It is often argued in almost deterministic terms that leaders have little influence over events because of the highly structured nature of contemporary institutions and the complexity of modern societies. Actually, this complexity has the opposite effect; since other groups and influences stalemate each other, there is often latitude for the leadership elite (i.e., the key figure and those immediately around him) to influence events heavily. A few dramatic examples from the recent past include the following: Johnson's decision to enter the Vietnam War and his Great Society programs; Nixon's move towards China and Watergate; de Gaulle's exit from Algeria and move towards the Arabs and away from Israel; Brandt's *Ostpolitik*; the support by King Carlos for democracy in Spain; Begin's willingness to withdraw from the Sinai totally and his declared intention to keep the West Bank; Thatcher's move in the Falklands and in her conservative approach to the British economy; Reaganomics; Mitterand's program of nationalization; Papandreou's suspicion of the United States; Nakasone's declared interest in an expanded Japanese military. These examples are especially dramatic cases, but in hosts of often ignored ways (e.g., the appointment of U.S. Supreme Court Justices) particular individuals at the head of any government make a critical difference in the conduct of politics and policies in their own societies which often last for years after they have left office.

However supportive the party or the coalition behind the President or the Prime Minister and his entourage may be, it is questionable in each case whether the same policies would have been pursued by other politicians had they been elected — even from the same party. Whatever the internal and external constraints on the team at the top — and they are always profound — decision-makers, even in highly institutionalized, industrialized societies, establish patterns, set trends, and, of course, act in crises that determine the direction in which their societies move. Even leaders who are unable to enunciate an ideology, a vision, or a set of principles and then put them into effective practice affect their societies by their failure.

The South: A Craving for Normalcy?

If under modern conditions this conclusion applies to the West, it certainly pertains more directly to the developing countries. Because of the large number of states emerging from colonial rule since World War II, much attention has been focused on the "revolutionary leader" who often symbolizes the aims and politics of the new era not only in the Western media, but in his own society as well. As Henry Kissinger has written, "The type of individual who leads a struggle for independence has been sustained in the risks and suffering of such a cause primarily by a commitment to a vision which enabled him to override conditions which had seemed overwhelmingly hostile. Revolutions are rarely initiated primarily by material considerations...."[6]

The "cult of personality" is typical of revolutionary eras as suggested by such names as Washington, Bolivar, Lenin, Mao, Gandhi and Khomeini. In reviewing the record of many of these revolutions, it is often doubtful whether they would have progressed similarly and with analogous results if these particular leaders and their associates had not been at the helm. Afterward, as in the United States, they are critical to creating national myths and mores which are often long followed.

Although revolutions in the post-1945 period have generally been of two types — struggles for independence against colonial regimes and revolutions which occur against an indigenous government — one revolutionary movement, represented by the Palestine Liberation Organization, has epitomized a third type. The PLO has sought to reverse a historical pattern by — in its stated aim — displacing the people present in one area in favor of another group. They have claimed to act on behalf of the rightful inhabitants of the territory of Palestine. This land-based orientation to revolutionary objectives represents the ultimate reversal of the American model. The Founding Fathers had sought to overthrow a colonial rule which had become burdensome by resorting to force of arms. They were fighting against an external party using mercenaries; neither side employed terror. In addition, the colonists fought in the name of a set of principles which propounded a new form of government. The PLO has been the reverse: it employed mercenaries and terror, operated from outside the territory in dispute, and the land itself — rather than a set of political principles — has become the focus of its objectives. Indeed, it has set out to wage war, not revolution, against Israel.

It is instructive of the role of successful revolutions that the Palestinians only began to achieve a measure of success after their spontaneous uprising on the West Bank and Gaza Strip. The intifada was more consistent with classic patterns in its claim to displace the Israelis as occupiers and not to challenge their existence. Its soldiers were now the populace of the West Bank and Gaza Strip, and not outsiders.

Similarly, all other revolutions in the modern era have been focused internally. In the violent conflicts for independence the form of government followed was determined by the ideology of the leadership group conducting the revolution, as in the Communism around Ho Chi Minh in Vietnam, the Marxism of the FLN around Ben Bella in Algeria, the capitalist/democratic thrust around Kenyatta in Kenya, and the socialist/democratic thrust around Nehru in India. In all of these situations the ideology of the new regime was peripheral to the force of nationalism. New institutions emerged only after independence. There was nothing inevitable about China or Vietnam becoming Communist (as the existence of alternative governments in Taiwan and South Vietnam confirmed). India and Kenya could have developed alternate types of governments (as Indira Gandhi's "Emergency" and Kenya's sorry descent into one-party rule suggest). The attainment of Namibian independence and the continued struggle of the African National Congress against the apartheid regime of South Africa are the latest examples of Third World struggles for self-determination. In each case where independence initially occurred, the new leadership — obviously affected by internal economic and political conditions — took the country in a particular direction which might have been different had another group captured the independence movement. In this sense the American revolutionary model of leadership has had continued applicability.

In the majority of countries, however, independence did not occur after an extended period of violence, a guerrilla campaign, or war. In many countries the colonial power left voluntarily, as in the Philippines, many states in Africa, and in the Middle East. In these cases the colonial power may have had greater influence over the initial rulers or the procedures by which they were chosen. In some cases these rulers or elites remained in power over extended periods, as in Jordan, Senegal, Guinea, Tanzania, the Ivory Coast, and Zambia. Despite these cases, whenever and however independence occurred in the Third World and however long it had previously existed, many countries have been affected by another round (often rounds) of revolution — the product of instability, poverty, population growth, corruption, and often sheer chaos.

It is actually these revolutions which have become distinctive of the current era in the Third World, and these later revolutions have been of a variety of types: many have simply been a succession of coups — one dictator replacing another in dizzying succession (Bolivia, Ghana, Syria before Assad). The military has been the most frequent base of revolutionary ferment in many contexts. Several regimes have been overthrown by army officers who offered new stability and a reformed polity and society (Egypt and Turkey), safety from Marxism (Indonesia and Chile), a more radical direction (Iraq, Libya, Ethiopia). Other revolutions — usually with a radical or Communist orientation — have occurred as a consequence of guerrilla campaigns (China, Yugoslavia, Cuba, Nicaragua). In Africa, tribal and ethnic differences and rival claims to equality or superiority is the basis of much of the turmoil in such areas as Zimbabwe, Ethiopia, the Sudan, Mozambique, and Angola; the attempt of the Ibos to secede from Nigeria and form Biafra was similarly rooted. We are reminded that these types of ethnic-based revolutions are not limited to Africa by such conflicts as the Tamil rebellion in Sri Lanka, the Kurdish rebellion — particularly active in Iraq, and the Kashmiri and Punjab protests in India. Finally, Iran represents a religion-based, fundamentalist revolution which seeks to alter the direction and orientation of its own and that of neighboring societies to a pure form of Islam, away from what it perceives as the corrupting influences of the West. Another revolution in neighboring Afghanistan against Soviet occupation and later a Soviet-backed government is also led by several Islamic fundamentalist groups.

As suggested by these cases, the American Revolution has become progressively irrelevant as a model for the succession of upheavals that have occurred throughout the Third World. The move to rid a country of its colonial yoke gave the American experience an affinity (often superficial) to foreign developments as diverse as Ireland, Algeria, India, Rhodesia (Zimbabwe), Namibia, and Indonesia. It is difficult to draw even the vaguest analogies with the types of changes which now regularly occur within Third World states.

Similarly, the leadership in many of these countries bears progressively less relationship to the American model. If the U.S. was founded by men who brought a combination of pragmatism and principle to their work, the first generation of leaders in many areas of the Third World seemed to be potentially following in their footsteps: names like Gandhi and Nehru, Sukarno, Nkrumah, Senghor, Kuanda, Ho Chi Minh, and Mugabe seemed then and some even seem now to be the Washingtons and Jeffersons of their societies. Each in his own way seemed to offer not only a dynamism, fervor, and inspiration associated with revolutionary leadership, but also to represent a set of principles peculiarly rooted in the demands and needs of his own people.

In the revolutions that have followed, many of the new movements have appeared (at least at first and at least to many Western intellectuals) to be similarly based. Many leaders have acquired an aura which has led them to be worshipped or despised both within and without their own countries — names like Nasser, Khadafi, Tito, Castro, Mao, and Khomeini have become identified with the politics of the age. Each is certainly the first new leader following a revolution, and each remained in power over an extended period of time.

Yet, analogies to the American Revolution seem hardly applicable, not only in image but in practice as well. It is distinctive of contemporary revolutionaries that of all those who have been mentioned in the course of this essay, only one, Leopold Senghor of Senegal, left office voluntarily before his death, and only after twenty years of rule. The precedent which Washington set of two terms of constitutionally elected government followed by voluntary retirement is totally missing from the current revolutionary record.

The American Revolution not only offered high quality leadership, but a large number of capable contributors to the new political experiment. It was Washington's eminent replaceability that serves as one of the distinguishing features of the American experience. The reliance on one man or a small clique around him is one of the prime tragedies of contemporary failures. Few, if any, contemporary leaders can in any sense be regarded as the George Washington of their countries, and even more states lack the Hamiltons, Burrs, Adams, Jeffersons, and Madisons to surround them. Revolution around personalities means that when the leader is removed, killed, or dies, his replacement will not be immediately apparent or logical unless he is able to gain and maintain power by resort to the use or threat of force. Not surprisingly, therefore, one of the critical tests of a successful revolution is the ability to institutionalize success past the first generation, as has occurred in very different contexts in both China and India. However, even in these cases the revolution did not succeed by following the inspiration or visionary content of the original model as symbolized by the rejection of non-violence in India and of the Cultural Revolution and Mao's philosophy of government in China.

The successor generations where revolutions have continued have presided over a thirsting for normalcy, as reflected in the increasing bureaucratization and colorless nature of the leadership of countries which had initially burst on the international scene boasting revolutionary idealism and activism, as in Egypt, Yugoslavia, Indonesia, Algeria, Vietnam, and even China.

Political instability and increasing economic failure have often led to more cautious leaders preoccupied largely with perpetuating their own rule. Indeed, in the 1980s developments within many Third World states where revolution occurred or independence was attained was the exact opposite of what was happening in the industrial states. The attraction of a visionary or an ideologue to the citizenry of the West in the 1980s was generally not matched in developing countries, where progressively the bureaucrat, the technocrat and, above all, the survivor ruled.

Certainly, the founding generation cannot continue indefinitely in office; in the United States, Martin Van Buren and John Tyler were not George Washington and Thomas Jefferson. What is striking in much of the Third World is how quickly bureaucratic leadership has taken charge — especially when it in turn has often been brought to power by coup or palace revolts. We see this pattern in such countries as Indonesia, Ghana, Yugoslavia, China, Vietnam, Kenya, and Algeria. The replacements for Sukarno, Nkrumah, Tito, Mao, Ho Chi Minh, Kenyatta, and Ben Bella have in each case lacked the revolutionary dynamism of the first generation, however long the first or second wave of leadership lasted in each country.

Egypt is a model of this progression. The first leader of the revolution, Nasser, sought to change the economic basis of the society internally and in foreign policy to forge a new dynamic role for his country as the leader of the Arab states. Egypt was unusual in that its second leader, Anwar Sadat, also served as a dynamic figure by pursuing an activist approach, changing the fundamental policies of his predecessor in both the domestic and foreign arenas. Sadat's successor, Hosni Mubarak, is more typical of leadership elsewhere in the Third World in his heavy reliance on bureaucratic modes. Egypt is still unusual in the orderly succession that has occurred since the original revolution in 1952, especially given the critical internal problems the regime faces.

Thus, whereas in the "North" the preference today is more and more frequently for the charismatic ideologue who projects a vision or a philosophy of the future and then tries in office to keep the vision alive, the inspiration of independence and revolution has progressively given way in the "South" to an arena of pragmatism which is directed almost solely simply to maintaining the reins of power no matter how depressed the internal economy may become. By the end of his life, Anwar Sadat was more popular in the West than at home, reflecting the contrasting appeals in North and South. If the Reagans, the Thatchers, and the Mitterands are some of the successful leaders in the North, by comparison the Suhartos, the Mobutus, the Saddam Husseins, and the Assads symbolize the new phase in the South. No conclusion could confirm more thoroughly the tragedy of what is happening in the Third World.

There were some exceptions to this sorry record of democratic decline, especially in Latin America, in the 1980s. The military returned to the barracks in such countries as Argentina, Brazil, Chile, Uruguay, and Bolivia. With the exception of Chile, severe economic problems have remained to promote social and political fragility. The shaky experiments in democratic rule in the Philippines, Pakistan, and Turkey are further examples of inherent instability in the new movements. There is no American model here. In each case significant political and social forces threaten the survival of the new regimes. None are certain to last until the turn of the century. Few of the conditions which created the success of the American revolution — commitment to peaceful change; social cohesion; a base of economic stability; democratic political culture; wise and creative leadership — are present. We can hope that democracy may take hold in many of these countries, but we cannot look to events in North America two hundred years ago for guidance.

This conclusion is not universal. That the American model can apply to countries in the twentieth century — although only in the most restricted and unusual of cases — is reflected in the Israeli experience. Here was a revolt against the same outside colonial power, the British, as in the thirteen colonies. Here, too, a particularly dynamic group of Founding Fathers remained in office over an extended period of time, while an elite of dynamic figures (many in conflict with each other) contributed to a rich combination of inspiring political philosophy and healthy pragmatism. Here, too, leaders have left office voluntarily and as a consequence of an orderly and democratic transfer of power. The conflict with the Arabs notwithstanding, unlike most other countries of the modern era, the analogy can at least be made with the American Revolution.

The East: A Craving for Democracy?

Whatever the complex trends of revolution and leadership in the West and South, it is the East which has recently provided the most fascinating potential examples of the American Revolution as a contemporary model. Unquestionably, Mikhail Gorbachev is the most important leader in the world today, the one leader whose actions have had the greatest impact on his own country's political evolution, on the fate of other nations, and on changes in the international system. Because of Gorbachev, the USSR has begun to experience the first signs of democratic government, the halting beginning of economic reform, the attempt to break down the stultifying chokehold of bureaucracy over society, and moves toward autonomy for individual peoples. Thanks to Gorbachev, the democratic movement in Eastern Europe has been possible, the Soviet role in the Third World been reduced, the acceptance of the USSR as a respectable member of the family of nations been enhanced in the West. Certainly, economic stagnation and a yearning for greater openness existed in the USSR before

Gorbachev assumed power. However, he was the one member of the Communist party who made these changes possible. There can be little question that the new era in the USSR would not have happened — at least not as it has and not as quickly — if Gorbachev had not been selected as head of the Community party.

We should not forget, however, that *glasnost* and *perestroika* are Russian words. Gorbachev's is no revolution on an American model. This is not an upheaval from the bottom up but, in typical Russian fashion, from the top down. Since the Bolshevik revolution, every Soviet leader has rejected the value of the achievements of his predecessor. In this respect, Gorbachev is no exception. Had Andropov or Chernenko lived, we would not today be celebrating the potential of a new USSR. We would not be concerned about the growing instability inside the country. We would not be seeing the gradual transformation of the Soviet Communist party, the attempts to alter the economic system, the declining reliance on the efficacy of military power, the expanded religious and political freedoms, or the limited experiments in representative democracy. This is leadership, and very significant leadership at that. It is change, and certainly significant change. In some ways it is a revolution. But it is not leadership on the American model, which accounts in part for the peculiar combination of fascination and discomfort with which he has been greeted by many Americans. Gorbachev may or may not survive, but his role as a "new reformist czar" understandably confuses Americans. The pattern, pace and prospects for change inside the USSR are so foreign to the American experience that it is difficult to assess the likelihood of permanent alterations in the structure of Soviet society and polity.

Nevertheless, there can be no question that if Gorbachev succeeds and reform moves forward, we will necessarily see examples of political pluralism and the public expression of differing views. This pluralism, however, will have been made possible by decisions at the pinnacle of power and in response to the economic stagnation and political corruption into which the Soviet Union has descended. Here is an entirely different set of circumstances than the Founding Fathers confronted in the 1770s.

By contrast, the pattern of events in East Europe is more familiar. The huge crowds demonstrating against Communist dictators once kept in power by the Soviet army remind Americans of their own struggles against a far less oppressive British master. The analogy with colonies being freed by a crumbling and self-doubting empire does not appear overly far-fetched. Of all the countries in the region, only Czechoslovakia has had experience with democracy. There are many dark clouds: the threat of fascist authoritarianism, return to Communist dictatorship, the impact of the German question on the politics of the region, and the growing dangers of ethnic strife and hostilities. Yet, the pattern of change in these countries is clearly closer to the American model than we have seen either in the USSR or in the bulk of the Third World. The end of Communist dictatorship and the move toward elections clearly express the popular will. The common goal of "life, liberty, and the pursuit of happiness" is apparent, for these are not revolutions imposed from above.

Of course, there are differences. We can be more optimistic about prospects in Czechoslovakia, Poland and Hungary than in Romania, Bulgaria, and Yugoslavia. In East Germany, reunification will undoubtedly lead to a democratic government dominated by the West Germans. But the emergence of legally accepted opposition groups in all these countries with a chance to participate in governance is a development which confirms the continuing relevance of the American model.

The notion of a popular opposition, so essential to the American concept of government, is matched by a leadership group, especially in Czechoslovakia, Poland, and Hungary, which holds open the prospect of innovation and ingenuity in moving from oppression to freedom, from dictatorship to democracy. In Poland, Lech Walesa and Solidarity — though obviously molded by a different country living under different conditions in a different era — remind us of the heroic activities of America's Founding Fathers. In Czechoslovakia, a formerly imprisoned playwright as President reminds us of Thomas Jefferson and James Madison. In Hungary, historic agreements with the opposition, the victory of reformers, and the determination to make a peaceful and successful transition to democracy are a further indication of the new politics in Eastern Europe. If democracy is to succeed in these countries, it will require a group of farsighted and ingenious Founding Fathers. The obvious courage and vision of many of the leaders who have emerged in the wake of the 1989 revolutions in all of these countries provides hope that they may indeed succeed despite the horrendous state of all of their respective economies.

However, the events of June 1989 in Tiananmen Square in Beijing are an ever-present reminder that the move from communism to democracy is not inevitable. Within the USSR there are also diverse developments. The Baltic states, similar to Eastern Europe, combine a move to democracy with an effort to shed the yoke of Russian dominance. As in Czechoslovakia, Hungary, and Poland, in each case there are signs of a leadership core which has emerged from a popular movement expressing a desire for a new form of government and a new independence.

In other parts of the USSR, however, unrest is more complex. The ethnic aspirations expressed by such diverse groups as Azerbaijanis, Armenians, Ukrainians, Moldavians, Georgians, and Tazhiks takes many forms. Separatist rivalries with other groups, anti-communism, religious fundamentalism all coexist uneasily. In the Baltics the American pattern of a skilled leadership guiding a popular revolt against foreign oppression is clearly present. Elsewhere in the Soviet empire, the content and goal of protest is still muddied. The democratic objective is as convoluted as the potential leaders who might direct it.

Revolution and the Current International System

The difficulty of drawing lessons from the American Revolution is further exacerbated by the nature of the current international system, with a hierarchy of states and huge gaps of power on the economic and military levels. In this system the Great Powers inevitably mix into the affairs of lesser states and regularly affect the course of revolutions. The decision of Great Powers on whether or not to intervene or how and whether to aid local revolutionaries has often been a hidden factor in assessing any revolution. Thus, without outside influence Korean history since 1945 would have been different and the country would undoubtedly have been united. Without Soviet intervention, revolutions would certainly have succeeded earlier in Eastern Europe and neither the Cuban nor the Afghani revolutions as we know them today would have progressed as they have. Similarly, Vietnamese intervention buried one Communist revolution and "created" another in Cambodia, while Cuba itself has affected the direction of politics in such countries as Ethiopia, Angola, and Grenada. Idi Amin was ousted by an internal upheaval backed by the troops of neighboring Tanzania. The French have been active in West Africa.

The United States has not been quiescent either, acting around the world (and especially in Latin America) to affect the direction of politics in many countries. Soviet and American agents have often competed to affect, if not determine, the fate of revolutionary

movements. Particularly dramatic American actions have occurred in Iran in 1953 to save the Shah, in the Dominican Republic
in 1965 to avoid a potential coup returning Juan Bosch to power, in
a murky — never totally explained — way in Chile in the early
1970s to prevent the continued rule of Salvador Allende's Marxist
government, in the intervention in Grenada in October 1983, in
Panama in December 1989, and in the Reagan administration's
support for the Nicaraguan Contras. The greatest failure of the period was the inability of the United States to prevent Communist
takeover throughout Indochina. The U.S. decision to cut off support for the Iraqi Kurds in 1975 and congressional disapproval the
same year of U.S. involvement in Angola rapidly weakened
American-backed rebel movements in both countries. In the
1980s, under Reagan, the UNITA (Union for National Independence Total of Angola) rebellion again received critical assistance from the U.S.

Despite Great Power efforts to influence events and their
mixed record of success and failure outside their immediate
spheres of influence in Central America, Eastern Europe, and
West Africa, the revolutions that have occurred have had their
origins in indigenous conflict and dissatisfaction. Even in each
of these three areas the predominant Great Power has had
increasing difficulty in totally controlling political developments, as recent events in Eastern Europe and Central America
dramatically confirm.

Nonetheless, revolutions no longer occur in relative isolation.
The French may have assisted the American revolutionaries, but
they did not determine the character of the revolution, nor were
they able to control the elite or to prevent the new American
leadership under Washington from opposing "entangling alliances." Today, economic interdependence and an advanced
technology which permits global involvements constrain the
freedom of action of new leaders and often make them subject to
outside influences that would not have been possible in an era of
more restricted communications. At the same time, these conditions tempt revolutionary leaders to seek the spread of their
movement either out of ideological motivations or in order to dis-
tract their populace from internal failures. Many revolutions of
the current period have at least passed through an active international phase: China, the Soviet Union, Egypt, Cuba, Algeria, Vietnam, Khomeini's Iran, Indonesia, Libya.

Thus, in the present era the revolutionary leader has not only played a role at home, but has become an international figure as well. The leader's function has been one of forming new alliances, of influencing politics in other countries, or even of serving as a symbol of fear or adulation to kindred movements elsewhere. Technology makes possible communication and transportation that often create events of global significance out of otherwise isolated developments.

The ultimate irony has been represented by Yassir Arafat — a revolutionary without a country, barely in control of a part of his movement, beholden to competing Arab governments, repeatedly suffering military setbacks at the hands of the Israelis and his Palestinian and Arab adversaries, yet able — thanks to television and the jet — to be known throughout the world, to meet international leaders from the Pope to the Commissars, to be received as a major figure wherever he visits. Prince Norodom Sihanouk, the deposed ruler of Cambodia, has played a similar role on a lesser scale. The international system, then, today presents a "revolution of mirrors," an image in world capitals not clearly related to actual events as they are transpiring in local regions.

In any revolution the new leaders who have emerged victorious are greeted by previously existing governments with suspicion or celebration, depending on their attitudes and ideology. But many revolutionary movements represent a challenge to the established order either globally (e.g., USSR until Gorbachev, China 1949-1976) or regionally (e.g., Vietnam, Cuba, Libya, Iran). In the modern era the acculturation of the new revolutionary elites into the framework of international politics is primarily affected by the high rate of personal contact that occurs among leaders. These contacts have assumed major proportions in the developed world where they now occur on a regular basis. A recent book by Lawrence Martin, *The Prime Ministers and the Presidents,* argues that the ups and downs in relations between the U.S. and Canada can be charted by reference to the personal relations between the nations' leaders.[7] Similarly, the lack of respect for Jimmy Carter among several European heads of state — especially Helmut Schmidt — helped to erode European-American relations in the late 1970s. By contrast, the close personal rapport that developed between Ronald Reagan and Helmut Kohl dominated German-American relations by 1985, as did the close personal relations between Reagan and Thatcher in the same period. Menachem Begin's problems with both Carter and Reagan helped to create a crisis in U.S.-Israeli relations that dissipated when he left office.

In the Third World the process of contacts among leaders is especially significant because of the fluidity of politics in this sector. Of particular importance for contacts among Third World leaders have been regional meetings — especially of the Organization of African Unity; of international gatherings — especially of the "nonaligned" states; of functional groups — e.g., OPEC (Organization of Petroleum Exporting Countries); of meetings among potential revolutionaries (as exemplified by terrorist training bases in Lebanon prior to the Israeli invasion in 1982); and of constant bilateral contacts among elites with similar goals. Jefferson warned against the danger of entangling alliances; today many revolutionary leaders are entangled long before they capture the reins of power.

In the East, revolutions have clearly had a domino effect. Each additional upheaval has impacted on its neighbors, emboldening the popular and opposition leaders, while weakening and ultimately destroying the entrenched Communist governments. Meanwhile, the Soviet imperium's willingness to acquiesce to change, indeed its support of the opposition, have served to accelerate the process of revolution in Eastern Europe. Every Soviet word of encouragement or demonstrable passivity in the wake of local rebellion has served as a motor for altering previous political patterns until opposition groups at home have themselves been encouraged to an extent not anticipated by those who promoted these developments abroad.

Conclusion

In sum, with the partial exception of Eastern Europe, the contemporary revolutionary movement is of an entirely different character than the American model. In the Third World, with almost all countries now having gained their independence, revolutions continue at a rapid pace, but they are aimed at indigenous governments, they are often entangled with outside parties, they almost always lack an elite that is capable of carrying forth the new approach to government combining principle and practice. Often reactions to economic desperation, or political oppression, or failure internationally, many contemporary revolutions are little more than palace coups. In many cases the rhetoric of revolutionary fervor has replaced the requirements of fundamental reforms. When revolutionary governments have continued, a bureaucratic leadership epitomized by the urge for survival has taken charge.

Max Weber recognized the tension between charismatic and bureaucratic leadership, the conflict between the romantic and the passionate hero, on the one hand, and the ever-pervasive encroachment of bureaucracy and large-scale organization on all spheres of modern life, on the other. The attraction of the politician as political hero in the industrialized world is, to a large degree, an attempt to escape from the routinized rationality and the impersonal objectivity of the complex modern bureaucratic state. The tragedy in the Third World, however, is that Walter Lippmann's definition of a truly great leader, who can leave behind him principles to be practiced by lesser figures later, has generally not been realized. The failure of Third World revolutions is that they have incorporated some of the advanced mechanisms of the bureaucratic state for use in political repression or corruption without creating the combination of political romance in the employment of practical necessities which was the genius of the American Revolution. Without that peculiar delicate mix their future is likely to be bleak indeed.

Only in Eastern Europe does the American model have a chance. It remains to be seen in each country whether a creative leadership expressing and encouraging democratic institutions will emerge or whether banal and corrupt regimes — dictatorships of the left or the right — which are typical of the Third World will prevail; we must be even more pessimistic about prospects inside the USSR itself.

In *Reflections on the Revolution in France*, Edmund Burke wrote "make the Revolution a parent of settlement, and not a nursery of revolutions."[8] The American Revolution was parent to a new order of government, but that kind of achievement has only rarely been attained in the current era.

Notes

1. Walter Lippman, "Roosevelt has Gone," April 14, 1945.
2. George Washington, *General Orders, Headquarters*, New York, July 2, 1776.
3. George Washington, *First Inaugural Address*, April 3, 1789.
4. George Washington, *Farewell Address*, April 30, 1796.
5. Thomas Jefferson, *First Inaugural Address*, March 4, 1801.
6. Henry Kissinger, *American Foreign Policy*, 3rd ed., (New York: W.W. Norton and Co., 1977), p. 39.
7. Lawrence Martin, *The Presidents and the Prime Ministers: Washington and Ottawa Face to Face: The Myth of Bilateral Bliss, 1867-1982* (Toronto: Doubleday, 1982).
8. Edmund Burke, *Reflections on the Revolution in France* (1790).

ABOUT THE AUTHORS

Daniel J. Elazar is Professor of Political Science and Director of the Center for the Study of Federalism at Temple University in Philadelphia, as well as Senator N.M. Paterson Professor of Intergovernmental Relations at Bar-Ilan University and President of the Jerusalem Center for Public Affairs, He is the author or editor of over 50 books including *The American Constitutional Tradition* and *Constitutionalism: The Israeli and American Experiences*.

Morton J. Frisch is Professor of Political Science at Northern Illinois University. He is the author of *Franklin D. Roosevelt: the Contribution of the New Deal to American Political Thought and Practice, Alexander Hamilton and the Political Order: An Interpretation of his Political Thought and Practice*, and co-editor of *American Political Thought: the Philosophic Dimension of American Statesmanship*.

The late J. David Greenstone, Professor of Political Studies at the University of Chicago, devoted his last years to studying Abraham Lincoln and the development of the American constitutional tradition in the nineteenth century. He was an Adjunct Scholar of the Center for the Study of Federalism.

Moshe Hazani is a Lecturer in the interdisciplinary Department of the Social Sciences at Bar-Ilan University and is a Fellow of the Jerusalem Center for Public Affairs. His current interests include the phenomenology of ideologically radical and deviant movements, including utopianism, messianism and political violence.

Forrest McDonald is Distinguished Research Professor at the University of Alabama and one of the foremost students of the American founding. His most recent books are *Novus Ordo Seclorum: The Intellectual Origins of the Constitution*, and *Requiem: Variations on Eighteenth-Century Themes*.

Rozann Rothman is Director of Applied Politics at Indiana University in Indianapolis and is an Adjunct Scholar of the Center for the Study of Federalism in Philadelphia. She has specialized in the American founding, the ambiguity of American federalism, and symbols and politics.

Gary J. Schmitt was Executive Director of the President's Foreign Intelligence Advisory Board during the Reagan Administration. He has authored articles on the presidency, executive-congressional relations, the intelligence oversight process, and American political thought.

Barry Schwartz teaches sociology at the University of Georgia. He is the author of *Vertical Classification: A Study in Structuralism and the Sociology of Knowledge, The Battle for Human Nature: Science, Morality and Modern Life,* and *George Washington: The Making of an American Symbol.*

Steven L. Spiegel is Professor of Political Science at the University of California, Los Angeles, and a Fellow of the Jerusalem Center for Public Affairs who specializes in U.S. policy in the Middle East. He is the author of *The Other Arab-Israeli Conflict: Making American Middle East Policy, From Truman to Reagan,* editor of *The Middle East and the Western Alliance,* and co-editor of *The Soviet-American Competition in the Middle East.*

Gary Wills teaches history at Northwestern University. He has written extensively on the American founding. He is the author of *Inventing America: Jefferson's Declaration of Independence, The Kennedy Imprisonment: A Meditation of Power,* and *Cincinnatus: George Washington and the Enlightenment.*

Books by Daniel J. Elazar

The American Partnership (1962)
American Federalism: A View From The States (1966; 1973; 1984)
The American System: A New View of Government in the United States
(ed.) (1966)
A Classification System for Libraries of Judaica (co-author) (1968; 1979)
The Politics of American Federalism (ed.) (1969)
Cooperation and Conflict: A Reader in American Federalism (co-editor)
(1969)
Cities of the Prairie (1970)
The Politics of Belleville (1971)
The Federal Polity (ed.) (1973; 1978)
The Ecology of American Political Culture (co-editor) (1975)
*Community and Polity: The Organizational Dynamics of American
Jewry* (1976)
Federalism and Political Integration (ed.) (1979; 1984)
Republicanism, Representation and Consent: Views of the Founding Era
(ed.) (1979)
Self-Rule/Shared Rule: Federal Solutions to the Middle East Conflict (ed.)
(1979; 1984)
Covenant, Polity and Constitutionalism (co-editor) (1980)
*Kinship and Consent: The Jewish Political Tradition and Its Contempo-
rary Uses* (ed.) (1981; 1983)
Governing Peoples and Territories (ed.) (1982)
Judea, Samaria and Gaza: Views on the Present and Future (ed.) (1982)
Jewish Communities in Frontier Societies (co-author) (1983)
From Autonomy to Shared Rule: Options for Judea, Samaria and Gaza
(ed.) (1983)
Balkan Jewish Communities: Yugoslavia, Bulgaria, Greece and Turkey
(co-author) (1984)
*The Jewish Communities of Scandinavia: Sweden, Denmark, Norway
and Finland* (co-author) (1984)
Understanding the Jewish Agency: A Handbook (co-editor) (1984; 1985)
*The Jewish Polity: Jewish Political Organization From Biblical Times to
the Present* (co-author) (1985)
Federalism and Consociationalism (ed.) (1985)
Jewish Political Studies: Selected Syllabi (co-editor) (1985)
Israel: Building a New Society (1986)
Cities of the Prairie Revisited: The Closing of the Metropolitan Frontier
(co-author) (1986)
Israel at the Polls, 1981 (co-editor) (1986)
*Building Cities in America: Urbanization and Suburbanization in a
Frontier Society* (1987)
Exploring Federalism (1987)
Project Renewal in Israel: Urban Revitalization Through Partnership (co-
author) (1987)
*Federalism as a Grand Design: Political Philosophers and the Federal
Principle* (ed.) (1987)
Canadian Federalism: From Crisis to Constitution (co-editor) (1987)
Local Government in Israel (co-editor) (1987; 1988)
The American Constitutional Tradition (1988)
The New Jewish Politics (ed.) (1988)
The Other Jews: The Sephardim Today (1989)
People and Polity: The Organizational Dynamics of World Jewry (1989)

Morality and Power: Contemporary Jewish Views (ed.) (1989)
Maintaining Consensus: The Canadian Jewish Polity in the Postwar World (co-author) (1990)
Constitutionalism: The Israeli and American Experiences (ed.) (1990)
Israel's Odd Couple: The 1984 Elections and the National Unity Government (co-editor) (1990)